THE RELIGIOUS PHILOSOPHY OF JOSIAH ROYCE

THE RELIGIOUS PHILOSOPHY OF

JOSIAH ROYCE

Edited, with an Introductory Essay, by

STUART GERRY BROWN

Professor of Citizenship and American Culture
Maxwell School of Citizenship
Syracuse University

The King's Library

GREENWOOD PRESS, PUBLISHERS
WESTPORT, CONNECTICUT

Library of Congress Cataloging in Publication Data

Royce, Josiah, 1855-1916.
The religious philosophy of Josiah Royce.

Reprint of the ed. published by Syracuse University
Press, Syracuse, N. Y.
CONTENTS: The possibility of error.--Individuality
and freedom.--The temporal and the eternal.--The concep-
tion of immortality.--Loyalty and religion. [etc.]
1. Religion--Philosophy--Addresses, essays, lectures.
I. Title.
[B945.R61B7 1976]   200'.9   76-4496
ISBN 0-8371-8810-5

Copyright 1952 Syracuse University Press

Originally published in 1952 by Syracuse University Press,
Syracuse

Reprinted with the permission of Syracuse University Press

Reprinted in 1976 by Greenwood Press,
a division of Williamhouse-Regency Inc.

Library of Congress Catalog Card Number 76-4496

ISBN 0-8371-8810-5

Printed in the United States of America

CONTENTS

꩜

INTRODUCTION

THE RELIGIOUS PHILOSOPHY OF JOSIAH ROYCE

To use a metaphor which I believe to be neither trivial nor unjust:
The gods, as man conceives the gods, live upon spiritual food; but, viewed
in the light of history, they appear as beings who must earn their bread
by supplying, in their turn, the equally spiritual sustenance which their
worshippers need. And unless they thus earn their bread, the gods die; and
the holy places that have known them, know them no more forever. Let
the ruins of ancient temples suggest the meaning that lies behind my
figure of speech.

—The Problem of Christianity

It was no accident that Josiah Royce's first book was called *The
Religious Aspect of Philosophy*. Though the catholic sweep of his
mind and the breadth of his idealist perspective included music and
literature, science and mathematics, economics and politics, his deepest
concerns were always with the relationships between the individual
human being and the social nexus of the individual life. The tone of
these concerns was always, in a pure sense, religious. Royce's early
investigations and speculations in metaphysics were carried on in the
hope of finding a rational basis for belief in the purposiveness of man
and of the world. Later, when his idealism was well formed, most of
his thought and writing were an attempt to draw the implications of
his metaphysics for ethical conduct, individual and social, and, more
particularly, for the devoted or consecrated life, which, regardless of
creed or church, could properly be called religious. In his last years
he turned his attention specifically to Christianity, endeavoring to reinterpret the Pauline doctrines by showing how the miraculous might
also be the human.

I

I

Royce was a clear, if somewhat laborious writer. His religious writings are lucid enough. But their essential continuity, as selected in this volume, may perhaps be illumined by some consideration of the two major theoretical formulations, one early and the other late, which underlay their progression. These are his arguments for the Absolute and his theory of a "community of interpretation." The former is thematic in all his work from his first book, through *The World and the Individual*, to *The Philosophy of Loyalty*, while the latter gives a somewhat different character to *The Problem of Christianity* and *The Hope of the Great Community*.

As both James and Santayana early pointed out, and Royce himself readily confessed, his argument for the Absolute was a distinctive variation on the medieval ontological formulation. The distinction lay in his emphasis on thought. While the "ontological proof" had been intended simply to demonstrate the existence of an unlimited *being*, which could then be equated with the God of Christianity, Royce wished to show that the Absolute Being was a mind, or better, Mind itself. And so he worked out his argument in terms of judgments rather than comparisons.

Starting with simple judgments, Royce argued that none could be true unless some were false. Error must be possible. At any rate no one would deny the proposition. But if errors occur, how do we know them? In practical situations we appeal to witnesses, chosen because they are believed to have better perspective. Thus if John and Thomas disagree, William is appealed to for arbitration. However, William's judgment may also be erroneous, so that it is necessary to appeal further. The process of appeal continues. Indeed, so long as error remains possible, it *must* continue until a mind is found which views simultaneously from *all* perspectives, and so, actually, contains all judgments. Such a mind would be without limit and therefore absolute. Its judgment would be final truth. Finite minds are seen to be minds at all only by their relation to Infinite Mind. The rejection of this argument, Royce maintained, involves the assumption that error is not possible, which is manifestly absurd.

This skeletal formulation, first set forth in "The Possibility of Error," is greatly enriched and considerably varied in Royce's later books. But the pattern of thought remains consistent. Thus, in *The World and the Individual*, the freedom of the individual man is seen as permanently limited by the infinite freedom of the Absolute. It is the fact of absolute freedom which makes individual, limited freedom a reality. In *The Philosophy of Loyalty*, all specific loyalties are found to be limited and subordinated to absolute Loyalty itself.

When applied to social relationships Royce's theory makes the individual dependent upon the family, the family upon the "province," the province upon the nation, and the nation upon the world. The individual and his community derive their meaning only from the Universal Community. He who rejects this insight, and its ethical implications, becomes a "lost" individual and is spiritually destroyed.

It is important to observe here, as I showed in my previous volume *The Social Philosophy of Josiah Royce*, that Royce has no interest in the Universal Community, or any other absolute, for its own sake. He is a thoroughgoing individualist. His whole philosophy of Absolute Mind is intended to show the meaning of individual minds, and his theory of the Community is directed to the problem of defining and giving genuine dignity to the individual personality. So far from adopting totalitarian views, Royce is a democrat who wishes to show the dependence of democracy upon individual responsibility. Individualism and freedom depend upon sacrifice. Both are lost through selfishness, which is denial of community.

And so it is with his religious philosophy. The whole purpose Royce set himself is to demonstrate the sacredness of personality and to find the road to salvation. He is a modernist in the sense that he cannot accept unsupported dogma or revelation. He is friendly to the findings and hopes of science and concerned to show that the enduring values of religion are not endangered by free inquiry. Indeed it is from the field of science that he draws his principal illustration of the second of his two distinctive formulations, the theory of interpretation.

II

As he gratefully acknowledged, Royce owed much to the theory of communication worked out by his friend Charles Sanders Peirce. From it he derived his own view of interpretation. The key to this view is the notion of mediation. In isolation an individual is capable of only two of three distinct forms of knowledge: perception and conception. He can receive the data of sense and he can formulate names for experiences. But he cannot bring his sense data and his concepts into harmonious intercourse with another individual unless *interpretation* takes place. Differences of experience and formulation will tend to prevent communication of ideas, even information, at one level, and at another level will lead to friction. Projected on the scale of society the same differences may cause wars between groups or nations. Thus a third person, or party, is required to serve as mediator. The mediator functions as interpreter, and so *interpretation* becomes a third form of knowledge, the crucial form. The three parties thus brought together form a "community of interpretation." It is precisely because such a community of interpretation exists among scientists that science progresses even when groups and nations are torn apart by tensions of feeling and interest. Universal peace would thus be a direct possibility of the universalizing of the interpretative function.

III

With these two doctrines as lodestones,—the doctrine of the Absolute Mind and the doctrine of the Community of Interpretation,—Royce finally approached the "problem" of Christianity. Why was Christianity, in his view, a problem? Briefly, Royce conceived the problem to lie in the fact that the essential notions of Christian doctrine had hitherto depended upon supernatural sanction. But science was rapidly casting doubt upon the validity of supernatural beliefs, at least in the older understanding of the term. Yet the notions thus undermined were the best men had ever devised for the maintenance and extension of order, freedom, civilization, and peace. If these cohesive principles were now to go by default man would indeed create for himself a living death. Hell would have a new and more terrible meaning. As Yeats later put it:

> Turning and turning in the widening gyre
> The falcon cannot hear the falconer;
> Things fall apart, the center cannot hold;
> Mere anarchy is loosed upon the world,
> The blood-dimmed tide is loosed, and everywhere
> The ceremony of innocence is drowned;
> The best lack all conviction, while the worst
> Are full of passionate intensity.[1]

1. "The Second Coming," ll. 1-8.

But, Royce insisted, the nature of man is social. Anarchy is impossible as a permanent condition. If the Christian synthesis is destroyed, some other will replace it. He did not live to watch the growth of the twin totalitarian evils of the twentieth century: fascism and communism. But he saw already in the mild authoritarianism of Imperial Germany a dark foreshadowing. If the free community were to die it would be succeeded by an unfree community.

The tragic aspect of the problem lay in the fact that the Christian essentials did not depend, in reality had never depended, upon unscientific or irrational sanctions. The prospects for civilization and peace were dark, so it seemed, only because people had been Christians for wrong reasons. Now they were giving up their hopes for the illusion of loss. Thus what was needed was to reinterpret Christianity in directly human terms. It would turn out that the human value rescued and re-established in the process was not the exclusive possession of the Christian churches. But it was necessary to begin with Christianity as the common inheritance of the free peoples of the West.

IV

In the context of Royce's whole work *The Problem of Christianity* is thus his central, as it is certainly his finest, book. In the course of the two volumes Royce examines and "humanizes" all of the more important doctrines of the Christian faith. However, the argument makes special use of three ideas: man as "fallen," the Church as the "Mystical Body of Christ," and the Atonement. The first is expressed in such a passage as this:

> The pith of the matter can be expressed, in terms of purely human psychology, thus: Man's fallen state is due to his nature as a social animal. This nature is such that you can train his conscience only by awakening his self-will. By self-will, I here mean, as Paul meant, man's conscious and active assertion of his own individual desires, worth, and undertakings, over against the will of his fellow, and over against the social will. Another name for this sort of conscious self-will is the modern term "individualism," when it is used to mean the tendency to prefer what the individual man demands to what the collective will requires. In general, and upon high levels of human intelligence, when you train individualism, you also train collectivism; that is, you train in the individual a respect for the collective will. And it belongs to Paul's very deep and searching insight to assert that these two tendencies—the tendency towards individualism, and that towards collectivism—do not exclude, but intensify and inflame each other.

Training, if formally successful in producing the skillful member of human society, breeds respect, although not love, for "the law," that is, for the expression of the collective will. But training also makes the individual conscious of the "other law" in "his members," which "wars against" the law of the social will. The result may be, for his outward conduct, whatever the individual's wits and powers make it. But so far as this result is due to cultivation in intelligent conduct, it inevitably leads to an inner division of the self, a disease of self-consciousness, which Paul finds to be the curse of all merely natural human civilization.[2]

Thus the "higher" the level of intellectual "civilization" men attain the more desperately do they become detached, lost, and miserable. The need for Christianity grows, not diminishes, with advancement of science and the arts. Christianity offers, through the church, a hard but possible way to salvation, a salvation which is necessary for the preservation of the very intellectual achievements which have rendered its need so urgent. For in the Church is to be found the meaning of Christ. In human terms the "mystical body" is the community, the Beloved Community or the Church Universal.

All morality, namely, is, from this point of view, to be judged by the standards of the Beloved Community, of the ideal Kingdom of Heaven. Concretely stated, this means that you are to test every course of action not by the question: What can we find in the parables or in the Sermon on the Mount which seems to us more or less directly to bear upon this special matter? The central doctrine of the Master was: "So act that the Kingdom of Heaven may come." This means: So act as to help, however you can, and whenever you can, towards making mankind one loving brotherhood, whose love is not a mere affection for morally detached individuals, but a love of the unity of its own life upon its own divine level, and a love of individuals in so far as they can be raised to communion with this spiritual community itself.[3]

In attempting to live by this standard is to be found the universal meaning of sacrifice. So the sacrifice of Christ is emulated by the death of each individual man,—death to selfishness. The death brings life to the spirit, rescue from the wilderness of isolation. As Eliot put it in his "Journey of the Magi":

All this was a long time ago, I remember,
And I would do it again, but set down
This set down

2. The Problem of Christianity, I, 176-177.
3. ibid., 356-357.

This: were wc led all that way for
Birth or Death? There was a Birth, certainly,
We had evidence and no doubt, I had seen birth and death,
But had thought they were different; this Birth was
Hard and bitter agony for us, like Death, our death.
We returned to our places, these Kingdoms,
But no longer at ease here, in the old dispensation,
With an alien people clutching their gods,
I should be glad of another death.[4]

The death thus died by membership in the Beloved Community, by sacrifice of individual desires in the interests of the ideal brotherhood of all the faithful, is Atonement.

Christianity interpreted in such terms is *true*, Royce argues, in the human sense, regardless of one's private opinions regarding matters of mystery and revelation. It is true by the pragmatic test of observing consequences.

V

In the forty years since Royce finished his work nothing has happened which would have led him to change his view. The free individual whom he was addressing is more lost than ever in the middle of the twentieth century. The world is further from peace than ever. The need for salvation and atonement is greater than ever. We may do well now to heed the prophetic statement with which he concluded his analysis of the Christian doctrine:

> The Christian virtues, then, will flourish in the civilization of the future, if indeed that civilization itself flourishes. For the more complex its constitution, and the swifter and vaster its social changes, the more will that civilization need love, and loyalty, and the grace of spiritual unity, and the will and the conscience which the Christian ideas have defined, and counselled, and that atoning conflict with evil wherein the noblest expression of the spirit must always be found.
>
> The Christian virtues will survive if humanity triumphs in its contest with its own deepest needs and in its struggle after its own highest goods.[5]

4. II. 32-43.
5. *The Problem of Christianity*, I, 385-386.

꧁

THE RELIGIOUS ASPECT OF PHILOSOPHY (1885)

THE POSSIBILITY OF ERROR

On ne sert dignement la philosophie qu'avecle même feu qu'on sent pour une maîtresse.—Rousseau, *Nouvelle Helöise*

I

The story of the following investigation shall first be very briefly told. The author had long sought, especially in the discussions of Kant's "Kritik," and in the books of the post-Kantians, for help in seeing the ultimate principles that lie at the basis of knowledge. He had found the old and well-known troubles. Experience of itself can give no certainty about general principles. We must therefore, said Kant, bring our own principles with us to experience. We know then of causation, because causation is a fundamental principle of our thought, whereby we set our experience to rights. And so long as we think, we shall think into experience the connection of cause and effect, which otherwise would not be there. But hereupon the questions arose that have so often been asked of Kant and the Kantians. Why just these principles and no others? "That is inexplicable," replies Kant. Very well, then, suppose we give up applying to experience those arbitrary principles of ours. Suppose we choose to stop thinking of experience as causally connected. What then? "But you cannot stop," says Kant, "Your thought, being what it is, must follow this one fashion forever." Nay, we reply, how knowests thou that, Master? Why may not our thought get a new fashion some day? And then what is now a necessary principle, for example, that every event has a cause, would become unnecessary or even nonsensical. Do we then know *a priori* that our *a priori* principles must always remain such? If so, how come we by this new knowledge?

So Kant leaves us still uncertain about any fundamental principles upon which a sure knowledge of the world can be founded.

Let us, then, examine a little deeper. Are there any certain judgments possible at all? If one is skeptical in a thorough-going way, as the author tried to be, he is apt to reach, through an effort to revise Kant's view, a position something like the following,—a provisional position of course, but one that results from the effort to accept nothing without criticism: "Kant's result is that our judgments about the real world are founded on an union of thought and sense, thought giving the appearance of necessity to our judgment, sense giving the material. The necessity of any judgment amounts then only to what may be summed up in the words: *So the present union of thought and sense makes things appear.* If either thought or sense altered its character, truth would alter. Hence every sincere judgment is indeed true for the moment in which it is made, but not necessarily true for other moments. We only postulate that it is true for other moments." "And so," to continue this view, "it is only by means of postulates that our thought even seems to have any unity from moment to moment. We live in the present. If our thought has other truth or falsity than this, we do not know it. Past and future exist not for this present. They are only postulated. Save as postulated, they have no present meaning."

When he held and expressed this view, the author is free to admit that he was not always clear whether he ought to call it the doctrine of the relativity of truth or not. It might have avoided the absurdities of total relativity by taking form as a doctrine that the present moment's judgment is really true or false, for a real past and future, but that we, being limited to present moments, can never compare our judgments with reality to find whether our judgments are true or false. But although this interpretation is possible, this view often did express itself for the author as the doctrine of the total relativity of truth. The latter doctrine to be sure has no real meaning, but the author used with many others to fancy that it had.

To apply the view to the case of causal relations. "We continually postulate," the author used to point out, "we demand, without being able to prove it, that nature in future shall be uniform." So, carrying out this thought, the author used to say: "In fact future nature is not given to us, just as the past is not given to us. Sense-data and thought unite at every instant afresh to form a new judgment and a new postulate. Only in the present has any judgment evident validity. And our postulate of causal relation is just a way of looking at this world of conceived past and future *data*. Such postulates avoid being absurd efforts to regulate independent facts of sense, because, and only because, we have in experience no complete series of facts of sense at all, only from moment to moment single facts, about which we make single judgments. All the rest we *must* postulate or else do without them." Thus one reaches a skepticism as nearly complete as is possible to any one with earnest activity of thought in him. From moment to moment one can be sure of each moment. All else is postulate.

From the depths of this imperfectly defined skepticism, which seemed to him provisionally the only view he could adopt, the author escaped only by asking the one question more: "If everything beyond the present is doubtful, then how can even that doubt be possible?" With this question that bare relativity of the present moment is given up. What are the conditions that make doubt logically intelligible? These conditions really transcend the present moment. Plainly doubt implies that the statement doubted may be false. So here we have at least one supposed general truth, namely, "All but the immediate content of the present moment's judgment, being doubtful, we may be in error about it." But *what then is an error?* This becomes at once a problem of exciting interest. Attacking it, the author was led through the wilderness of the following argument.

II

Yet before we undertake this special examination of the nature of error, the reader must pardon us for adding yet another explanatory word. The difficulty of the whole discussion will lie in the fact that we shall be studying the possibility of the plainest and most familiar of commonplaces. Common sense hates to do such things, because common sense thinks that the whole matter is sure from the outset. Common sense is willing to ask whether God exists, but unwilling to inquire how it is possible that there can exist an error about anything. But foreseeing that something is to follow from all this, we must beg common sense to be patient. We have not the shadow of a doubt ourselves about the possibility of error. That is the steadfast rock on which we build. Our inquiry, ultra-skeptical as it may at moments seem, is into the question: *How* is the error possible? Or, in other words: *What is an error?* Now there can be little doubt that common sense is not ready with any general answer to such a question. Error is a word with many senses. By error we often mean just a statement that arouses our antipathy. Yet we all admit upon reflection, that our antipathy can neither make nor be used to define real error. Adam Smith declares, with common sense on his side, in his "Theory of the Moral Sentiments,"[1] that: "To approve or disapprove of the opinions of others is acknowledged, by everybody, to mean no more than to observe their agreement or disagreement with our own." Yet no one would accept as a definition of error the statement that: *Error is any opinion that I personally do not like.* Error has thus a very puzzling character. For common sense will readily admit that if a statement is erroneous, it must appear erroneous to every "right mind" that is in possession of the facts. Hence the personal taste of one man is not enough to define it. Else there might be as many sorts of error as there are minds. It is only the "right mind" whose personal taste shall decide what is an error in any particular case. But what then is a normal mind? Who is the right-minded judge? There seems to be danger that common sense shall run at this point into an infinite regress. I say: *That opinion is an error.* What do I mean? Do I mean that I do not like that opinion? Nay, I mean more. I mean that *I ought not to like or to accept it.* Why ought I not? *Because the ideally right-minded person would not,* seeing the given facts, hold that opinion about them. But who is the ideally right-minded person? Well, common sense may answer, *It is my ideal person, the right-minded man as I conceive him.* But why is my ideal the true ideal? *Because I like it?*—Nay, *because, to the ideal judge, that kind of mind would seem the ideal.* But who is the ideal judge? And so common sense is driven from point to point, unable to get to anything definite.

So much, then, to show in general that common sense does not know what an error is, and needs more light upon the subject. Let common sense not disturb us, then, in our further search, by the constant and indignant protest that error must somehow exist, and that doubt on that subject is nonsense. Nobody has any doubts on that subject. We ask only *how* error exists and how it can exist.

For the rest, what follows is not any effort to demonstrate in fair and orderly array, from any one principle or axiom, what must be the nature of error, but to use every and any device that may offer itself, general analysis, special example, comparison and contrast of cases,—anything that shall lead us to the insight into what an error is and implies. For at last, immediate insight must decide.

We shall study our problem thus. We shall take either some accepted

1. Part I., sect. i., chap. iii., near the beginning.

definition of error, or some special class of cases, and we shall ask: How is error in that case, or in accordance with that definition, possible? Since error plainly is possible in some way, we shall have only to inquire: *What are the logical conditions* that make it possible? We shall take up the ordinary suppositions that common sense seems to make about what here determines the possibility of error. We shall show that these suppositions are inadequate. Then the result will be that, on the ordinary suppositions, error would be impossible. But that result would be absurd, if these were the only possible suppositions. Hence the ordinary suppositions must somehow be supplemented. When, therefore, we seem to say in the following that error is impossible, we shall mean only, impossible under the ordinary suppositions of common sense. What supplement we need to these suppositions, our argument will show us. In sum we shall find the state of the case to be this: Common sense regards an assertion as true or as false apart from any other assertion or thought, and solely in reference to its own object. For common sense each judgment, as a separate creation, stands out alone, looking at its object, and trying to agree with it. If it succeeds, we have truth. If the judgment fails, we have error. But, as we shall find, this view of common sense is unintelligible. A judgment cannot have an object and fail to agree therewith, unless this judgment is part of an organism of thought. Alone, as a separate fact, a judgment has no intelligible object beyond itself. And therefore the presuppositions of common sense must be supplemented or else abandoned. Either then there is no error, or else judgments are true or false only in reference to a higher inclusive thought, which they presuppose, and which must, in the last analysis, be assumed as Infinite and all-inclusive. This result we shall reach by no mystical insight, by no revelation, nor yet by any mere postulate such as we used in former discussions, but by a simple, dry analysis of the meaning of our own thought.

The most formidable opponent of our argument will be, after all, however, not common sense, but that thought mentioned in the last chapter,—the thought that may try to content itself with somewhat plausible jargon, and to say that: *"There is no real difference between truth and error at all, only a kind of opinion or consensus of men about a conventional distinction between what they choose to call truth and what they choose to call error."* This view, as the author has confessed, he once tried to hold. Still this meaningless doctrine of relativity is not the same as the view that contents itself with the postulates before discussed. That view might take, and for the author at one time did take, the possible and intelligible form thus expressible: *"Truth and error, though really distinguishable, are for us distinguished only through our postulates, in so far as relates to past and future time."* Such views, while not denying that there is real truth, despair of the attainability for us of more than momentary truth. But the doctrine of Total Relativity, this view above expressed, differs from genuine skepticism. It tries to put even skepticism to rest, by declaring the opinion, *that there is error*, to be itself an error. This is not merely a moderate expression of human limitations, but jargon, and therefore formidable, because jargon is always unanswerable. When the famous Cretan declared all statements made by Cretans to be in all cases lies, his declaration was hard to refute, because it was such honest-seeming nonsense. Even so with the statement that declares the very existence of error to be an erroneously believed fancy. No *consensus* of men can make an error erroneous. We can only find or commit an error, not create it. When we commit an error, we say what was an error already. If our skeptical view in previous chapters seemed to regard truth and error as mere objects of our postulates, that was only because, to our skepticism, the real truth, the real error, about any real past and future, seemed beyond our reach, so that we had to content ourselves with postulates. But that real error exists is absolutely indubitable.

This being the case, it is evident that even the most thorough-going skepticism is full of assumptions. If I say, "There may be no money in the purse yonder," I assume the existence of the purse yonder in order to make just that particular doubt possible. Of course, however, just that doubt may be rendered meaningless by the discovery of the actual non-existence of that particular purse. If there is no purse yonder, then it is nonsensical either to affirm or to deny that it contains money. And so if the purse of which I speak is an hallucination of mine, then the doubt about whether, as an actually existent purse, it has money in it, is deprived of sense. My real error in that case would lie in supposing the purse itself to exist. If, however, I abandon the first doubt, and go on to doubt the real existence of the purse, I equally assume a room, or some other environment, or at all events the universe, as existent, in order to give sense to my question whether the purse has any being in this environment or in this universe. But if I go yet further, and doubt whether there is any universe at all outside of my thought, what does my doubt yet mean? If it is to be a doubt with any real sense, it must be a doubt still with an object before it. It seems then to imply an assumed order of being, in which there are at least two elements, my lonely thought about an universe, and an empty environment of this thought, in which there is, in fact, no universe. But this empty environment, whose nature is such that my thought does wrong to suppose it to be an universe, what is that? Surely if the doubt is to have meaning, this idea needs further examination. The absolute skepticism is thus full of assumptions.

The first European thinker who seems to have discussed our present problem was Plato, in a too-much-neglected passsage of the "Theætetus,"[1] where Socrates, replying to the second definition of knowledge given by Theætetus, namely, *knowledge is True Opinion*, answers that his great difficulty has often been to see how any opinion can possibly be false. The conclusion reached by Plato is no very definite one, but the discussion is deeply suggestive. And we cannot do better here than to pray that the shade of the mighty Greek may deign to save us now in our distress, and to show us the true nature of error.

III

Logicians are agreed that single ideas, thoughts viewed apart from judgments, are neither true nor false. Only a judgment can be false. And if a reasoning process is said to be false, the real error lies still in an actual or suppressed assertion. A fallacy is a false assertion that a certain conclusion follows from certain premises. Error is therefore generally defined as a judgment that does not agree with its object. In the erroneous judgment, subject and predicate are so combined as, in the object, the corresponding elements are not combined. And thus the judgment comes to be false. Now, in this definition, nothing is doubtful or obscure save the one thing, namely, the *assumed relation between the judgment and its object*. The definition assumes as quite clear that a judgment has an object, wherewith it can agree or not agree. And what is meant by the agreement would not be obscure, if we could see what is meant by the object, and by the possession of this object implied in the pronoun *its*. What then is meant by *its object?* The difficulties involved in this phrase begin to appear as soon as you look closer. First then the object of the assertion is as such supposed to be neither the subject nor the predicate thereof. It is external to the judgment. It has a nature of its own. Furthermore, not all judgments have the same object, so that objects are very numerous. But from the infinity of real or of possible objects the judg-

1. Plato, *Th.*, p. 187 *sqq.*

ment somehow picks out its own. Thus then for a judgment to have an object, there must be something about the judgment that shows what one of the external objects that are beyond itself this judgment does pick out as its own. But this something that gives the judgment its object can only be the intention wherewith the judgment is accompanied. A judgment has as object only what it intends to have as object. It has to conform only to that to which it wants to conform. But the essence of an intention is the knowledge of what one intends. One can, for instance, intend a deed or any of its consequences only in so far as he foresees them. I cannot be said to intend the accidental or the remote or even the immediate consequences of anything that I do, unless I foresaw that they would follow; and this is true however much the lawyers and judges may find it practically necessary to hold me responsible for these consequences. Even so we all find it practically useful to regard one of our fellows as in error in case his assertions, as we understand them, seem to us to lead to consequences that we do not approve. But our criticisms of his opinions, just like legal judgments of his acts, are not intended to be exact. Common sense will admit that, unless a man is thinking of the object of which I suppose him to be thinking, he makes no real error by merely failing to agree with the object that I have in mind. If the knights in the fable judge each other to be wrong, that is because each knight takes the other's shield to be identical with the shield as he himself has it in mind. In fact neither of them is in error, unless his assertion is false for the shield as he intended to make it his object.

So then judgments err only by disagreeing with their intended objects, and they can intend an object only in so far forth as this object is known to the thought that makes the judgment. Such, it would seem, is the consequence of the common-sense view. But in this case a judgment can be in error only if it is knowingly in error. That also, as it seems, follows from the common-sense suppositions. Or, if we will have it in syllogistic form:—

Everything intended is something known. The object even of an erroneous judgment is intended. ∴. The object even of an error is something known.

Or: Only what is known can be erred about. Nor can we yet be content with what common sense will at once reply, namely, that our syllogism uses *known* ambiguously, and that the object of an erroneous judgment is known enough to constitute it the object, and not enough to prevent the error about it. This must no doubt be the fact, but it is not of itself clear; on the contrary, just here is the problem. As common sense conceives the matter, the object of a judgment is not as such the whole outside world of common sense, with all its intimate interdependence of facts, with all its unity in the midst of diversity. On the contrary, the object of any judgment is just that portion of the then conceived world, just that fragment, that aspect, that element of a supposed reality, which is seized upon for the purposes of just this judgment. Only such a momentarily grasped fragment of the truth can possibly be present in any one moment of thought as the object of a single assertion. Now it is hard to say how within this arbitrarily chosen fragment itself there can still be room for the partial knowledge that is sufficient to give to the judgment its object, but insufficient to secure to the judgment its accuracy. If I aim at a mark with my gun, I can fail to hit it, because choosing and hitting a mark are totally distinct acts. But, in the judgment, choosing and knowing the object seem inseparable. No doubt somehow our difficulty is soluble, but we are here trying first to show that it is a difficulty.

To illustrate here by a familiar case, when we speak of things that are solely matters of personal preference, such as the pleasure of a sleigh-ride, the taste of olives, or the comfort of a given room, and when we only try to tell how these things appear to us, then plainly our judgments, if sincere, cannot be in error. As these things are to us, so they are. We are their measure. To doubt our truthfulness in these cases is to doubt after the fashion of the student who wondered whether the star that the astronomers call Uranus may not be something else after all, and not really Uranus. Surely science does not progress very far or run into great danger of error so long as it employs itself in discovering such occult mysteries as the names of the stars. But our present question is, How do judgments that can be and that are erroneous differ in nature from these that cannot be erroneous? If astronomers would be equally right in case they should agree to call Uranus Humpty Dumpty, why are not all judgments equally favored? Since the judgment chooses its own object, and has it only in so far as it chooses it, how can it be in that partial relation to its object which is implied in the supposition of an erroneous assertion?

Yet again, to illustrate the difficulty in another aspect, we can note that not only is error impossible about the perfectly well-known, but that error is equally impossible, save in the form of direct self-contradiction, about what is absolutely unknown. Spite of the religious awe of some people in presence of the Unknowable, it is safe to say, somewhat irreverently, that about a really Unknowable nobody could make any sincere and self-consistent assertions that could be errors. For self-consistent assertions about the Unknowable would of necessity be meaningless. And being meaningless, they could not well be false. For instance, one could indeed not say that the Unknowable contemplates war with France, or makes sunspots, or will be the next Presidential candidate, because that would be contradicting one's self. For if the Unknowable did any of these things, it would no longer be the Unknowable, but would become either the known or the discoverable. But avoid such self-contradiction, and you cannot err about the Unknowable. For the Unknowable is simply our old friend *Abracadabra*, a word that has no meaning, and by hypothesis never can get any. So if I say that the Unknowable dines *in vacuo* with the chimera, or is Humpty Dumpty, I talk nonsense, and am therefore unable to make a mistake. Nonsense is error only when it involves self-contradiction. Avoid that, and nonsense cannot blunder, having no object outside of itself with which it must agree. But all this illustrates from the other side our difficulty. Is not the object of a judgment, in so far as it is unknown to that judgment, like the Unknowables for that judgment? To be in error about the application of a symbol, you must have a symbol that symbolizes something. But in so far as the thing symbolized is not known through the symbol, how is it symbolized by that symbol? Is it not, like the Unknowable, once for all out of the thought, so that one cannot just then be thinking about it at all, and so cannot, in this thought at least, be making blunders about it? But in so far as the thing symbolized is, through the symbol, in one's thought, why is it not known, and so correctly judged? All this involves that old question of the nature of symbols. They are to mean for us more than we know that they mean. How can that be? No doubt all that is really possible, but how?

IV

We follow our difficulty into another department. Let us attempt a sort of provisional psychological description of a judgment as a state of mind. So regarded, a judgment is simply a fact that occurs in somebody's thought. If we try to describe it as an occurrence, without asking whence it came, we shall perhaps find in it three elements,—elements which are in some fashion described in Ueberweg's well-known definition of a judgment as the "Consciousness about the objective validity of a subjective union of ideas." Our interpretation of them shall be this: The elements are: The *Subject*, with the accompanying shade of curiosity about it; the *Predicate*, with the accompanying sense of its worth in satisfying a part of our curiosity about the subject; and the *Sense of Dependence*, whereby we feel the value of this act to lie, not in itself, but in its agreement with a vaguely felt Beyond, that stands out there as Object.

Now this analysis of the elements of a judgment is no explanation of our difficulties; and in fact for the moment only embarrasses us more. But the nature of the difficulty may come home to us somewhat more clearly, if we try to follow the thread of this analysis a little further. Even if it is a very imperfect account, it may serve to lead us up to the true insight that we seek into the nature of error. Let us make the analysis a little more detailed.

In its typical form then, the judgment as a mental state seems to us to begin with a relatively incomplete or unstable or disconnected mass of consciousness, which we have called the Subject, as it first begins to be present to us. This subject idea is attended by some degree of effort, namely, of attention, whose tendency is to complete this incomplete subject by bringing it into closer connection with more familiar mental life. This more familiar life is represented by the predicate-idea. If the effort is successful, the subject has new elements united to it, assumes in consciousness a definiteness, a coherency with other states, a familiarity, which it lacked at the outset of the act of judgment; and this coherency it gets through its union with the predicate. All this is accompanied further by what one for short may call a sense of dependence. The judgment feels itself not alone, but looks to a somewhat indefinite object as the model after which the present union of ideas is to be fashioned. And in this way we explain how the judgment is, in those words of Ueberweg's definition, "the consciousness about the objective validity of a subjective union of ideas."

Now as a mere completion of subject-ideas through the addition of a predicate-idea, the judgment is simply a mental phenomenon, having interest only to the person that experiences it, and to a psychologist. But as true or as false the judgment must be viewed in respect to the indefinite object of what we have called the sense of dependence, whereby the judgment is accompanied. Seldom in any ordinary judgment does this object become perfectly full and clear; for to make it so would often require many, perhaps an infinite, series of judgments. Yet, for the one judgment, the object, whether full and clear or not, exists as object only in so far forth as the sense of dependence has defined it. And the judgment is true or false only with reference to this undefined object. The intention to agree with the object is contained in the sense of dependence upon the object, and remains for this judgment incomplete, like the object itself. Somewhat vaguely this single act intends to agree with this vague object.

Such being the case, how can the judgment, as thus described, fairly be called false? As mere psychological combination of ideas it is neither true nor false. As accompanied by the sense of dependence upon an object, it would be false if it disagreed with its imperfectly defined object. But, as described, the only object that the judgment has is this imperfectly defined one. With this, in so far as it is for the moment defined, the judgment must needs agree. In so far as it is not defined, it is however not object for this judgment at all, but for some other one. What the imperfect sense of dependence would further imply if it existed in a complete instead of in an incomplete state, nobody can tell, any more than one can tell what towns would grow up by a given rain-pool, if it were no pool, but a great lake. The object of a single judgment, being what it is, namely, a vaguely defined object, present to this judgment, is just what it is for this judgment, and the judgment seems once for all to be true, in case it is sincere.

Some one may here at once answer that we neglect in this description the close interdependence of various judgments. Thought, some one may say, is an organic unity. Separated from all else but its own incompletely defined object, a single judgment cannot be erroneous. Only in the organic unity of a series of judgments, having a common object, is the error of one of them possible. We reply that all this will turn out to be just our result. But the usual supposition at the outset is that any judgment has by itself its own object, so that thereby alone, apart from other judgments, it stands or falls. And thus far we have tried to show that this natural supposition leads us into difficulty. We cannot see how a single sincere judgment should possibly fail to agree with its own chosen object. But enough of our problem in general. We must consider certain classes of errors more in detail. Let us see how, in these special classes of cases, we shall succeed in verifying the natural presupposition of common sense, which regards error as possible only when our object is not wholly present to mind, and which assumes that a judgment can have an object that is yet only partially present to mind. In choosing the classes of cases, we shall first follow common sense as to their definition.

We shall take just the assumptions of daily life, and shall show that they lead us into difficulty. We are not for the first bound to explain why these assumptions are made. That common sense makes them is enough. But let the reader remember: The whole value of our argument lies in its perfect generality. However much we dwell on particular classes of errors, we care nothing for the proof that just those errors are inexplicable, but only for the fact that they illustrate how, without some entirely new hypothesis, absolutely all error becomes impossible. This or that class of judgments may be one in which all the judgments are relative, but the total relativity of our thought implies an incomprehensible and contradictory state of things. Any hypothesis about error that makes total relativity the only admissible view, must therefore give place to some new hypothesis. And our illustrations in the following are intended to show that just what constitutes the difficulty in respect of these illustrations, makes the existence of any error inexplicable without some new hypothesis.

V

The class of errors that we shall first take seems, to common sense, common enough. It is the class known as errors about our neighbor's states of mind. Let us then, for argument's sake, assume without proof that our neighbors do exist. For we are not here concerned to answer Solipsism, but merely to exemplify the difficulties about the nature of error. If our neighbors did not exist, then the nature of the error that would lie in saying that they do exist would present almost exactly the same difficulties. We prefer, however, to begin with the common-sense assumption about ourselves and our neighbors as separate individuals, and to ask how error can then arise in judging of our neighbors' minds.

In the first place then: Who is my neighbor? Surely, on the assumptions that we all make, and that we made all through the ethical part of our discussion, he is no one of my thoughts, nor is any part of him ever any part of my thought. He is not my object, but, in Professor Clifford's phrase, an "eject," wholly outside of my ideas. He is no "thing in my dream," just as I am not in his dream.

Yet I make judgments about him, and he makes them about me. And when I make judgments about him, I do so by having in my thought some set of my own ideas that, although not himself, do yet, as I say, represent him. A kind of dummy, a symbol, a graven image of my own thought's creation, a phantom of mine, stands there in me as the representative of his mind; and all I say about my neighbor's inner life refers directly to this representative. The Scottish philosophy has had much to say to the world about what it calls direct or presentative, as opposed to representative, knowledge of objects. But surely the most obstinate Scottish philosopher that ever ate oatmeal cannot hold so tenaciously by his national doctrine as to say that I have, according to common sense, anything but a representative knowledge of my neighbor's thoughts and feelings. That is the only sort of knowledge that common sense will regard as possible to me, if so much as that is possible. But how I can know about this outside being is not now our concern. We notice only that our difficulty about error comes back to us in a new form. For how can I err about my neighbor, since, for this common-sense view, he is not even partly in my thoughts? How can I intend that as the object of my thought which never can be object for me at all?

But not everybody will at once feel the force of this question. We must be more explicit. Let us take the now so familiar suggestion of our great humorist about the six people that take part in every conversation between two persons. If John and Thomas are talking together, then the real John and Thomas, their respective ideas of themselves, and their ideas of each other, are all parties to the conversation. Let us consider four of these persons, namely the real John, the real Thomas, John as Thomas conceives him, and Thomas as John conceives him. When John judges, of whom does he think? Plainly of that which can be an object to his thoughts, namely, of *his* Thomas. About whom then can he err? About *his* Thomas? No, for he knows him too well. His conception of Thomas is his conception, and what he asserts it to be, that it is for him. About the real Thomas? No, for it should seem, according to common sense, that he has nothing to do with the real Thomas in his thought, since that Thomas never becomes any part of his thought at all. "But," says one, "there must be some fallacy here, since we are sure that John *can* err about the real Thomas." Indeed he can, say we; but ours is not this fallacy. Common sense has made it. Common sense has said: "Thomas never is in John's thought, and yet John can blunder about Thomas." How shall we unravel the knot?

One way suggests itself. Mayhap we have been too narrow in our definition of *object*. Common sense surely insists that objects are outside of our thought. If, then, I have a judgment, and another being sees both my judgment and some outside object that was not in my thought, and sees how that thought is unlike the object in some critical respect, this being could say that my assertion was an error. So then with John and Thomas. *If Thomas could know John's thoughts about him*, then Thomas could possibly see John's error. That is what is meant by the error in John's thought.

But mere disagreement of a thought with any random object does not make the thought erroneous. The judgment must disagree with *its chosen* object. If John never has Thomas in thought at all, how *can* John choose the real Thomas as his object? If I judge about a penholder that is in this room, and if the next room is in all respects like this, save for a penholder in it, with which my assertion does not agree, who, looking at that penholder in that other room, can say that my judgment is false? For I meant not that penholder when I spoke, but this one. I knew perhaps nothing about that one, had it not in mind, and so could not err about it. Even so, suppose that outside of John there is a real Thomas, similar, as it happens, to John's ideal Thomas, but lacking some thought or affection that John attributes to his ideal Thomas. Does that make John's notion an error? No, for he spoke and could speak only of his ideal Thomas. The real Thomas was the other room, that he knew not of, the other side of the shield, that he never could conceive. His Thomas was his phantom Thomas. This phantom it is that he judges and thinks about, and his thoughts may have their own consistency or inconsistency. But with the real other person they have nothing to do. The real other is not his object, and how can he err about what is not object for him?

Absurd, indeed, some one will reply to us. John and Thomas have to deal with representative phantoms of each other, to be sure; but that only makes each more apt to err about the real other. And the test that they can err is a very simple one. Suppose a spectator, a third person, to whom John and Thomas were both somehow directly present, so that he as it were included both of them. Then John's judgment of his phantom Thomas would be by this spectator at once compared with the real Thomas, and even so would Thomas's judgment of John be treated. If now John's phantom Thomas agreed with the real Thomas, then John's ideas would be declared in so far truthful; otherwise they would be erroneous. And this explains what is meant by John's power to err about Thomas.

The explanation is fair enough for its own purpose, and we shall need it again before long. But just now we cannot be content with it. For what we want to know is not what the judgment of a third thinker would be in case these two were somehow not independent beings at all, but things in this third being's thought. For we have started out with the supposition of common sense that John and Thomas are not dreams or thoughts of some higher third being, but that they are independent beings by themselves. Our supposition may have to be given up hereafter, but for the present we want to hold fast to it. And so John's judgment, which we had supposed to be about the independently existing Thomas, has now turned out to be only a judgment about John's idea of Thomas. But judgments are false only in case they disagree with their intended objects. What, however, is the object of John's judgment when he thinks about Thomas? Not the real Thomas, who could not possibly be an object in another man's thoughts. John's real object being an ideal Thomas, he cannot, if sincere, and if fully conscious of what he means by Thomas, fail to agree in his statements with his own ideal. In short, on this our original supposition, John and Thomas are independent entities, each of which cannot possibly enter in real person into the thoughts of the other. Each may be somehow represented in the other's thoughts by a phantom, and only this phantom can be intended by the other when he judges about the first. For unless one talks nonsense, it should seem as if one could mean only what one has in mind.

Thus, like the characters in a certain Bab ballad, real John, real Thomas, the people in this simple tale, are total strangers to each other. You might as well ask a blind man to make true or false judgments about the real effects of certain combinations of colors, as to ask either John or Thomas, defined as common sense defines them, to make any judgments about each other. Common sense will assert that a blind man can learn and repeat verbally correct statements about color, or verbally false statements about color, but, according to the common-sense view, in no case can he err about color-ideas as such, which are never present to him. You will be quite ready to say that a dog can make mistakes about the odors of the numberless tracks on the highway. You will assure us, however, that you cannot make mistakes about them because these odors do not exist for you. According to the common-sense view, a mathematician can make blunders in demonstrating the properties of equations. A Bushman cannot, for he can have no ideas corresponding to equations. But how then can John or Thomas make errors about each other, when neither is more present to the other than is color to the blind man, the odor of the tracks on the highway to the dog's master, or the idea of an equation to a Bushman? Here common sense forsakes us, assuring us that there is such error, but refusing to define it.

The inconsistency involved in all this common-sense view, and the consequences of the inconsistency, will appear yet better with yet further illustration. A dream is false in so far as it contains the judgment that such and such things exist apart from us; but at least in so far as we merely assert in our dreams about the objects as we conceive them, we make true assertions. But is not our actual life of assertions about actual fellow-beings much like a dream to which there should happen to correspond some real scene or event in the world? Such correspondence would not make the dream really "true," nor yet false. It would be a coincidence, remarkable for an outside observer, but none the less would the dreamer be thinking in his dream not about external objects, but about the things in his dream. But is not our supposed Thomas so and only so in the thought of John as he would be if John chanced to dream of a Thomas that was, to an external spectator, like the real one? Is not then the phantom Thomas, John's only direct object, actually a thing in John's thought? Is then the independent Thomas an object for John in any sense?

Yet again. Let us suppose that two men are shut up, each in a closed room by himself, and for his whole life; and let us suppose that by a lantern contrivance each of them is able at times to produce on the wall of the other's room a series of pictures. But neither of them can ever know what pictures he produces in the other's room, and neither can know anything of the other's room, as such, but only of the pictures. Let the two remain forever in this relation. One of them, A, sees on his wall pictures, which resemble more or less what he has seen in his own room at other times. Yet he perceives these to be only pictures, and he supposes them to represent what goes on in another room, which he conceives as like his own. He is interested, he examines the phenomena, he predicts their future changes, he passes judgment upon them. He may, if you like to continue the hypothesis, find some way of affecting them, by himself acting in a way mysterious to himself so as to produce changes in B's actual room, which again affect the pictures that the real B produces in A's room. Thus A might hold what he would call communication with his phantom room. Even so, B lives with pictures before him that are produced from A's room. Now one more supposition, namely, that A and B have absolutely no other means of communication, that both are shut up altogether and always have been, that neither has any objects before him but his own thoughts and the changing pictures on the wall of his room. In this case what difference does it make whether or no the pictures in A's room are actually like the things that could be seen in B's room? Will that make A's judgments either true or false? Even if A, acting by means that he himself cannot understand, is able to control the pictures on his wall by some alteration that he unconsciously produces in B's room and its pictures, still A cannot be said to have any knowledge of the real B and his room at all. And, for the same reason, A cannot make mistakes about the real room of B, for he will never even think of that real room. He will, like a man in a dream, think and be able to think only of the pictures on his wall. And when he refers them to an outside cause, he does not mean by this cause the real B and his real room, for he has never dreamed of the real B, but only of the pictures and of his own interpretation of them. He can therefore make no false judgments about B's room, any more than a Bushman can make false judgments about the integral calculus.

If to our present world there does correspond a second world somewhere off in space, a world exactly like this, where just the same events at every instant do actually take place, still the judgments that we make about our world are not actually true or false with reference to that world, for we *mean* this world, not that one, when we judge. Why are not John's Thomas and the real Thomas related like this world and that second world in distant space? Why are not both like the relation of A's conceived phantom room and B's real room? Nothing of either real room is ever present to the other. Each prisoner can make true or false judgments if at all, then, only about the pictures on his wall; but neither has even the suggestion that could lead him to make a blunder about the other's real room, of which he has and can have not the faintest idea.

One reason why we fail to see at once this fact lies in the constant tendency to regard the matter from the point of view of a third person, instead of from the point of view that we still implicitly attribute to A and B themselves. If A could get outside of his room once and see B's room, then he could say: "My picture was a good one," or the reverse. But, in the supposed case, he not only never sees B's room, but he never sees anything but his own pictures, never gets out of his room at all for any purpose. Hence, his sole objects of assertion being his pictures, he is innocent of any power to err about B's room as it is in itself, even as the man born blind is innocent of any power to err about the relations of colors.

Now this relation of A and B, as they were supposed to dwell in their perpetual imprisonment, is essentially like the relation that we previously postulated between two independent subjects. If I cannot have you in my thought at all, but only a picture produced by you, I am in respect to you like A confined to the pictures produced from B's room. However much I may fancy that I am talking of you, I am really talking about my idea of you, which for me can have no relation whatever to the real you. And so John and Thomas remain shut up in their prisons. Each thinks of his phantom of the other. Only a third person, who included them both, who in fact treated them as, in the Faust-Epilogue, the *Pater Seraphicus* treats the *selige Knabe* (*Er nimmt sie in sich*, says the stage direction)—only such an inclusive thought could compare the phantoms with the real, and only in him, not in themselves, would John and Thomas have any ideas of each other at all, true of false.

This result is foreign to our every-day thought, because this every-day thought really makes innocent use of two contradictory views of the relations of conscious beings. On the one hand we regard them as utterly remote from one another, as what Professor Clifford called ejects; and then we speak of them as if the thoughts of one could as such become thoughts of the other, or even as if one of them could as an independent being still become object in the thought of the other. No wonder that, with such contradictory assumptions as to the nature of our relations to our neighbors, we find it very easy to make absurd statements about the meaning of error. The contradiction of common sense has in fact just here much to do with the ethical illusion that we called the illusion of selfishness. To clear up this point will be useful to us, therefore, in more ways than one.

VI

Disappointed once more in our efforts to understand how error is possible, we turn to another class of cases, which lie in a direction where, at least for this once, all will surely be plain. Errors about matters of fact or experience are certainly clear enough in nature. And as this class of errors is practically most important, the subtleties of our previous investigation may be dismissed with light heart so soon as we have gotten rid of the few little questions that will now beset us. It is to be noted that all errors about material objects, about the laws of nature, about history, and about the future, are alike errors about our actual or possible experiences. We expect or postulate an experience that at the given time, or under the given conditions, turns out to be other than it was postulated or expected to be. Now since our experiences not now present are objective facts, and capable of clear definition, it would seem clear that error concerning them is an easily comprehensible thing. But alas! again we are disappointed. That errors in matters of experience are common enough is indubitable, but equally evident becomes the difficulty of defining what they are and how they are possible. Take the case of error about an expected future. What do we mean by a future time? How do we identify a particular time? Both these questions plunge us into the sea of problems about the nature of time itself. When I say, *Thus and so will it be at such and such a future moment*, I postulate certain realities not now given to my consciousness. And singular realities they are. For they have now no existence at all. Yet I postulate that I can err about them. This their non-existence is a peculiar kind of non-existence, and requires me to make just such and such affirmations about it. If I fail to correspond to the true nature of this non-existent reality, I make an error; and it is postulated not merely that my present statement will in that case hereafter turn out false or become false, but also that it is now false, is at this moment an error, even though the reality with which it is to agree is centuries off in the future. But this is not all the difficulty. I postulate also that an error in prediction can be discovered when the time comes by the failure of the prediction to verify itself. I postulate then that I can look back and say: Thus and thus I predicted about this moment, and thus and thus it has come to pass, and this event contradicts that expectation. But can I in fact ever accomplish this comparison at all? And is the comparison very easily intelligible? For when the event comes to pass, the expectation no longer exists. The two thoughts, namely, expectation and actual experience, are separate thoughts, far apart in time. How can I bring them together to compare them, so as to see if they have the same object? It will not do to appeal to memory for the purpose; for the same question would recur about the memory in its relation to the original thought. How can a past thought, being past, be compared to a present thought to see whether they stand related? The past thought lived in itself, had its own ideas of what it then called future, and its own interpretation thereof. How can you show, or intelligently affirm, that the conception which the past expectation had of its future moment is so identical with the conception which this present thought has of this present moment, as to make these two conceived moments one and the same? Here in short we have supposed two different ideas, one of an expected future, the other of an experienced present, and we have supposed the two ideas to be widely separated in time, and by hypothesis they are not together in one consciousness at all. Now how can one say that in fact they relate to the same moment at all? How is it intelligible to say that they do? How, in fine, can a not-given future be a real object of any thought; and how, when it is once the object thereof, can any subsequent moment be identified with this object?

A present thought and a past thought are in fact separate, even as were John and Thomas. Each one means the object that it thinks. How can they have a common object? Are they not once for all different thoughts, each with its own intent? But in order to render intelligible the existence of error about matters of fact, we must make the unintelligible assumption, so it would seem, that these two different thoughts have the same intent, and are but one. And such is the difficulty that we find in our second great class of cases.

VII

So much for the problem, both in general and in some particular instances. But now may not the reader insist, after all, that there can be in this wise no errors whatever? Contradictory as it seems, have we not, after all, put our judgments into a position whence escape for us is impossible? If every judgment is thus by its nature bound up in a closed circle of thought, with no outlook, can any one come afterwards and give it an external object? Perhaps, then, there is a way out of our difficulty by frankly saying that our thoughts may be neither truths nor errors beyond themselves, but just occurrences, with a meaning wholly subjective.

We desire the reader to try to realize this view of total relativity once more in the form in which, with all its inherent absurdities, it now comes back to us for the last time. It says, "Every judgment, A is B, in fact does agree and can agree only with its own object, which is present in mind when it is made. With no external object can it agree or fail to agree. It stands alone, with its own object. It has neither truth nor error beyond itself. It fulfills all its intentions, and is true, if it agrees with what was present to it when it was thought. Only in this sense is there any truth or falsity possible for our thought."

But once more, this inviting way out of the difficulty needs only to be tried to reveal its own contradictions. The thought that says, "No judgment is true beyond itself," is that thought true beyond itself or not? If it is true beyond itself, then we have the possibility of other truth than the merely subjective or relative truth. If it is false, then equally we have objective falsity. If it is neither true nor false, then the doctrine of relativity has not been affirmed at all as a truth. One sets up an idea of a world of separate, disorganized thoughts, and then says, "Each of them deals only with its own object, and they have no unity that could make them true or false." But still this world that one thus sets up must be the true world. Else is there no meaning in the doctrine of relativity. Twist as one will, one gets not out of the whirlpool of thought. Error must be real, and yet, as common sense arranges these judgments and their relations to one another, error cannot be real. There is so far no escape.

The perfectly general character of the argument must be understood. One might escape it if it applied to any one class of errors only. Then one would say: "In fact, the class of cases in question may be cases that exclude the possibility of both truth and error." But no, that cannot be urged against us, for our argument applies equally to all possible errors. In short, either no error at all is possible, or else there must be possible an infinite mass of error. For the possibilities of thought being infinite, either all thought is excluded once for all from the possibility of error, or else to every possible truth there can be opposed an infinite mass of error. All this infinite mass is at stake upon the issue of our investigation. Total relativity, or else an infinite possibility of truth and error; that is the alternative before us. And total relativity of thought involves self-contradiction.

Every way but one has been tried to lead us out of our difficulty. Shall we now give up the whole matter, and say that error plainly exists, but baffles definition? This way may please most people, but the critical philosophy knows of no unanswerable problem affecting the work of thought in itself considered. Here we need only patience and reflection, and we are sure to be some day rewarded. And indeed our solution is not far off, but very nigh us. We have indicated it all along. To explain how one could be in error about his neighbor's thoughts, we suggested the case where John and Thomas should be present to a third thinker whose thought should include them both. We objected to this suggestion that thus the natural presupposition that John and Thomas are separate self-existent beings would be contradicted. But on this natural presupposition neither of these two subjects could become object to the other at all, and error would here be impossible. Suppose then that we drop the natural presupposition, and say that John and Thomas are both actually present to and included in a third and higher thought. To explain the possibility of error about matters of fact seemed hard, because of the natural postulate that time is a pure succession of separate moments, so that the future is now as future non-existent, and so that judgments about the future lack real objects, capable of identification. Let us then drop this natural postulate, and declare time once for all present in all its moments to an universal all-inclusive thought. And to sum up, let us overcome all our difficulties by declaring that all the many Beyonds, which single significant judgments seem vaguely and separately to postulate, are present as fully realized intended objects to the unity of an all-inclusive, absolutely clear, universal, and conscious thought, of which all judgments, true or false, are but fragments, the whole being at once Absolute Truth and Absolute Knowledge. Then all our puzzles will disappear at a stroke, and error will be possible, because any one finite thought, viewed in relation to its own intent, may or may not be seen by this higher thought as successful and adequate in this intent.

How this absolute thought is to be related to individual thoughts, we can in general very simply define. When one says: "This color now before me is red, and to say that it is blue would be to make a blunder," one represents an including consciousness. One includes in one's present thought three distinct elements, and has them present in the unity of a single moment of insight. These elements are, first, the perception of red; secondly, the reflective judgment whose object is this perception, and whose agreement with the object constitutes its own truth; and, thirdly, the erroneous reflection, *This is blue*, which is in the same thought compared with the perception and rejected as error. Now, viewed as separate acts of thought, apart from the unity of an including thought, these three elements would give rise to the same puzzles that we have been considering. It is their presence in a higher and inclusive thought that makes their relations plain. Even so we must conceive the relation of John's thought to the united total of thought that includes him and Thomas. Real John and his phantom Thomas, real Thomas and his phantom John, are all present as elements in the including consciousness, which completes the incomplete intention of both the individuals, constitutes their true relations, and gives the thought of each about the other whatever of truth or of error it possesses. In short, error becomes possible as one moment or element in a higher truth, that is, in a consciousness that makes the error a part of itself, while recognizing error.

So far then we propose this as a possible solution for our puzzles. But now we may insist upon it as the only possible solution. *Either there is no such thing as error, which statement is a flat self-contradiction, or else there is an infinite unity of conscious thought to which is present all possible truth.* For suppose that there is error. Then there must be an infinite mass of error possible. If error is possible at all, then as many errors are possible as you please, since, to every truth, an indefinite mass of error may be opposed. Nor is this mere possibility enough. An error is possible for us when we are able to make a false judgment. But in order that the judgment should be false when made, it must have been false before it was made. An error is possible only when the judgment in which the error is to be expressed always was false. Error, if possible, is then eternally actual. Each error so possible implies a judgment whose intended object is beyond itself, and is also the object of the corresponding true judgment. But two judgments cannot have the same object save as they are both present to one thought. For as separate thoughts they would have separate subjects, predicates, intentions, and objects, even as we have previously seen in detail. So that every error implies a thought that includes it and the corresponding truth in the unity of one thought with the object of both of them. Only as present to an including thought are they either true or false. Thus then we are driven to assume an infinite thought, judging truth and error. But that this infinite thought must also be a rational unity, not a mere aggregate of truths, is evident from the fact that error is possible not only as to objects, but as to the relations of objects, so that all the possible relations of all the objects in space, in time, or in the world of the barely possible, must also be present to the all-including thought. And to know all relations at once is to know them in absolute rational unity, as forming in their wholeness one single thought.

What, then, is an error? An error, we reply, is an incomplete thought, that to a higher thought, which includes it and its intended object, is known as having failed in the purpose that it more or less clearly had, and that is fully realized in this higher thought. And without such higher inclusive thought, an assertion has no external object, and is no error.

VIII

If our argument were a Platonic dialogue, there would be hereabouts an interruption from some impatient Thrasymachus or Callicles or Polus, who would have been watching us, threatening and muttering, during all of the latter part of our discussion. At last, perhaps, ... he would spring upon us, and would say: "Why, you nonsense-mongers, have you not bethought you of the alternative that represents the reality in this question of yours? Namely, an error is an error, neither to the thought that thinks it, nor of necessity to any higher inclusive thought, but only to a *possible* critical thought that should undertake afterwards to compare it with its object. An error is a thought such that *if* a critical thought *did* come and compare it with its object, it *would be* seen to be false. And it has an object for such a critical thought. This critical thought need not be real and actually include it, but may be only a *possible* judge of its truth. Hence your Infinite all-knower is no reality, only a logical possibility; and your insight amounts to this, that if all *were* known to an all-knower, he *would judge* error to be mistaken. And so error is what he would perceive to be error. What does all that amount to but worthless tautology?"

This argument of our Thrasymachus is the only outwardly plausible objection that we fear to the foregoing analysis, because it is the only objection that fully expresses the old-established view of common sense about such problems. Though common sense never formulates our present difficulty, common sense still dimly feels that to some possible (not actual) judge of truth, appeal is made when we say that a thing is false not merely for us, but in very truth. And this possible judge of common sense we have now unhesitatingly declared to be an Infinite Actuality, absolutely necessary to *constitute* the relation of truth and error. Without it there is for our view no truth or error conceivable. The words, *This is true,* or *This is false,* mean nothing, we declare, unless there is the inclusive thought for which the truth is true, the falsehood false. No barely possible judge, who *would* see the error *if* he were there, will do for us. He must be there, this judge, to constitute the error. Without him nothing but total subjectivity would be possible, and thought would then become purely a pathological phenomenon, an occurrence without truthfulness or falsity, an occurrence that would interest anybody if it could be observed; but that, unfortunately, being only a momentary phantom, could not be observed at all from without, but must be dimly felt from within. Our thought needs the Infinite Thought in order that it may get, through this Infinite judge, the privilege of being so much as even an error.

This, it will be said, is but reassertion. But how do we maintain this view against our Thrasymachus? Our answer is only a repetition of things that we have already had to say, in the argument for what we here reassert. If the judgment existed alone, without the inclusive thought to judge it, then, as it existed alone, it either had an object, or had none. But if it had none, it was no error. If it had one, then either it knew what its object actually was, or it did not know what its object was, or it partially knew and partially did not know what its object actually was. In the first case the judgment must have been an identical one, like the judgment *A pain is a pain*. Such a judgment knows its own object, therefore cannot fail to agree with it, and cannot be an error. If the judgment knew not its own object at all, then it had no meaning, and so could not have failed to agree with the object that it had not. If, however, this separate judgment knew its object enough to intend just that object, but not enough to insure agreement with it, all our difficulties return. The possible judge cannot give the judgment its complete object until he becomes its actual judge. Yet as fair judge he must then give it the object that it already had without him. Meanwhile, however, the judgment remains in the unintelligible attitude previously studied at length. It is somehow possessed of just the object it intends, but yet does not know in reality what it does intend, else it would avoid error. Its object, in so far as unknown to it, is no object for it; and yet only in so far as the object is thus unknown can it be erred about. What helps in all this the barely possible judge? The actual judge must be there; and for him the incomplete intention must be complete. He knows what is really this judgment's object, for he knows what is imperfectly meant in it. He knows the dream, and the interpretation thereof. He knows both the goal and the way thither. But all this is, to the separate judgment as such, a mystery.

In fact, the separate judgments, waiting for the possible judge to test them, are like a foolish man wandering in a wood, who is asked whether he has lost his way. "I may have lost it," he answers. "But whither are you going?" "That I cannot tell?" "Have you no goal?" "I may have, but I have no notion what it is." "What then do you mean by saying that you may have lost the way to this place that you are not seeking? For you seem to be seeking no place; how then can you have lost the way thither?" "I mean that some possible other man, who was wise enough to find whither I am trying to go, might possibly, in his wisdom, also perceive that I am not on the way to that place. So I may be going away from my chosen goal, although I am unaware what goal it is that I have chosen." Such a demented man as this would fairly represent the meaningless claim of the separate judgment, either to truthfulness, or to the chance of error.

In short, though the partial thought may be, as such, unconscious of its own aim, it can be so unconscious only in case it is contained in a total thought as one moment thereof.

It will be seen that wherever we have dealt in the previous argument with the possibility of error as a mere possibility, we have had to use the result of the previous chapter concerning the nature of possibility itself. The idea of the barely possible, in which there is no actuality, is an empty idea. If anything is possible, then, when we say so, we postulate something as actually existent in order to constitute this possibility. The conditions of possible error must be actual. Bare possibility is blank nothingness. If the nature of error necessarily and with perfect generality demands certain conditions, then these conditions are as eternal as the erroneousness of error itself is eternal. And thus the inclusive thought, which constitutes the error, must be postulated as existent.

So finally, let one try to affirm that the infinite content of the all-including mind does not exist, and that the foregoing idealism is a mere illusion of ours. He will find that he is involved in a circle from which there is no escape. For let him return to the position of total relativity and so say: "The infinite thought is unreal for me, and hence you are wrong." But then also he admits that we are right, for in affirming this infinite we affirm, according to this doctrine of total relativity itself, something that is just as true as it seems to us to be true. The opposing argument is thus at each moment of its progress involved in a contradiction. Or again, let him insist that our doctrine is not only relatively, but really false. Then however he will fail to show us what this real falsity is. In fact he says what all our previous examination shows to mean, this, namely, that an infinite thought does exist, and does experience the truth, and compares our thought with the truth, and then observes this thought of ours to be false, that is, it discovers that itself is non-existent. Whoever likes this result may hold it if he can.

IX

Now that our argument is completed as an investigation, let us review it in another way. We started from the fact of Error. That there is error is indubitable. What is, however, an error? The substance of our whole reasoning about the nature of error amounted to the result that in and of itself alone, no single judgment is or can be an error. Only as actually included in a higher thought, that gives to the first its complete object, and compares it therewith, is the first thought an error. It remains otherwise a mere mental fragment, a torso, a piece of drift-wood, neither true nor false, objectless, no complete act of thought at all. But the higher thought must include the opposed truth, to which the error is compared in that higher thought. The higher thought is the whole truth, of which the error is by itself an incomplete fragment.

Now, as we saw with this as a starting-point, there is no stopping-place short of an Infinite Thought. The possibilities of error are infinite. Infinite then must be the inclusive thought. Here is this stick, this brick-bat, this snow-flake: there is an infinite mass of error possible about any one of them, and notice, not merely possible is it, but actual. All the infinite series of blunders that you could make about them not only would be blunders, but in very truth now are blunders, though you personally could never commit them all. You cannot in fact *make* a truth or a falsehood by your thought. You only *find* one. From all eternity that truth was true, that falsehood false. Very well then, that infinite thought must somehow have had all that in it from the beginning. If a man doubts it, let him answer our previous difficulties. Let him show us how he can make an error save through the presence of an actual inclusive thought for which the error always was error and never became such at all. If he can do that, let him try. We should willingly accept the result if he could show it to us. But he cannot. We have rambled over those barren hills already too long. Save for Thought there is no truth, no error. Save for inclusive Thought, there is no truth, no error, in separate thoughts. Separate thoughts as such cannot then know or have the distinction between their own truth and their own falsity in themselves, and apart from the inclusive thought. There is then nothing of truth or of error to be found in the world of separate thoughts as such. All the thoughts are therefore in the last analysis actually true or false, only for the all-including Thought, the Infinite.

We could have reached the same result had we set out from the problem, *What is Truth?* We chose not to do so because our skepticism had the placid answer ready: "No matter *what* truth is, for very likely there is little or no truth at all to be had. Why trouble one's mind to define what a fairy or a brownie is?" "Very well, then," we said to our skepticism, "if that is thy play, we know a move that thou thinkest not of. We will not ask thee of truth, if thou thinkest there is none. We will ask thee of error, wherein thou revelest." And our skepticism very cheerfully, if somewhat incoherently, answers, that, "if there be little or no truth here below, there is at least any amount of error, which as skeptics we have all been detecting ever since we first went to school." "We thank thee for that word, oh friend, but now, what is an error?" Blessed be Socrates for that question. Upon that rock philosophy can, if it wants, build we know not yet how much.

It is enough for the moment to sum up the truth that we have found. It is this: "*All reality must be present to the Unity of the Infinite Thought.*" There is no chance of escape. For all reality is reality because true judgments can be made about it. And all reality, for the same reason, can be the object of false judgments. Therefore, since the false and the true judgments are all true or false as present to the infinite thought, along with their objects, no reality can escape. You and I and all of us, all good, all evil, all truth, all falsehood, all things actual and possible, exist as they exist, and are known for what they are, in and to the absolute thought; are therefore all judged as to their real character at this everlasting throne of judgment.

This we have found to be true, because we tried to doubt everything. We shall try to expound in the coming chapter the religious value of the conception. We can however at once see this in it: The Infinite Thought must, knowing all truth, include also a knowledge of all wills, and of their conflict. For him all this conflict, and all the other facts of the moral world, take place. He then must know the outcome of the conflict, that Moral Insight of our first book. In him then we have the Judge of our ideals, and the Judge of our conduct. He must know the exact value of the Good Will, which for him, like all other possible truth, must be an actually realized Fact. And so we cannot pause with a simply theoretical idealism. Our doctrine is practical too. We have found not only an infinite Seer of physical facts, but an infinite Seer of the Good as well as of the Evil. He knows what we have and what we lack. In looking for goodness we are in no wise looking for what the real world does not contain.

This, we say, we have found as a truth, because we tried to doubt everything. We have taken the wings of the morning, and we have fled; but behold, we are in the midst of the Spirit. Truly the words that some people have thought so fantastic ought henceforth to be put in the text-books as commonplaces of logical analysis:—

"They reckon ill that leave me out;
When me they fly, I am the wings,
I am the doubter and the doubt."—

Everything finite we can doubt, but not the Infinite. That eludes even our skepticism. The world-builders, and the theodicies that were to justify them, we could well doubt. The apologetic devices wearied us. All the ontologies of the realistic schools were just pictures, that we could accept or reject as we chose by means of postulates. We tried to escape them all. We forsook all those gods that were yet no gods; but here we have found something that abides, and waxes not old, something in which there is no variableness, neither shadow of turning. No power it is to be resisted, no plan-maker to be foiled by fallen angels, nothing finite, nothing striving, seeking, losing, altering, growing weary; the All-Enfolder it is, and we know its name. Not heart, nor Love, though these also are in it and of it; Thought it is, and all things are for Thought, and in it we live and move.

꩜

THE WORLD AND THE INDIVIDUAL (1899)

INDIVIDUALITY AND FREEDOM

I

No accusation is more frequent than that an Idealism which has once learned to view the world as a rational whole, present in its actuality to the unity of a single consciousness, has then no room either for finite individuality, or for freedom of ethical action. It was for the sake of preparing the way for a fair treatment of this very problem that we from the beginning defined the nature of ideas in terms at once of experience and of will. As we later passed to the assertion of the unity of the world from the final point of view, we have never lost sight of the fact that this is the unity of a divine Will, or, if you please, of a divine Act, at the same time as it is the unity of the divine Insight. The word "Meaning" has for us, from the outset, itself possessed a twofold implication,—not because we preferred ambiguity, but because, once for all, the facts of consciousness warrant, and in fact demand, this twofold interpretation. Whoever is possessed of any meaning, whoever faces truth, whoever rationally knows, has before his consciousness at once, that which *possesses the unity of a knowing process*, and that which *fulfils a purpose*, or in other words, that which constitutes what we have from the outset called an act of will as well as an act of knowledge. It is essential to our entire understanding of our Fourth Conception of Being, that we should remember the truth in both of these aspects, not dividing the aspects themselves, nor confounding their significance.

A few words of purely psychological analysis may then be, at this point, useful, to clarify the precise relations between intellectual and voluntary processes in our ordinary consciousness.

Popular psychology long since far too sharply sundered the Intellect and the Will in the empirical processes of the finite human mind. Viewing the intellect as a passive reception of the truth, defining the will as the power to alter facts, the popular psychology was forced, almost from the outset, to make an effort to reunite the powers that it had thus falsely separated. For a very little consideration shows not only that we can will to know, but also that we are in general guided, in our intellectual processes, by the very interests which popular psychology refers to the will. On the other hand, our voluntary processes, if they are conscious, are themselves matters of knowledge. For our conscious volition implies that we know what we will. In consequence of these obvious considerations, a more modern psychology has been led to its well-known doctrine that all such psychological divisions are rather distinctions between different aspects of the same process, than means for telling us of naturally sundered or even of separable processes. If we regard the human subject, in the ordinary psychological way, as a being whose conscious life runs parallel with the highest physical processes of his organism, we get a view of the relation between the intellect and the will which is far more just, at once to the natural history of the mind, and to the deeper meaning of the inner life of our consciousness. View man as a natural being, and you find him adjusting himself to his environment, acting, as they say, in response to stimuli. The world influences his senses, only to awaken him to such functions as express his interest in this world. Now the whole life of the organism is precisely the life of adjustment. The physical activities accompanying consciousness so take place that the organism preserves itself, and expresses its natural bearing toward its world. And the whole life of consciousness, accompanying these adjustments, constitutes a more or less accurate knowledge of what the adjustments are. The life of our consciousness is therefore a life of watching our deeds, of estimating our deeds, of predicting our deeds, and of interpreting our whole world in terms of deeds. We observe no outer facts without at the same time more or less clearly observing our attitude towards those facts, our estimate of their value, our response to their presence, our intentions with respect to our future relations with these facts.

But, within the circle of this general unity of our consciousness, various distinctions indeed arise. Sometimes the outer fact, viewed more or less in abstraction from its value to ourselves, more completely fills the field of our consciousness, and then we are likely to talk of a state of relatively pure Knowledge. If our state is one in which an idea explicitly appears as attempting to correspond to the presupposed object of its own External Meaning, or to its own Other, we call the process one of Thought about External Reality. Sometimes, however, our acts themselves, viewed as efforts to alter the outside facts, come more clearly before us either for deliberate estimate, or for impulsive decision; and in such cases we find the narrow view of our consciousness more clearly taken up by what we call Will. But facts are never known except with reference to some value that they possess for our present or intended activities. And on the other hand, our voluntary activities are never known to us except as referring to facts to which we attribute in one way or another an intellectually significant Being,—a reality other than what is present to us at the moment.

It follows that when, for general purposes, we study, not the psychology, but, as at present, the total significance of our conscious life, we are much less interested in the separation between knowledge and will than in that unity which psychology already recognizes, and which philosophy finds of still more organic importance. Consequently, when, at the outset of these discussions, we pointed out the element of will in the constitution of ideas, we were dwelling upon precisely what for the psychologist appears as the intimate connection between the knowing process of the mind and the motor responses of the organism to its environment. When we know, we have in the first place present to our minds certain contents, certain data, certain facts, it may be of the outer senses, it may be of the memory and the imagination. But if rational knowledge takes place, these data are not merely present, but they also take on forms; they constitute ideal structures; they fulfil our own purposes. These purposes consciously correspond either to what an ordinary observer would call our visible responses to our environment, or to what a psychologist, who looks closer than an ordinary observer, would find also to involve memories, or hints, or fragments, of former adjustments. The result is, so far, that, when we know, the facts both of sense and of imagination unite in our minds, into the expression of a Plan of Action. And thus the knowing process is a process partially embodying our own will. Upon such an analysis of the nature of ideas all the foregoing discussion has been founded; and now we deliberately repeat and emphasize this interpretation in order to make way for a final statement of the place of the will in our doctrine of being.

From this point of view, then, the contrast between knowledge and will, *within* our own conscious field, is so far this; viz., that we speak of our conscious process as a Knowing, in so far as all the data are woven into one unity of consciousness; while we speak of this same process as Will, in so far as this unity of consciousness involves a fulfilment or embodiment of a purpose. The word "Meaning" very properly lays stress upon both of these aspects at once. For what we call a Meaning is at once something observed with clearness as an unity of many facts, and something also intended as the result which fulfils a purpose. But when we take account of *External* Meanings, we speak of Thought in so far as we seek correspondence to our presupposed Other, and of Will in so far as we seek to produce the Other that shall correspond to the Internal Meaning. Yet here the distinction, as we have already seen, is wholly relative to the point of view.

But now it next becomes us to take special note of this latter aspect of the will,—an aspect upon which the popular consciousness lays great stress. For the will is usually regarded as primarily the Cause of something which but for the will would not come into existence. We have already spoken of *acts* of will; and the popular view declares that we are conscious of an activity which *causes states of consciousness to exist within ourselves, and acts to come into existence outside of ourselves,* and which is therefore responsible for the actual production of new Being in the universe. But if, with reference to the scientific value of this popular view, we turn to psychology for advice, we find at the present time, in that science, decidedly opposed interpretations of the sense in which the human will can be regarded as a cause. According to one of these interpretations the word "act" is properly to be applied merely to the physical process by which our organism gets adjusted to its environment. The causes of precisely such physical acts are, from this psychological point of view, themselves physical causes. Our consciousness, according to this same view, is not itself a cause, either of the physical act whereby we express our will, or of the states of mind themselves which constitute our inner intent. Our will merely accompanies our adjustment to the environment, and constitutes our own consciousness of the meaning of a certain portion of this adjustment. Our will is not itself one of the forces or powers of nature.

On the other hand, a traditional doctrine, which has won for itself no small hearing in psychology, regards the volitional, or active, side of our consciousness, not merely as a fact in itself, but as a cause of other facts, both physical and mental. From this point of view, the distinction between intellect and will acquires a fresh importance, and declines to be reduced to that mere distinction of aspects which we have emphasized in the foregoing account. For, as is often said, man, in so far as he is a mere knower, accomplishes nothing; he merely observes. But as doer, as voluntary agent, he is the source of new being; he is an originator. Will, for this view, is nothing if not efficacious. A process that merely accompanies and reflects, without affecting, the adjustments of my organism to its environment, would be no true will. A sort of consciousness which merely observes that from moment to moment my inner life, for me, seems to have meaning, would, as this view asserts, in the end deprive my life of its most important meaning. For above all, as they say, what I mean to be is an originator of facts, and of facts that but for me would not exist. The true problem regarding the place of the will in the universe arises, according to this view, precisely at the point where one asks, Is the will the cause of any existence other than itself?

The two views about the will as cause thus brought into opposition have justly played a great part, both in the psychological and the metaphysical controversies of all periods, ever since the meaning of life began seriously to be considered. And the relation of this whole controversy to the deepest interest of metaphysics is as unquestionable as it is easy to misinterpret. For the word "cause" is a term of very various meaning. So ambiguous and obscure, in fact, is the idea of cause as customarily used, that I have deliberately preferred to avoid even defining the issue about the causality of the will until our concept of Being had first assumed in general a definite form. Moreover, even at the present stage of our inquiry, although we must indeed deal with one aspect of the issue upon its own substantial merits, we shall do best to avoid, on the present occasion, any thorough-going discussion of the varieties of meaning of the word "cause." We shall do best merely to state the sense in which we ourselves regard the Being of facts as *due to the will*, be that will human or divine. We shall then postpone, until our second course of lectures, a more precise distinction of the various forms of causation, which we shall learn to recognize as present in nature and in mind. For the concept of cause, properly regarded, is rather a cosmological than a fundamentally metaphysical conception.

To metaphysics in general belongs, above all, the question that we have been considering,—the question what it is to be. To metaphysics also belongs the problem, What fundamentally different kinds of Being are there? And in this connection the relation between God and the individual is indeed of essential importance. From the metaphysician you may also expect the answer to the question, To what principles is the actual constitution of the world of conscious volition, and of ethically significant life, due? But it is within the realm of what we call Nature,—

namely, within the realm of finite experience, with its various phenomenal distinctions of organic and inorganic, of apparently living and apparently lifeless beings,—it is, I say, in case of Nature, that the diversified processes, present to our ordinary experience, arouse questions as to the special kinds of causal linkage that, in any particular case, bind one fact to another. It is in this world,—the phenomenal or natural, the essentially fragmentary world, the realm which cannot contain its whole truth within itself,—it is in this realm, I say, that the special problems concerning physical and mental causation, concerning active and inactive beings, concerning the relation of physical organism and mental phenomena, most properly arise. And we shall do well to keep separate the study of the whole constitution of the universe (conceived in accordance with the general principles of our theory of Being), from a study of the special problems of the phenomenal world. It is not my present purpose, then, to exhaust the theory of the sense in which will is, and is not, an active cause in the natural world. What can at present be asked from us is a general statement of the sense in which what exists expresses, on the one hand, the will of God; and, on the other hand, that individual will which you find at any moment present in a fragmentary way in your own finite consciousness. I shall maintain that both God's will and our own finite will get consciously expressed in the world, and that no contradiction results from this statement.

II

At any moment your ideas, in so far as they are rational, embody a purpose. That we have asserted from the outset. Our original example, that of the melody sung, for the sake of the mere delight in singing, remains for us typical of the entire life of what one may call consciously free and internally unrestricted finite ideas. Now what we in the first place have asserted in regard to such ideas, is that, precisely in so far as they are whole ideas, they stand before our consciousness as present fulfilments of purpose.

Any mere purpose, so far as it is still relatively fragmentary, or is, so to speak, disembodied, or is a mere striving, begins, in any such empirical case, the little drama that is acted within the momentary limits of a finite consciousness. In saying that this, as first disembodied purpose, becomes expressed, whenever any consciousness of such an act passes from its earlier to its later temporal stages,—I merely report what happens. I make as yet simply no assertion with regard to any psychological or physical causation. I assert as yet, in such a case, no effective force. I mention nothing of the nature of a physical or psychical tendency such that, by the mere necessity of its nature, it must work itself out. What my consciousness finds when I sing or speak is that a certain meaning actually gets expressed. My act of singing takes place. At once, then, there are data present, there are facts of consciousness, and there is this significance which these facts embody. Whether the facts could have come into existence in this way unless a given nervous organism or a given psychical entity, endowed with specific powers, subject to general laws, were already in existence, of all that my finite consciousness in the present moment tells me nothing. To assert any such thing is so far to assert a mere psychological or cosmological theory. The basis of such an assertion, if it has any basis, must be sought outside of any one moment's experience. On the other hand, in vain would any psychologist, in vain would any realistic metaphysician, attempt to rob my finite consciousness of the significance which this my own moment of singing or speaking has, for me, embodied. This significance is a matter of my experience. Whatever your system of metaphysics, the singer can say: Here at least the world has meaning, for lo! *I sing.*

Now, as a metaphysical theory, our idealistic doctrine with regard to Being in its wholeness has simply maintained that, without any regard to a doctrine of causation, without regard in the least to any specific view as to the psychology of mental process, *the whole universe, precisely in so far as it is, is the expression of a meaning, is the conscious fulfilment of significance in life,* precisely as the melody present at a given moment to the singer is for his consciousness the momentary expression of a meaning. And so our theory of Being is not founded upon any prior doctrine of causation. Cause and effect, laws mechanical or laws psychological, fate or freedom, in so far as any of these have Being, are from our point of view subject to the prior conditions of the very concept of Being itself. If nothing can be *except* what embodies a meaning, we are not first required to explain how anything whatever comes into Being, or how anything whatever is caused. For the cause of Being would itself have Being, and could itself exist, if our analysis is correct, only as the actual expression of a meaning.

The unhappy slavery of the metaphysics of the past to the conception of causation has been responsible for some of the most fatal of the misfortunes of religion and of humanity. That the existence of God was to be proved only by the means of the concept of causation, was one of the most characteristic of the presuppositions of an earlier theology, and was often supposed to be maintained on the basis of the authority of Aristotle. As a fact, this method of dealing with the theory of Being was false to the deepest spirit of Aristotle himself. For Aristotle's God is primarily the All-perfect Being, and is only secondarily the subject of which causation could be predicated in any form whatever. But however that may be, the theology which conceives the relation between God and the world, and between the world and the individual, as primarily a causal relation, subordinates the universal to the particular in theory, and the significant to the relatively insignificant in practical doctrine. The inevitable results of any such inversion of the rational order is a world where either fate reigns, or absolute mysteries are the final facts; or where both these unhappy results are combined. That just because the universe is through and through transparently significant, it may later prove to be worth while to regard my will as in this or that respect a cause of certain special results, is intelligible enough. But the genuine significance of my voluntary process is always an affair of my own consciousness regarding the present meaning of my life. You will in vain endeavor to deduce that meaning from the distinctly lower category of causal efficacy. That lower category of causation always implies a comment which somebody else, viewing my act in a relatively external way, may pass upon me from without.

It is indeed metaphysically just to assert that in certain aspects of my life I must needs be regarded as a cause, because I am already known to possess conscious significance, and because some aspects of this significance turn out to be causal. But you can never, on the other hand, discover wherein consists my significance by merely asserting that I am somehow or other a powerful cause. And precisely so it is in the case of God. You can indeed say that this or that fact in the world must be viewed as a result of laws whose source lies in the divine nature. But in asserting this you merely lay stress upon a result of that conscious significance which first of all attaches to the Being of all things, and to the life of God in its wholeness.

I cannot, then, too strenuously insist upon the thought that our own theory of Being places the very significance, both of the whole world and of the individual life, in the actual conscious fulfilment of meaning. Such fulfilment, from our own point of view, is the only reality. We therefore do not explain the existence of meaning in the world by looking, in the end, beyond any meaning for the cause which has brought the significant world to pass. To view the matter in that way would be of the very essence of Realism, and would involve all the contradictions which have already led us to reject the realistic interpretation of Being. Causation will find its place in our world, but as a mere result,—a partial aspect,—a mere item of the very significance of that world itself. For causal connections have a place only as expressing their own aspect of the meaning of things. On the other hand, the mere part, causation, will never appear in our account as the source of the whole; nor will this causation, which is but a very special form of Being, or a name for various special forms of Being, ever appear as that to which either the Being, or the wholeness of the meaning of the world, is due. And so much, then, for the mere causal efficacy, either of God or of man.

In consequence of these considerations, our primary question in regard to the finite human individual, in his relation to the divine life, is merely the question, In what sense does the finite Being retain, despite the unity of the whole divine life, any individual significance of his own, and what is the relation of this finite significance to the meaning and plan of the whole? But for the answer to this, our really important question, we may now be prepared, if we next lay new stress upon certain aspects of the Fourth Conception of Being, to which we have made repeated reference.

III

We have said that a meaning gets wholeness and individuality of expression precisely in so far as it gets, at the same time, conscious determination. An imperfect idea is vague. It is general. But it is so, in our own finite consciousness, in *two* senses. (1) Any finite idea, as we have seen, sends us to some other experience to furnish us yet further instances that are needed for its whole expression. This reference to another for the remainder of itself is characteristic of even the clearest and most precise of our finite ideas, just in so far as they are general. Thus, in counting, the single numbers refer us, further on in the number-series, for the rest of what the counting process implies. If one merely counts the first ten numbers, there are still other numbers to count. A complete consciousness of the whole meaning of the number-series would complete this process of seeking Another by presenting the whole individual meaning of the number concept in a finished form. We have, so far, altogether postponed the discussion of those difficulties about the quantitative Infinite which the conception of a completed knowledge of numbers seems to involve. We have asserted only that the arithmetical or mathematical Being of the number-series cannot be consistently expressed, either in realistic form or in the form of mere valid possibilities of experience. We have consequently asserted that even the realm of mathematical Being involves facts which only our Fourth Conception can adequately express. In what way the whole experience in question gets realized, we have pointed out only in the general fashion indicated in the foregoing lecture. The whole Being in question, as we have said, must be present to the final consciousness in its complete form, or in such wise that no other, beyond, remains to be sought. So much, then, for the first inadequacy of our finite general ideas.

(2) But our finite passing consciousness is incomplete or inadequate to its own purposes not merely by lack of contents adequate to express its wholeness, but by reason of vagueness with regard to its own momentarily conscious purposes. The principal source of actual error, in finite consciousness, we have already found to be the indetermination of our purposes at any stage in their realization. Now the presupposition of our whole view is that the final expression of purpose is not merely complete as to its contents, *but* absolutely determinate as to what meaning these contents fulfil. Now the finite process, whereby our own consciousness passes from an indeterminate to a relatively determinate state of purpose, of intention, of seeking for contents, is known to us in its psychological manifestations as a process of Selective Attention, growing more and more definite as it proceeds. Precisely in so far as we are conscious of a definite meaning at any instant, we are conscious of contents selected, as it were, from the background of our own finite consciousness, selected as the contents which are such that no other contents would definitely tend to express our will. Now it is the law of conscious growth in ourselves, that greater determination of purpose, and greater wealth of presented contents, are the correlative aspects of any gradual fulfilment of meaning. The more we know and the more richly we find our will fulfilled, the more exclusive and determinate becomes our purpose. The vague purpose is so far not at the instant clear as to whether *this or that* would better fulfil its meaning. The precise purpose selects this *instead* of that. Precise decision is exclusive as well as inclusive. And when I speak of this fact, I refer once more directly to our consciousness as my warrant. I presuppose nothing as to the causal basis, or as to the psycho-

logical or physical origin, of attention. I say that one who rationally finds a meaning fulfilled, discovers at once a wealth of contents, and a very sharply specific exclusiveness of interest fulfilled by these contents. A satisfied will, a fully expressed meaning, would involve, then, the twofold consciousness that we may express by the two phrases, (1) I have all that I seek, and need no other; (2) I need precisely these contents, and so select them as to permit no other to take here and for this purpose their place. As a matter of fact, then, a will satisfied, a precisely determinate meaning expressed in facts, is as selective and exclusive on the one hand, as, on the other hand, it is possessed of an exhaustive wealth of contents which meet its selection.

Now it is this selective character of every rational conscious process, a character as manifest to consciousness as it is ultimately significant for the constitution of all Being,—it is this character, I say, which to my mind is responsible above all for the Individuality which we have already characterized as belonging to the whole of Being, and which we shall now find as equally characteristic of every region of finite Being. Strange as it may at first seem, a closer examination of the nature of truth makes easily manifest that what is, quite apart from any causal theory, must be viewed by the consciousness that faces Being as a selection from abstractly possible contents. The nature of these contents in general is recognized, and is so far present, at the very moment when the realization of this nature in the single shape selected from amongst all possible shapes is, at the same time, experienced.

This general view, that what is, is a selection from possibilities, is in another form as characteristic of Realism, and even in a sense of Mysticism, as it is of our own view of Being.

The discovery that the affirmation of reality is logically based upon the exclusion of the barely possible, is constantly made by common sense, is constantly illustrated by daily experience, and is popularly exemplified by that well-known destruction of possibilities which characterizes the passing of youth, the course of history, the reproduction of every species through relatively chance union of the members of that species, and by countless other instances. The Darwinian theory of the genesis of species by natural selection, is only a single instance of the application of this general concept that the real is a selection from amongst possibilities.

In elementary logic, as we earlier showed, it becomes manifest that all universal judgments are at once, as they say, negatively existential, and involve a destruction of logically possible classes of objects. Thus, let there be what the logicians call an Universe of Discourse, that is, a world of possible beings of which you are discoursing. Into that world let two classes of objects, A and B, be introduced. Then in your universe of discourse it becomes logically possible that there should be four sub-classes of beings, namely, the things which are both A and B, the things which are A but not B, the things which are not A but which are B, and finally the things which are neither A nor B. Thus, for example, if your universe of discourse is to contain righteous men and happy men, there are possible the four sub-classes of men who are righteous and happy, who are righteous and unhappy, who are unrighteous but happy, and who are neither righteous nor happy. Now begin to make universal assertions about the relations amongst these classes. Assert that all the righteous are happy. At once, as we saw in our seventh lecture, this assertion appears as a negative existential assertion, and as the destruction of a possibility. For you can express it by saying that in your universe the sub-class, otherwise possible, of righteous men who are unhappy, has vanished from existence. Your universe has now reduced its realized possibilities to the existence of three sub-classes. The example is trivial. It is but one of a countless number. To know facts is to destroy mere possibilities. To know that there is even a single righteous man in your universe of discourse, is to destroy so far the abstractly possible alternative that that individual man is unrighteous. This result so far holds with absolute generality, and without regard to your special definition of the concept of Being. Accordingly every realist regards the real as the selection from the possible. And in this we too agree with him.

Spinoza, in his curious compromise between realistic and mystical motives, undertook indeed to deny this selective function of reality; and asserted that from the divine point of view all that is possible is real. In vain, however, would one attempt to carry out this doctrine, except by expressly substituting for all other conceptions of being the Third Conception, viz., that of the real as the valid. But even this conception itself is obliged to distinguish between the relatively determinate genuine possibilities of experience, and the absolutely unrestricted products of any passing fancy. For one who develops even his most general ideas so that they have any relative wholeness of meaning, some possibilities seem to be at once excluded. Thus we already saw that in the mathematician's realm numerous abstract possibilities are excluded whenever a specific theorem is demonstrated. Our rejection, however, of the Third Conception of Being as inadequate was due in the end to a recognition of the fact that, so long as you define mere universals, mere general natures of things, you define neither the Being of objects nor the truth of ideas.

But now, as a fact, our whole experience with the concept of Being has shown us that this exclusion of bare or abstract possibilities by the presence of determinate facts does *not* tend to impoverish, but rather to enrich, our consciousness of what is real; for it is by exclusion of vain possibilities that we become able at once to define a conscious purpose and to get it fulfilled in a precise way. The life in which anything whatever can consistently happen, and in which any purpose can be fulfilled in any way, has in so far no character as a life. So far the experience of such a life is the experience of nothing in particular,—of no meaning. It is indeed true that an object which we regard as possible in the sense that it is still lacking, but is needed for a specific purpose, is precisely the object which our finite experience seeks, longs to possess, regards as beyond itself, calls therefore the desired Other. The absence of such an object is indeed a lack, a relative defeat of the finite purpose. And from our own point of view, the Fourth Conception of Being does indeed involve the thesis that there are no valid possibilities which are to remain in the end, and for God, merely possible and unfulfilled in *this* sense, namely in the sense that while they are needed for a specific purpose, they are still regarded as absent or as non-existent. But, on the other hand, we have also found that what a given finite purpose desires includes its own specific definition, as this one purpose rather than another, as this specific way of selecting facts. Now the more determinate the consciousness of such a purpose becomes, the more does such consciousness involve a selection of some facts rather than others, or an exclusion from Being of what is now regarded as merely and vainly or abstractly possible.

If you ask what manner of partial Being, from the point of view of our Fourth Conception, such abstractly conceived but concretely excluded facts possess, I answer, precisely the fragmentary sort of Being which the consciousness of a specific purpose, that is the consciousness of a particular attentive selection, consciously assigns to them. They are known *as* the excluded facts. They are defined by consciousness only in relatively general terms. As mere kinds of experience, the facts which attention thus excludes are themselves part of the very consciousness which forbids them to have any richer and more concrete Being than this character of remaining mere aspects of the whole. In this sense, but in this only, are they facts whose nature is experienced. And once more, in saying this, I refer to consciousness and to nothing else as my warrant for the meaning that I intend to convey. When one attends, when one chooses, when one finds a meaning at once specific and fulfilled, one actually observes, as an aspect of one's experience, that which one defines as the exclusion of a generally conceived possibility. One's experience of the general nature of this possibility is itself a part of the contents of one's whole present consciousness. The realization of the whole present meaning is known by virtue of this very consciousness that one is excluding from complete expression facts whose general nature one still experiences.

Now what I assert is that our Fourth Conception of Being, in conceiving the real as the present fulfilment of meaning, experienced as such fulfilment from the absolute point of view, still expressly recognizes that every such fulfilment involves conscious selection and exclusion. The facts which fulfil the meaning are at once such that no other beyond is still needed to supply a lack, while, on the other hand, no other facts could take their place without precisely a failure to fulfil the purpose. And in this twofold sense is the world of the fulfilled meaning an individual world, a world whose place no other could take. A consciousness which faced a collection of mere possibilities, without selection, would face neither wholeness nor determination of life. The very perfection of experience involves then, as an element, the exclusion of another, whose general nature is indeed a part of the very experience in question. Just as formal logic and traditional Realism have already recognized that to be real involves the exclusion of bare possibilities, so our own conception also expressly recognizes that the life which is, in its wholeness, is exclusive as well as inclusive; and that in this sense, once more, the realm of Being has the character of the complete, but for this very reason of the determinate, Individual. So much then for Exclusion and Selection as aspects of will both in God and in man. We next pass on toward more special comparisons between Absolute and Finite Individuality. For Individuality, as we now begin to see, is, in one aspect, the expression of Selective Interest. Yet for a moment we must still treat of Individuality in general.

IV

The concept of the logical Individual, viewed apart from the question as to the distinctions of the various grades of individuality, finite or infinite, is a problem that frequently has received far too indefinite a treatment in logical discussions. What shall the word "individual" in general mean? As we have often already indicated, the technical answer to this question runs: By an individual being, whatever one's metaphysical doctrine, one means an unique being, that is, a being which is alone of its own type, or is such that no other of its class exists. Now, as we saw in an earlier lecture, our human knowledge begins with immediate data, and with vague ideas. But mere colors and sounds, as such, may indeed indicate individual beings; but they are not yet known as individuals; while our early ideas, in their twofold vagueness, both as ideas needing further determination in order to define their purpose, and as ideas needing further embodiment to complete their expression, are far from being consciously adequate ideas of individual entities. A very little examination of our popular conceptions shows how very general all such conceptions are. A very little study of concrete science reveals how hard it is for any man to get a clear idea of what his science regards as the constitution of any of its individual objects. It is far easier to know something about the circulation of the blood, than to have any adequate knowledge of the medical aspects of the case of an individual man whose circulation is in any way deranged by disease. It is precisely the individual case that constitutes the goal of the physician's knowledge. In general a real knowledge of individual facts is the ideal aim of science, rather than the beginning of any form of human insight; and this one can observe to be true, quite apart from any metaphysical conception of what constitutes individuality.

Yet it is indeed perfectly true that, long before we have any scientific approach to a knowledge of the individual facts of the natural world, we all of us somehow believe that the world contains individual beings. And the historical prominence of the thesis that whatever is, is individual, the prominence, I say, of this thesis in the metaphysics of all ages, is due to deep reasons which seldom come to the clear consciousness of those who are accustomed to talk glibly about individuality. Only our Fourth Conception of Being is able to make the conception at once rational and explicit. It is, so we have asserted, precisely as the final and satisfactory expression of the whole will of an idea that any object can be regarded as unique. But what makes the presupposition that objects are individual precisely in so far as they are real appear so early in human thought, and exercise such a controlling influence over the development of science, is precisely that demand of the finite idea for wholeness of expression, which we have just analyzed in both of its contrasted aspects. Long before we can ever say, with even a shadow of plausibility, that we ourselves have known and experienced the unique presence of any single fact, as such, our restless finite will itself has demanded that the real world wherein our will seeks, and logically speaking, ultimately finds, its fulfilment, shall be altogether determinate, both in so far as nothing further is needed to complete it, and in so far as nothing else would meet the needs which constitute finite ideas.

But owing to our finitude, will, in our own case, far anticipates its own fulfilment. The individual, therefore, as a conceived object of inquiry, of desire, and of knowledge, appears in our finite human thought as something that we early define much more in terms of selective exclusion than of empirically observed completeness. We presuppose the individual in both the foregoing senses; viz., as selected and as complete. But, if you look closely at that region of our consciousness where first we come nearest to facing what we take to be an experience of individuality, you find, I think, that it is our selective attention, especially as embodied in what one may call our exclusive affections, which first brings home to us what we mortals require an individual being to be. How in fact should a finite being, whose experience constantly passes from one partial fulfilment to another, from one vague general idea to another instance of the same generality,—how should such a being, I say, come to be so sure as most of us are that he has actually stood in the presence of individuals, and has faced beings that are unique? Yet every man supposes, to take perfectly ordinary instances, that his own father and mother are real individuals, and that other men, too, even where their individuality has been far less closely scrutinized, are still in themselves somehow individuals. Every man also early believes that the world as a whole, whether he regards it as one or as many, is at all events an individual collection of individuals. Yet to make this assertion is in any case far to transcend any man's actual experience, regarded merely as that experience comes to us. For what we find in our finite wanderings are always cases of types, instances of imperfectly fulfilled meanings. In observing my father, what I each time experience must necessarily be merely the presence to my mind of a certain kind of experience. That the object of this experience is unique, that in all the universe there is no other like it, how should I myself ever experience this fact? That this theorem about individuality is itself true, is precisely what our Fourth Conception of Being has now asserted. For whatever the relation between the finite idea and the whole world may be, this we already know from our Fourth Conception, namely that the world in its unity is an individual whole, such that no other could take its place as an expression of this one purpose.

Our idea of individuality comes to our finite consciousness, therefore, rather on the selective side of this consciousness than upon the side of its present fulfilment. It is not so much what I already know about an individual as what my affections determine to regard as unique in the value of my object, that first brings home to me, in the case of my father or my mother or my home or my personal possessions, or my own life, and later only in the case of indifferent beings, the uniqueness of the object in question. Affection first says in presence of an object, imperfectly presented in experience, not only that there shall be further experience completing and fulfilling this meaning, but also that there shall be in this further experience such unity as constitutes an unique object. Affection first declares that there shall be no other object capable of fulfilling this meaning, beyond the single object whose Being I now presuppose. It is thus, for instance, that the lover says, There shall be none like my beloved. It is thus, too, that the mother says, There shall be no child like my child. It is thus that the loyal friend says, There shall be no friend like my friend. It is thus that the finite Self says, No life shall have precisely the meaning that my life has. It is thus also that the ethical consciousness says, My duty shall be that which nobody but myself can conceivably do. In brief, in our finite life, the sense of the determinate selection of the single object that we shall regard as the fulfilment of our meaning, comes earlier to our consciousness than any specific hope that, in our finite capacity, we shall ever live to see this specific meaning wholly fulfilled.

Now this disposition of our finite will, this tendency to a selection of our objects as unique, is precisely the character which our Fourth Conception regards as also belonging to that Absolute Will which faces the final meaning and fulfilment of the world. For the world as a whole is, from our point of view, an individual fact, not merely by virtue of the completeness of the contents of the Absolute Experience, but by reason of the definiteness of the selection of that object which shall be permitted to fulfil the final meaning. No significant purpose, no element of meaning that finite ideas demand as necessary for their own fulfilment, could indeed be, according to our thesis, wholly ignored from the absolute point of view. But, on the other hand, the very perfection of the fulfilment would logically require of the divine will the sort of determination of purpose of which we too are conscious when we deal with the objects of the exclusive affection. It is will, then, in God and in man, that logically determines the consciousness of individuality. The individual is, primarily, the object and expression of an exclusive interest, of a determinate selection.

From this point of view, the world in its wholeness might indeed be regarded as, so to speak, an only begotten son of the central purpose,—an unique expression,—unique not merely by reason of its wealth, but of its exclusiveness. And thus the category of individuality would be fulfilled in the whole precisely in the sense in which our finite affection presupposes its fulfilment in individual cases.

V

We have thus gradually prepared ourselves to define the relation between the Finite and the Absolute Will. We have studied as aspects of will, both selective attention and the nature of individuality. We have indicated, too, the sense in which, for our Fourth Conception, the world is the fulfilment of purpose. And now, to sum up so far, we do not say that any purpose, divine or human, first existing as a merely separate power, thereupon *causes* its own fulfilment. On the contrary, we say as to God, that from the absolute point of view, the genuine knowledge of the absolute purpose, as an empirical fact, is its own fulfilment. For, according to our central thesis, except as consciously fulfilling a purpose, nothing can, logically speaking, exist at all. In the second place we have also maintained that the fulfilment of the divine purpose is twofold, involving at once wealth of experience conforming to the one meaning, and selection both of the facts which express the meaning, and of the precise and individual determination of the meaning itself. The world that thus expresses meaning appears, from the absolute point of view, as an unique whole, but as also an unique selected whole, such that neither for the whole nor for any of the parts could any other fact be substituted, without failure in the realization of precisely this totality of determinate meaning. And consequently, quite apart from any causal theory, that selective aspect which common sense already regards as essential to the will does indeed appear in our account as a real and logically required character of the divine or absolute will. In the third place, however, we find a similarly selective character belonging to our own will, and an experience of such selection we find in that sort of exclusive interest whereby, even in advance of knowledge, we undertake to define the individuality which we presuppose in all the objects of our more exclusive affection.

If you ask, from this point of view, in what sense the world is to be called rather the expression of the Divine Will, and in what sense it is rather the expression of the Divine Knowledge, I reply that while we have by no means separated these two aspects of the universe, we can now easily see the convenience from many points of view of distinguishing them. The Divine or Absolute Knowledge this world expresses, by virtue of the unity of consciousness in which all its facts are linked, and by virtue too of that universality of meaning which joins all various ideas, in such wise that every finite idea, in so far as it merely refers to another, or has external reference, is general, while the whole expression of these ideas is unique and individual. In this same sense we can also speak of the world, quite accurately, as the expression, or embodiment, or fulfil-ment, of the Divine Thought. Will, on the other hand, this world ex-presses, not as if the Divine Will were an external power causing the world, but in so far as the unity of the whole is teleological, is such as ideas intend; or again, in so far as the world attains wholeness, and needs no fact beyond it for its completion; and finally, in so far as this whole-ness and uniqueness of the world is the expression of an ideal selection, whose nature is well exemplified by our own exclusive interests, and whose type of fulfilment we all observe whenever we win a rational ideal goal.

Now all these considerations might seem once more to deprive any finite portion, or aspect, of this conscious universe, of any distinguishable private significance. On the contrary, however, precisely the opposite is the true result. For consider. If the whole world is at once the complete expression of a plan, and also the unique expression of such plan, then every fact in it, precisely in so far as we *distinguish* that fact from other facts, and consider its internal meaning, is also inevitably unique, sharing in so far the uniqueness of the whole. For, to illustrate, if in the ordinary empirical world of space, this room is unique, so that by hypothesis there shall be no other room like it in the world, then any definable part of the unique room, by virtue of the very fact that it is different from all the other parts of this same room, has its own unique individuality as opposed to any other fact in the universe.

Or again, let A be any fact. First suppose A to be merely an abstract universal, a general type. Then suppose A to be an individual. If A is as a whole merely a case of a type, so that there are other cases like it, then any part of A is in so far also only a case of a type, and is not unique. But if A is an individual, unique and elsewhere unexampled, then every fragment of A has its part in the individuality of the whole, just as a play of Shakespeare, as this particular expression of the individuality of the poet, has its own uniqueness by sharing in his.

Now, by hypothesis, the world exists only as *such* an expression of the meaning of the divine system of ideas, that no other life than this of the present world could express precisely this system. But suppose that you lay stress upon the facts of any finite life. You have a right to do so, for these facts exist for the Absolute precisely as much as for you. Then you have, in the first place, facts that exist only as an expression of a meaning. If you ask of what meaning they are the expression, the answer is, of the meaning of the very ideas and of the very will, that, in the finite consciousness, accompany these very facts.

Take, for instance, one of your own acts. In part, it expresses one of your own purposes. Now our theory does indeed unite both your act and the idea that your act expresses, along with all other acts and ideas, in the single unity of the absolute consciousness. But this single unity of the absolute consciousness, as we already saw at the last time, is nothing that merely absorbs your individuality, in such wise that you vanish from amongst the facts of the world. You remain from the absolute point of view precisely what you now know yourself to be, namely, the possessor of just this ideal purpose, whose internal meaning is embodied in just so much of conscious life as is yours. Our very theory insists that your internal meanings, your ideas viewed as internally significant, your selections and expressions, are typical instances of facts, and of precisely the facts of whose unity the world consists. Now if the whole world is, as whole, the unique expression of the divine purpose, it follows that every finite purpose, precisely in so far as it is, is a partial expression and attainment of the divine will; and also that every finite fulfilment of purpose, precisely as we finite beings find it, is a partial fulfilment of the divine meaning. For from our point of view, while all finite ideas, in so far as concerns their external meaning, are indeed general, still no fact exists *merely* as a case of a type, or merely as an instance of an universal. The very simplest view of any finite fact already makes it a positive part of the unique divine experience, and therefore, as this part, itself unique. A still deeper view recognizes any finite will, say your own present will, as a stage or case of the expression of the divine purpose at a given point of time; but this expression, too, is once more unique. And this expression is also in one aspect no other than what you find it to be, to wit, your own conscious will and meaning.

Thus the individuality of the whole in such wise dwells in the parts, the individuality of the unique divine purpose is in such wise present in each finite purpose, that no finite purpose, viewed merely as an internal meaning, could have its place taken by another without a genuine alteration of the whole; while, on the other hand, it is equally true that the whole would not be what it is were not precisely this finite purpose left in its own uniqueness to speak precisely its own word—a word which no other purpose can speak in the language of the divine will. In brief, then, our view leaves all the unique meaning of your finite individual life just as rich as you find it to be. You are in God; but you are not lost in God. If every finite pulsation of life, despite its aspect of mere generality, its external meaning, has something unique about it, and if this unique aspect of the finite life expresses an internal meaning, then the meaning of every such fact itself is unique. Or to apply the matter once more to yourself: if every instance of your life expresses a will that is to be found expressed in precisely this way nowhere else in all the world, and if this will is the will of which you are now conscious, then we can say that the verdict of your own consciousness when it regards your life as the expression of your individual will is in no wise refuted, but is only confirmed by our Fourth Conception of Being.

Thus it is then that we deal, in case of the finite will and the divine will, with the problem of the One and the Many. A realistic union of the many different beings in one being we long since found to be impossible. For our present point of view, however, the realistic difficulty of the Many and the One has been wholly set aside. It is not indeed for us a question of how many *things* could become one *thing*. For us the unity of the world is the unity of consciousness. The variety of the world is the internal, but none the less wealthy and genuine, variety of the purposes and embodiments of purpose present within this unity of the one divine consciousness. Now with regard to the ultimate unity and consequent harmony of all this variety, our Fourth Conception has given us indeed a general formula. The Many must, despite their variety, win harmony and perfection by their cooperation. But this principle, so far, gives us no limit either to the empirical variety of will, or of interest and of experience in the absolute, nor any limit to the relative independence which the uniqueness of the individual elements makes possible. What we see, however, is that every distinguishable portion of the divine life, in addition to all the universal ties which link it to the whole, expresses its own meaning. We see, too, that this meaning is unique, and that this meaning is precisely identical with what each one of us means by his own individual will, so far as that will is at any time determinate, uniquely selected, and empirically expressed. So much then for the general relations of Absolute and of Finite will.

VI

Two expressions, familiar to common sense in speaking of finite will, receive herewith their sufficient and, I believe, their only possible justification. Common sense first asserts that, when my will gets expressed, I individually am *active*. Common sense also, in the second place, asserts that when my will gets inwardly expressed in my choice, I individually am *free*. Now into the endless discussions as to the causal relations of this or that aspect of the human will we have declined in this discussion to go. We have declined, because we have said that all causation, whatever it is, is but a special instance of Being, and never can explain any of the ultimate problems about Being. But when we have asserted, as we have now done, that every moment of every finite consciousness has some unique character, and when we have asserted, as we have also done, that in our rational life our momentary will and its finite expression belong to this very unique aspect of our finite life, we have indeed found, in our finite will, an aspect which *no* causation could ever by any possibility explain. For whatever else causation may be, it implies the explanation of facts by their general character, and by their connections with other facts. Whatever is unique, is as such not causally explicable. The individual as such is never the mere result of law. In consequence, the causal explanation of an object never defines its individual and unique characters as such, but always its general characters. Consequently, *if* the will and the expression of that will in any moment of our finite life possess characters, namely, precisely these individual and uniquely significant characters which no causal explanation can predetermine, then such acts of will, as significant expressions of purpose in our life, constitute precisely what ethical common sense has always meant by free acts. If your finite purpose is now different from that of any other finite being, and if your

finite purpose now in any sense uniquely expresses, however inadequately, its own determinate meaning, in its own way, then, you can indeed
assert: I alone, amongst all the different beings of the universe, will this
act. That it is true that God here also wills in me, is indeed the unquestionable result of the unity of the divine consciousness. But it is equally
true that this divine unity is here and now realized by me, and by me
only, through my unique act. My act, too, is a part of the divine life
that, however fragmentary, is not elsewhere repeated in the divine consciousness. When I thus consciously and uniquely will, it is I then who
just here *am* God's will, or who just here consciously act for the whole.
I then am so far free.

The other popular conception, in addition to the conception of freedom, which belongs in this connection, is that very conception of Activity which I have just employed. By the term "activity" I regard our ethical common sense as meaning precisely the very fact that our present
will, as the will of an individual, is unique. By our activity, then, I mean
just the unique significance of the present expression of our will. If a
general law,—a merely universal type,—if our characters or tempera-
ments, or some other such universal nature of things, are expressed in
our present experience, then, in so far, we are indeed mere cases of
types. In so far we do not act. But if this my present expression of my
meaning is in such wise unique that, but for this meaning, this expression
would have no place in the whole realm of Being, then indeed I may call
my present expression of meaning my act. As my act this my present will
is as unique as is the whole divine life, as free as is the whole meaning of
which the whole world is an expression. *Not* by virtue then of any supposed causal efficacy is the divine will as a power the producer of the
world. And just so, not by virtue of its potency as a physical agent is our
human action a free cause.

To our later series of lectures must be altogether left the discussion of
any sort of causation in its real, but in its extremely subordinate, place in
the constitution of reality. But what we at present say to the finite being
is: You are at once an expression of the divine will, and by virtue of that
very fact the expression here and now, in your life, of your *own* will,
precisely in so far as you find yourself acting with a definite intent, and
gaining through your act a definite empirical expression. We do not say,
Your individuality causes your act. We do not say, Your free will creates your life. For Being is everywhere deeper than causation. What you
are is deeper than your mere power as a physical agent. Nothing what-

ever besides yourself determines either causally or otherwise just what constitutes your individuality, for you are just this unique and elsewhere unexampled expression of the divine meaning. And here and now your individuality in your act *is* your freedom. This your freedom is your unique possession. Nowhere else in the universe is there what here expresses itself in your conscious being. And this is true of you, not in spite of the unity of the divine consciousness, but just because of the very uniqueness of the whole divine life. For all is divine, all expresses meaning. All meaning is uniquely expressed. Nothing is vainly repeated; you too, then, as individual are unique. And (here is the central fact) just in so far as you consciously will and choose, you then and there in so far know what this unique meaning of yours is. Therefore are you in action Free and Individual, just because the unity of the divine life, when taken together with the uniqueness of this life, implies in every finite being just such essential originality of meaning as that of which you are conscious. Arise then, freeman, stand forth in thy world. It is God's world. It is also thine.

THE WORLD AND THE INDIVIDUAL (1901)

THE TEMPORAL AND THE ETERNAL

I

Time is known to us, both perceptually, as the psychologists would say, and conceptually. That is, we have a relatively direct experience of time at any moment, and we acknowledge the truth of a relatively indirect conception that we possess of the temporal order of the world. But our conception of time far outstrips in its development and in its organization anything that we are able directly to find in the time that is known to our perceptions. Much of the difficulty that appears in our metaphysical views about time is, however, due to lack of naïveté and directness in viewing the temporal aspects of reality. We first emphasize highly artificial aspects of our conception of time. Then we wonder how these various aspects can be brought into relation with the rest of the real world. Our efforts to solve our problem lead very easily to contradictions. We fail to observe how, in case of our more direct experience of time and of its meaning, various elements are woven into a certain wholeness,—the very elements which, when our artificial conception of time has sundered them, we are prone to view as irreconcilable with one another and with reality.

Our more direct perceptions of time form a complex sort of consciousness, wherein it is not difficult to distinguish several aspects. For the first, some Change is always occurring in our experience. This change may belong to the facts of any sense, or to our emotions, or to our ideas; but for us to be conscious is to be aware of change. Now this changing character of our experience is never the whole story of any of our clearer and more definite kinds of consciousness. The next aspect of the matter lies in the fact that our consciousness of change, wherever it is definite and wherever it accompanies definite successive acts of attention, goes along with the consciousness that for us something comes first, and something next, or that there is what we call a Succession of events.

Of such successions, melodies, rhythms, and series of words or of other simple acts form familiar and typical examples. An elementary consciousness of change without such definite successions we can indeed have; but where we observe clearly what a particular change is, it is a change wherein one fact succeeds another.

A succession, as thus more directly experienced by us, involves a certain well-known relation amongst the events that make up the succession. Together these events form a temporal sequence or order. Each one of them is over and past when the next one comes. And this order of the experienced time-series has a determinate direction. The succession passes *from* each event *to* its successor, and not in the reverse direction; so that herein the observed time relations notoriously differ from what we view as space relations. For if in space *b* is next to *a*, we can read the relation equally well as a coexistence of *a* with *b*, and as a coexistence of *b* with *a*. But in case *b* succeeds *a*, as one word succeeds another in a spoken sentence, then the relation is experienced as a passing from *a* to *b*, or as a passing over of *a* into *b*, in such wise that *a* is past, as an event, before *b* comes. This direction of the stream of time forms one of its most notable empirical characters. It is obviously related to that direction of the acts of the will whose logical aspect interested us in connection with the consideration of our discriminating consciousness.

But side by side with this aspect of the temporal order, as we experience this order, stands still another aspect, whose relation to the former has been persistently pointed out by many psychological writers, and as persistently ignored by many of the metaphysical interpreters of the temporal aspect of the universe. When we more directly experience succession,—as, for instance, when we listen to a musical phrase or to a rhythmic series of drum-beats,—we not only observe that any antecedent member of the series is over and past before the next number comes, but also, and without the least contradiction between these two aspects of our total experience, we observe that this whole succession, with both its former and later members, so far as with relative directness we apprehend the series of drum-beats or of other simple events, is present *at once* to our consciousness, in precisely the sense in which the unity of our knowing mental life always finds present at once many facts. It is, as I must insist, true that for my consciousness *b* is experienced as following *a*, and also that both *a* and *b* are *together* experienced as in this relation of sequence. To say this is no more contradictory than to say that while I experience two parts of a surface as, by virtue of their spatial position, mutually exclusive each of the other, I also may experience the fact that both these mutually exclusive parts go together to form one whole surface. The sense in which they form one surface is, of course, not the sense in which, as parts, they exclude each other, and form different surfaces. Well, just so, the sense in which *b*, as successor of *a*, is such, in the series of events in question, that *a* is over and gone when *b* comes, is not the sense in which *a* and *b* are together elements in the whole experienced succession. But that, in *both* of these senses, the relation of *b* to its predecessor *a* is an experienced fact, is a truth that any one can observe for himself.

If I utter a line of verse, such as

"The curfew tolls the knell of parting day,"

the sound of the word *day* succeeds the sound of the word *parting*, and I unquestionably experience the fact that, for me, every earlier word of the line is over and past before the succeeding word or the last word, *day*, comes to be uttered or to be heard. Yet this is unquestionably not my whole consciousness about the succession. For I am certainly *also* aware that the *whole* line of poetry, as a succession of uttered sounds (or, at all events, a considerable portion of the line), is present to me at once, and as this one succession, when I speak the line. For only by virtue of experiencing this wholeness do I observe the rhythm, the music, and the meaning of the line. The sense in which the word *parting* is over before the word *day* comes, is like the sense in which one object in space is *where* any other object is *not*, so that the spatial *presence* of one object excludes the presence of another at that same part of space. Precisely so the presence of the word *day* excludes the presence of the word *parting* from its own place in the temporal succession. And, in our experience of succession, each element is *present* in a particular point of the series, in so far as, with reference to that point, other events of the series are either *past*, that is, over and done with, or are *future*, that is, are later in the series, or are *not yet when* this one point of the series is in *this* sense present. Every word of the uttered line of poetry, viewed in its reference to the other words, or to previous and later experiences, is *present* in its own place in the series, is *over and done with* before later events can come, or when they are present, and is *not yet* when the former events of the succession are present. And that all this is true, certainly is a matter of our experience of succession.

But the sense in which, nevertheless, the whole series of the uttered words of the line, or of some considerable portion of the line, is presented to our consciousness *at once*, is precisely the sense in which we apprehend this line as one line, and this succession as one succession. The whole series of words has for us its rhythmic unity, and forms an instance of conscious experience, whose unity we overlook at one glance. And unless we could thus overlook a succession and view at once its serially related and mutually exclusive events, we should never know anything whatever about the existence of succession, and should have no problem about time upon our hands.

This extremely simple and familiar character of our consciousness of succession,—this essentially double aspect of every experience of a present series of events,—this inevitably twofold sense in which the term *present* can be used in regard to our perception of temporal happenings, —this is a matter of the most fundamental importance for our whole conception of Time, and, as I may at once add, for our conception of Eternity. Yet this is also a matter very frequently obscured, in discussion, by various devices often used to express the nature of the facts here in question. Sometimes, for the sake of a laudable attempt to define the term *present* in a wholly unambiguous way, those who are giving an account of our experience of time are led to assert that, since every part or element of any series of temporal events can be *present* only when all the other elements of the series are temporally non-existent, *i.e.* are either past or future, it must therefore be quite impossible for us to be conscious, *at once*, of a present succession involving a series of such elements. For how, they say, can I be conscious of the presence of all the successive words of the verse of poetry, when only one word is actually and temporally present at any one time? To comprehend how I can become in any sense aware of the series of successive words that constitutes the line of verse, such students of our problem are accustomed to say that when any one word as *passing*, or *day*, is present to my mind, the other words, even of the same line, can be present to consciousness *only* as coexistent memories or images of the former words, or as images of the expected coming words. From this point of view, I never really observe any sequence of conscious events as a sequence at all. I merely apprehend each element by itself; and I directly conclude from the images which in my experience are coexistent with this element, that there have been antecedent, and will be subsequent events in the series.

This interpretation of our consciousness of time is, however, directly counter to our time-experience, as any one may observe it for himself. For we do experience succession, and *at once* we do take note of facts that are in different times. For, I ask you, What word of mine is it that, as this single present word, you just *now* hear me speaking? If I pause a little, you perhaps dwell upon the last word that I utter before pausing, and call that the one present word. Otherwise, however, as I speak to you, you are conscious of series of successive words, of whole phrases, of word groups, of clauses. Within each one of these groups of words, you are indeed more or less clearly aware that every element has its own temporal place; and that, *in so far as* each element is taken by itself as present, the other elements either precede or succeed it, and in *this* sense are not in one time with it. But this very fact itself you know merely in so far as you actually experience series, each of which contains several successive words. These series come to you not merely by virtue of remembered facts, but also as experienced facts.

And in truth, were this not so, you could indeed have no experience of succession at all. You would then experience, at any one moment, merely the single word, or something less than any single word, together with the supposed coexistent and contemporaneous images of actually past or of coming words. But how, in that case, would your experience of time-sequences come to seem to you different from any experience whatever of coexistence? Nor is even this the only difficulty about the doctrine which supposes you to be unable to view a series of successive events as all at once presented to your consciousness. A still deeper difficulty results from such an effort to evade the double sense in which the facts of succession are known in your experience. If you can have present to you only *one* event at a time in a series of successive events, how long, or rather how short, must an event be to contain within itself no succession at all, or no difference between former and latter contents? In vain do you suppose that, at any time, you have directly present to your consciousness only one of the successive words that you hear me speak. Not thus do you escape our difficulty. For a spoken word is itself a series of temporally successive sounds. Can you hear at once the whole spoken word, or can you grasp at once this whole series? If so, my own foregoing account is in principle admitted. For then, in this presence of the facts of succession to your consciousness, there are our two former aspects, both of them, involved. *Each* element of the succession (namely, in this case, the elementary sounds that to your consciousness make up the word) is temporally present just when it occurs, but *not* before or afterwards, in so far as it follows previous elements and succeeds later elements; and also *all* the elements are, in the other sense of the term, *present at once* to consciousness, as constituting this whole succession which you call the word. If, however, you deny that you actually hear, apart from memory or from imagery, any single whole word at once, I shall only the more continue to ask you, What is the least or the simplest element of succession that is such as to constitute a merely present experience, with *no* former or latter contents within it? What apart from any memory or any imagery, and wholly apart from ideas of the past or the future of your experience, is present to you, in an indivisible time instant, just *Now?* The question is obviously unanswerable, just because an absolutely indivisible instant of mathematical time, with no former and latter contained within it, neither constitutes nor contains any temporal event, nor presents to you any fact of temporal experience whatever, just as an indivisible point in space could contain no matter, nor itself ever become, in isolation, an object of spatial experience. On the other hand, an event such that in it you were unable to perceive any succession, would help you in no whit to get the idea of time until you experienced it along with other events. What is now before you is a succession, within which are parts; and of these parts each, when and in so far as once your attention fixes it, and takes it in its time relations, is found as a present that in time both precedes and succeeds other facts, while these other facts are also just as truly before you as the observed element called the temporally present one is itself before you. And thus you cannot escape from our twofold interpretation of the experience of temporal succession. You are conscious of a series of successive states presented to you as a whole. You are also aware that each element of the succession excludes the others from its own place in time.

There is, to be sure, another frequent way of describing our consciousness of succession,—and a way that on the whole I find unsatisfactory. According to this view, events come to us in succession in our experience,—let us say the words of a spoken verse,—and *then* something often called the synthetic activity of the mind supervenes, and later binds together into unity, these successive facts, so that when this binding has taken place we *then* recognize the whole fagot of experience as a single succession. This account of the temporal facts, in terms of an activity called a synthesis, helps me, as I must confess, no whit. What I find in consciousness is that a succession, such as a rhythm of drum-beats, a musical phrase, a verse of poetry, comes to me as one present whole, present in the sense that I know it all at once. And I also find that this succession is such that it has *within* it a temporal distinction, or order, of earlier and later elements. While these elements are at once known, they are *also* known as such that at the briefer instant *within* the succession when any one of them is to be temporally viewed as a present fact, none of the others are contemporaneous with that fact, but all are either *no longer* or *not yet* when, and in so far as, that element is taken as the present one. And I cannot make this datum of experience any more definite by calling it a synthesis, or the mere result of a synthesis.

I have now characterized the more directly given features in our consciousness of succession. You see, as a result, that we men experience what Professor James, and others, have called our "specious present," as a serial whole, *within* which there are observed temporal differences of former and latter. And this our "specious present" has, when measured by a reference to time-keepers, a length which varies with circumstances, but which appears to be never any very small fraction of a second, and never more than a very few seconds in length. I have earlier referred to this length of our present moments as our characteristic "time-span" of consciousness, and have pointed out how arbitrary a feature and limitation of our consciousness it is. We shall return soon to the question regarding the possible metaphysical significance of this time-span of our own special kind of consciousness.

But it remains here to call closer attention to certain other equally important features of our more direct experience of time-succession. So far, we have spoken, in the main, as if succession were to us a mere matter of given facts, as colors and sounds are given. But all our experience also has relation to the interests whose play and whose success or defeat constitute the life of our will. Every serial succession of which we are conscious therefore has for us some sort of meaning. In it we find our success or our failure. In it our internal meanings are expressed, or hindered, thwarted or furthered. We are interested in life, even if it be, in idle moments, only the dreary interest of wondering what will happen next, or, in distressed moments, the interest in flying from our present fortune, or, in despairing moments, of wishing for the end; still more then if, in strenuous moments, our interest is in pursuing our ideal. And our interest in life means our conscious concern in passing on from any temporal present towards its richer fulfilment, or away from its relative insignificance. Now that Direction of temporal succession of which I before made mention, has the most intimate relations to this our interest in our experience. What is earlier in a given succession is related to what is later as being that *from* which we pass *towards* a desired fulfilment, or in search of a more complete expression of our purpose. We are never content in the temporal present in so far as we view it as temporal, that is, as an event in a series. For such a present has its meaning as a transition from its predecessors towards its successors.

Our temporal form of experience is thus peculiarly the form of the Will as such. Space often seems to spread out before us what we take to be the mere contents of our world; but time gives the form for the expression of all our meanings. Facts, in so far as, with an abstractly false Realism, we sunder them from their meanings, therefore tend to be viewed as merely in relations of coexistence; and the space-world is the favorite region of Realism. But ideas, when conscious, assume the consciously temporal form of inner existence, and appear to us as constructive processes. The visible world, when viewed as at rest, therefore interests us little in comparison with the same world when we take note of its movements, changes, successions. As the kitten ignores the dead leaves until the wind stirs them, but then chases them—so facts in general tend to appear to us all dead and indifferent when we disregard their processes. But in the movements of things lies for us, just as truly as in her small way for the kitten, all the glory and the tragedy, all the life and the meaning of our observed universe. This concern, this interest in the changing, binds us then to the lower animals, as it doubtless also binds us to beings of far higher than human grade. We watch the moving and tend to neglect the apparently changeless objects about us. And that is why narrative is so much more easily effective than description in the poetic arts; and why, if you want to win the attention of the child or of the general public, you must tell the story rather than portray coexistent truths, and must fill time with series of events, rather than merely crowd the space of experience or of imagination with manifold but undramatic details. For space furnishes indeed the stage and the scenery of the universe, but the world's play occurs in time.

Now all these familiar considerations remind us of certain of the most essential characters of our experience of time. Time, whatever else it is, is given to us as that within whose successions, in so far as for us they have a direct interest and meaning, every event, springing from, yet forsaking, its predecessors, aims on, towards its own fulfilment and extinction in the coming of its successors. Our experience of time is thus for us essentially an experience of longing, of pursuit, of restlessness.

And this is the aspect which Schopenhauer and the Buddhists have found so intolerable about the very nature of our finite experience. Upon this dissatisfied aspect of finite consciousness we ourselves dwelt when, in the former series of lectures, we were first learning to view the world, for the moment, from the mystic's point of view. As for the higher justification of this aspect of our experience, that indeed belongs elsewhere. But as to the facts, every part of a succession is present in so far as when it is, that which is *no longer* and that which is *not yet* both of them stand in essentially significant, or, if you will, in essentially practical relations to this present. It is true, of course, that when we view relatively indifferent time-series, such as the ticking of a watch or the dropping of rain upon the roof, we can disregard this more significant aspect of succession; and speak of the endless flight of time as an incomprehensible brute fact of experience, and as in so far seemingly meaningless. But no series of experiences upon which attention is fixed is wholly indifferent to us; and the temporal aspect of such series always involves some element of expectancy and some sense of something that no longer is; and both these conscious attitudes color our interest in the presented succession, and give the whole the meaning of life. Time is thus indeed the form of practical activity; and its whole character, and especially that direction of its succession of which we have spoken, are determined accordingly.

II

I have dwelt long upon the time consciousness of our relatively direct experience, because here lies the basis for every deeper comprehension of the metaphysics both of time and of eternity. Our ordinary conception of time as an universal form of existence in the external world, is altogether founded upon a generalization, whose origin is in us men largely and obviously social, but whose materials are derived from our inner experience of the succession of significant events. The conceived relations of Past, Present, and Future in the real world of common-sense metaphysics, appear indeed, at first sight, vastly to transcend anything that we ourselves have ever observed in our inner experience. The infinite and irrevocable past that no longer is, the expected infinite future that has as yet no existence, how remote these ideal constructions, supposed to be valid for all gods and men and things, seem at first sight from the brief and significant series of successive events that occur within the

brief span of our actual human consciousness. Yet, as we saw in the
ninth lecture of our former Series, common sense, as soon as questioned
about special cases, actually conceives the Being of both the past and
future as so intimately related to the Being of the present that every
definite conception of the real processes of the world, whether these
processes are viewed as physical or as historical or explicitly as ethical,
depends upon taking the past, the present, and the future as constituting
a single whole, whose parts have no true Being except in their linkage.
As a fact, moreover, the term *present*, when applied to characterize a
moment or an event in the time-stream of the real world, never means,
in any significant application, the indivisible present of an ideal mathematical time. The present time, in case of the world at large, has an unity
altogether similar to that of the present moment of our inner consciousness. We may speak of the present minute, hour, day, year, century. If
we use the term *present* regarding any one of these divisions of time, but
regard this time not as the experienced form of the inner succession of
our own mental events, but as the time of the real world in which we
ourselves form a part, then we indeed conceive that this present is world-
embracing, and that suns move, light radiates between stars, the deeds of
all men occur, and the minds of all men are conscious, in this same present time of which we thus make mention. Moreover, we usually view the
world-time in question in terms of the conceptions of the World of
Description, and so we conceive it as infinitely divisible, as measurable by
various mathematical and physical devices, and as a continuous stream
of occurrence. Yet in whatever sense we speak of the real present time
of the world, this present, whether it is the present second, or the present
century, or the present geological period, it is, for our conception, as
truly a divisible and connected whole region of time, within which a succession of events takes place, as it is a world-embracing and connected
time, within whose span the whole universe of present events is com-
prised. A mathematically indivisible present time, possessing no length,
is simply no time at all. Whoever says, "In the universe at large only
the present state of things is real, only the present movement of the
stars, the present streamings of radiant light, the present deeds and
thoughts of men are real; the whole past is dead; the whole future is not
yet,"—any such reporter of the temporal existence of the universe may
be invited to state how long his real present of the time-world is. If he
replies, "The present moment is the absolutely indivisible and ideal
boundary between present and future,"—then one may rejoin at once

that in a mathematically indivisible instant, having no length, no event happens, nothing endures, no thought or deed takes place,—in brief, nothing whatever temporally exists,—and that, too, whatever conception you may have of Being. But if the real present is a divisible portion of time, then it contains within itself succession, precisely as the "specious present" of psychological time contains such internal succession. But in that case, within the real present of the time-world, there are already contained the distinctions that, in case of the time of experience, we have heretofore observed. If, in what you choose to call the present moment of the world's history, deeds are accomplished, suns actually move from place to place, light waves traverse the ether, and men's lives pass from stage to stage, then *within* what you thus call the present there are distinguishable and more elementary events, arranged in series, such that when any conceived element, or mere elementary portion of any series is taken in relation to its predecessors and successors, it is *not yet* when its antecedents are taken as temporally present, and is *past and gone* when its successors are viewed as present. The world's time is thus in all respects a generalized and extended image and correspondent of the observed time of our inner experience. In the time of our more direct experience, we find a twofold way in which we can significantly call a portion of time a present moment. The present, in our inner experience, means a whole series of events grasped by somebody as having some unity for his consciousness, and as having its own single internal meaning. This was what we meant by the present experience of this musical phrase, this spoken line of verse, this series of rhythmic beats. But, in the other sense of the word, an element within any such whole is present in so far as this element has antecedents and successors, so that they are *no longer* or *not yet* when it is temporally viewed as present, while in turn, in so far as any one of them is viewed as the present element, this element itself is either *not yet* or *no longer*. But precisely so, in the conceptual time of our real world, the Present means any section of the time-stream in so far as, with reference to anybody's consciousness, it is viewed as having relation to this unity of consciousness, and as in a single whole of meaning with this unity. Usually by "our time," or "the real time in which we now live," we mean no very long period of the conceived time-stream of the real world. But we never mean the indivisible *now* of an ideal mathematical time, because, in such an indivisible time-instant, nothing could happen, or endure, or genuinely exist. But within the present, if conceived as a section of the time-stream, there are internal differences of present, past, and future.

For, in a similar fashion, as the actual or supposed length of the "specious present" of our perceptual time is something arbitrary, determined by our peculiar human type of consciousness, so the length of the portion of conceptual time which we call the *present*, in the first sense of that term, namely, in the sense in which we speak of the "present age," is an arbitrary length, determined in this case, however, by our more freely chosen interest in some unity which gives relative wholeness and meaning to this present. If usually the "present age" is no very long time, still, at our pleasure, or in the service of some such unity of meaning as the history of civilization, or the study of geology, may suggest, we may conceive the present as extending over many centuries, or over a hundred thousand years. On the other hand, within the unity of this first present, any distinguishable event or element of an event is *present*, in the second, and more strictly temporal sense in so far as it has predecessors and successors, whereof the first are *no longer*, and the latter *not yet*, when this more elementary event is viewed as happening.

Nor does the parallelism between the perceptual and the conceptual time cease here. The perceptual time was the form in which meaning, and the practically significant aspects of consciousness, get their expression. The same is true of the conceptual time, when viewed in its relations to the real world. Not only is the time of human history, or of any explicitly teleological series of events, obviously the form in which the facts win their particular type of conceived meaning; but even the time of physical science gets its essential characters, as a conception, through considerations that can only be interpreted in terms of the Will, or of our interest in the meaning of the world's happenings.

For the conceived time-series, even when viewed in relation to the World of Description, still differs in constitution from the constitution of a line in space, or from the characters belonging to a mathematically describable physical movement of a body, in ways which can only be expressed in terms of significance. Notoriously, conceptual time has often been described as correspondent in structure to the structure of a line, or as correspondent again, in character, to the character of an uniformly flowing stream, or of some other uniform movement. But a line can be traversed in either direction, while conceptual time is supposed to permit but one way of passing from one instant to another in its course. An uniform flow, or other motion, has, like time, a fixed direction, but might be conceived as returning into itself without detriment to its uniformity. Thus an ideally regular watch "keeps time," as we say, by virtue of the uniformity of its motion; but its hands return ever again to the same places on the face; while the years of conceptual time return not again. And finally, if one supposed an ideally uniform physical flow or streaming in one rectilinear direction only, and in an infinite Euclidean space, the character of this movement might so far be supposed to correspond to that of an ideally conceived mathematical time; except for one thing. The uniformity and unchangeableness of the conceived physical flow would be a merely given character, dependent, perhaps, upon the fact that the physical movement in question was conceived as meeting with no obstacle or external hindrance; but the direction of the flow of time is a character essential to the very conception of time. And this direction of the flow of time can only be expressed in its true necessity by saying that in case of the world's time, as in the case of the time of our inner experience, we conceive the past as leading towards, as aiming in the direction of the future, in such wise that the future depends for its meaning upon the past, and the past in its turn has its meaning as a process expectant of the future. In brief, only in terms of Will, and only by virtue of the significant relations of the stages of a teleological process, has time, whether in our inner experience, or in the conceived world order as a whole, any meaning. Time is the form of the Will; and the real world is a temporal world in so far as, in various regions of that world, seeking differs from attainment, pursuit is external to its own goal, the imperfect tends towards its own perfection, or in brief, the internal meanings of finite life gradually win, in successive stages, their union with their own External Meaning. The general justification for this whole view of the time of the real world is furnished by our idealistic interpretation of Being. The special grounds for regarding the particular Being of time itself as in this special way teleological, are furnished by the foregoing analysis of our own experience of time, and by the fact that the conceptual time in terms of which we interpret the order of the world at large, is fashioned, so to speak, after the model of the time of our own experience.

III

Having thus defined the way in which the conceptual time of the real world of common sense corresponds in its structure to the structure of the time known to our inner perception, we are prepared to sketch our theory both of the sense in which the world of our idealistic doctrine appears to be capable of interpretation as a Temporal order, and of the sense in which, for this same theory, this world is to be viewed as an Eternal order. For, as a fact, in defining time we have already, and inevitably, defined eternity; and a temporal world must needs be, when viewed in its wholeness, an eternal world. We have only to review the structure of Reality in the light of the foregoing analysis in order to bring to our consciousness this result.

And so, first, the real world of our Idealism has to be viewed by us men as a temporal order. For it is a world where purposes are fulfilled, or where finite internal meanings reach their final expression, and attain unity with external meanings. Now in so far as any idea, as a finite Internal Meaning, still seeks its own Other, and consciously pursues that Other, in the way in which, as we have all along seen, every finite idea does pursue its Other, this Other is in part viewed as something beyond, *towards* which the striving is directed. But our human experience of temporal succession is, as we have seen, just such an experience of a pursuit directed towards a goal. And such pursuit demands, as an essential part or aspect of the striving in question, a consciousness that agrees in its most essential respect with our own experience of time. Hence, our only way of expressing the general structure of our idealistic realm of Being is to say that wherever an idea exists as a finite idea, still in pursuit of its goal, there appears to be some essentially temporal aspect belonging to the consciousness in question. To my mind, therefore, time, as the form of the will, is (in so far as we can undertake to define at all the detailed structure of finite reality) to be viewed as the most pervasive form of all finite experience, whether human or extra-human. In pursuing its goals, the Self lives in time. And, to our view, every real being in the universe, in so far as it has not won union with the ideal, is pursuing that ideal; and, accordingly, so far as we can see, is living in time. Whoever, then, is finite, says, "not yet," and in part seeks his Other as involving what, to the seeker, is still future. For the finite world in general, then, as for us human beings, the distinction of past and future appears to be coextensive with life and meaning.

I have advisedly used, however, the phrase that the time-consciousness is a "part" or "aspect" of the striving. For from our point of view, the Other, the completion that our finite being seeks, is not *merely* something beyond the present, and is not merely a future experience, but is also inclusive of the very process of the striving itself. For the goal of every finite life is simply the totality whereof this life, in its finitude, is a fragment. When I seek my own goal, I am looking for the whole of myself. In so far as my aim is the absolute completion of my Selfhood, my goal is identical with the whole life of God. But, in so far as, by my whole individual Self, I mean my whole Self in contrast with the Selves of my fellows,—then the completion of my individual expression, in so far as I am this individual and no other,—*i.e.* my goal, as this Self, is still not any one point of experience in my life, nor any one stage of my life, but the totality of my individual life viewed as in contrast with the lives of other individuals. Consequently, while it is quite true that every incomplete being, every finite striving, regards itself as aiming towards a future, because its own goal is not yet attained; we have, nevertheless, to remember that the attainment of the goal involves more than any future moment, taken by itself, could ever furnish. For the Self in its entirety is the whole of a self-representative or recurrent process, and not the mere last moment or stage of that process. As we shall see, there is in fact no last moment. A life seeking its goal is, therefore, indeed, essentially temporal,—but is so just as music is temporal,—except indeed that music is not only temporal, but temporally finite. For every work of musical art involves significant temporal series, wherein there is progression, and passage from chord to chord, from phrase to phrase, and from movement to movement. But just as any one musical composition has its value not only by virtue of its attainment of its final chord, but also at every stage of the process that leads towards this conclusion; and just as the whole musical composition is, as a whole, an end in itself; so every finite Internal Meaning wins final expression, not merely through the last stage of its life (if it has a last stage), but through its whole embodiment. And, nevertheless, as the music attains wholeness only through succession; so every idea that is to win its complete expression, does so through temporal sequences.

Since, at all events, no other than such a temporal expression of meaning in life is in any wise definable for our consciousness, our Idealism can only express its view of the relation of finite and absolute life by viewing the whole world, and in particular the whole existence of any individual Self, as such a temporal process, wherein there is expressed, by means of a Well-Ordered Series of stages, a meaning that finally belongs to the whole life, but that at every temporal stage of the process in question appears to involve, in part, a beyond,—a something not yet won,—and so a distinction both of the past and the future of this Self from the content of any one stage of the process when that stage is viewed as the present one.

In this sense, therefore, our doctrine is obliged to conceive the entire world-life as including a temporal series of events. When considered with reference to any one of these events, the rest of the events that belong to the series of which any one finite Self take account, are past and future, that is, they are *no longer* and *not yet;* just as, when viewed with reference to any one chord or phrase in the musical composition, all the other successive elements of the composition are either past or future.

The infinite divisibility of the time of our ordinary scientific conceptions is indeed due to that tendency of our own discriminating attention to an endless interpolation of intermediary stages,—a tendency which we studied in connection with our general account of the World of Description. We have, however, seen reasons, which, applied to time, would lead us to declare that an absolute insight would view the temporal order as a discrete series of facts ordered as any succession of facts expressing one purpose would be ordered, viz. like the whole numbers. On the other hand, we have no reason to suppose that our human consciousness distinctly observes intervals of time that in brevity anywhere nearly approach to the final truth about the temporal order. Within what is for us the least observable happening, a larger insight may indeed discriminate multitudes of events. In dealing with the concept of Nature, we shall see what significant use may be made of the hypothesis that there exists or may exist, finite consciousness for which the series of events that we regard as no longer distinguishable from merely elementary and indivisible happenings, are distinguished so minutely as to furnish content as rich as those which, from our point of view, occupy æons of the world's history. Our right to such hypotheses is incontestable, provided only that they help us to conceive the true unity of experience. Nevertheless, in the last analysis, the Absolute Will must be viewed as expressed in a well-ordered and discrete series of facts, which from our point of view may indeed appear, as we shall still further see, capable of discrimination *ad infinitum.*

But now secondly, and without the least conflict with the foregoing theses, I declare that this same temporal world is, when regarded in its wholeness, an Eternal order. And I mean by this assertion nothing whatever but that the whole real content of this temporal order, whether it is viewed from any one temporal instant as past or as present or as future, is *at once* known, *i.e.* is consciously experienced as a whole, by the Absolute. And I use this expression *at once* in the very sense in which we before used it when we pointed out that to your own consciousness, the whole musical phrase may be and often is known *at once, despite* the fact that each element of the musical succession, when taken as the temporally present one, excludes from its own temporal instant the other members of the sequence, so that they are either *no longer* or *not yet*, at the instant *when* this element is temporally the present one. As we saw before, it is true that, in one sense, each one of the elements or partial events of a sequence excludes the former and the latter elements from being at the time *when* this particular element exists. But that, in another and equally obvious and empirical sense, *all* the members of an actually experienced succession are *at once* to any consciousness which observes the whole succession as a whole, is equally true. The term *present*, as we saw, is naturally used both to name the temporally present when it is opposed to whatever precedes or succeeds this present, and also to name the observed facts of a succession in so far as they are experienced as constituting one whole succession. In so far the term is indeed ambiguous. But even this ambiguity itself is due to the before-mentioned fact that, if you try to find an absolutely simple present temporal fact of consciousness, and still to view it as an event in time, you are still always led, in the World of Description, to observe or to conceive that this temporal fact is a complex event, having a true succession *within* itself. So that the *now* of temporal expression is never a *mere* now, unless indeed it be viewed either as the ideal mathematical instant within which *nothing* takes place, or else as one of the finally simple stages of the discrete series of facts which the absolute insight views as the expression of its Will.

As to the one hypothesis, an absolute instant in the mathematical sense is like a point, an ideal limit, and never appears as any isolated fact of temporal experience. Every *now* within which something happens is therefore *also* a succession; so that every temporal fact, every event, so far as we men can observe it, has to be viewed as present to experience in *both* the senses of the term present; since this fact *when* present may be contrasted with predecessors that are *no longer* and with successors that are *not yet*, while this same fact, when taken as an event occupying time, is viewed as a presented succession with former and latter members contained within it. As to the other hypothesis, it seems clear that we human beings observe no such ultimate and indivisible facts of experience just because, so far as we observe and discriminate fact, we are more or less under the bondage of the categories of the World of Description.

But, in view of the correspondence between the universal time of the world-order, as we conceive it, and the time of our internal experience, as we observe it, the temporal sequences must be viewed as having in the real world, and for the Absolute, the same twofold character that our temporal experiences have for ourselves. *Present*, in what we may call the inclusive sense of the term, is any portion of real time with all its included events, in so far as there is any reason to view it as a whole, and as known in this wholeness by a single experience. *Present*, in what we may by contrast call the exclusive sense, is any one temporal event, in so far as it is contrasted with antecedent and subsequent events, and in so far as it excludes them from coexistence with itself in the same portion of any succession. These two senses of the term *present* do not contradict each other in case of the world-order any more than they do in case of our own inner experience. Both senses express inevitably distinct and yet inseparable connected aspects of the significant life of the conscious will, whether in us, or in the universe at large. Our view declares that all the life of the world, and therefore all temporal sequences, are present at once to the Absolute. Our view also maintains that, without the least conflict with this sense in which the whole temporal order is known at once to the Absolute, there is another sense in which any portion of the temporal sequence of the world may be taken as present, when viewed with reference to the experience of any finite Self whose present it is, and when contrasted with what for this same point of view is the past and the future of the world. Now the events of the temporal order, when viewed in this latter way, are divided, with reference to the point of view of any finite Self, into what *now* is, and what *no longer* is, and what *is to be*, but is *not yet*. These same events, however, in so far as they are viewed at once by the Absolute, are for such view, all equally present. And this their presence is the presence of all time, as a *totum simul*, to the Absolute. And the presence in this sense, of all time at once to the Absolute, constitutes the Eternal order of the world,—eternal, since it is inclusive of all distinctions of temporal past and temporal future,—eternal, since, for this very reason, to totality of temporal events thus present at once to the Absolute has no events that precede, or that follow it, but contains all sequences within it,—eternal, finally, because this view of the world does not, like our partial glimpses of this or of that relative whole of sequence, pass away and give place to some other view, but includes an observation of every passing away, of every sequence, of every event and of whatever in time succeeds and follows that event, and includes all the views that are taken by the various finite Selves.

In order to conceive what, in general, such an eternal view of the temporal order involves, or to conceive in what sense the temporal order of the real world is also an eternal order, we have, therefore, but to remember the sense in which the melody, or other sequence, is known at once to our own consciousness, despite the fact that its elements when viewed merely in their temporal succession are, in so far, *not* at once. As we saw before, the brief span of our consciousness, the small range of succession, that we can grasp at once, constitutes a perfectly arbitrary limitation of our own special type of consciousness. But in principle a time-sequence, however brief, is already viewed in a way that is not *merely* temporal, when, despite its sequence, it is grasped at once, and is thus grasped not through mere memory, but by virtue of actual experience. A consciousness related to the whole of the world's events, and to the whole of time, precisely as our human consciousness is related to a single melody or rhythm, and to the brief but still extended interval of time which this melody or rhythm occupies,—such a consciousness, I say, is an Eternal Consciousness. In principle we already possess and are acquainted with the nature of such a consciousness, whenever we do experience any succession as one whole. The only thing needed to complete our idea of what an actually eternal consciousness is, is the conceived removal of that arbitrary limitation which permits us men to observe indeed at once a succession, but forbids us to observe a succession at once in case it occupies more than a very few seconds.

IV

This definition of the relations of the Temporal and the Eternal accomplishes all the purposes that are usually in mind when we speak of the divine knowledge as eternal. That eternity is a *totum simul*, the scholastics were well aware; and St. Thomas develops our present concept with a clearness that is only limited by the consequences of his dualistic view of the relation of God and the world. For after he has indeed well defined and beautifully illustrated the inclusive eternity of the divine knowledge, he afterwards conceives the temporal existence of the created world as sundered from the eternal life which belongs to God. And hereby the advantages of an accurate definition of the eternal are sacrificed for the sake of a special dogmatic interest.

Less subtle forms of speculation have led to uses of the word *eternal*, whose meaning is often felt to be far deeper than such usages can render explicit. But as these subtle usages are often stated, they are indeed open to the most obvious objections. An eternal knowledge is often spoken of as if it were one for which there is *no* distinction whatever between past, and present, and future. But such a definition is as absurd as if one should speak of our knowledge of a whole musical phrase or rhythm, when we grasped such a whole at once, as if the *at once* implied that there were for us no temporal distinction between the first and the last beat or note of the succession in question. To observe the succession *at once* is to have present with perfect clearness *all* the time-elements of the rhythm or of the phrase just as they are,—the succession, the tempo, the intervals, the pauses,—and yet, without losing any of their variety, to view them at once as one present musical idea. Now for our theory, that is precisely the way in which the eternal consciousness views the temporal order,— not ignoring one jot or tittle of its sharp distinctions of past or of future, of succession or of duration,—but still viewing the whole time-process as the expression of a single Internal Meaning. What we now call past and future are not merely the *same* for God; and, nevertheless, they are viewed *at once*, precisely as the beginning and the end of the rhythm are not the same for our experience, but are yet at once seen as belonging to one and the same whole succession.

Or again, an eternal knowledge is often supposed to be one that abstracts from time, or that takes no account of time; so that, for an eternal point of view it is as if time were not at all. But to say this is as if one were to speak of observing at once the meaning or character of the whole phrase or rhythm by simply failing to take any note at all of the succession as such. The meaning is the meaning of the succession; and is grasped only by observing this succession as something that involves former and latter elements, while these elements in time exclude one another, and therefore follow, each one *after* its predecessor has temporally ceased, and *before* its successor temporally appears. Just so, we assert that the eternal insight observes the whole of time, and all that happens therein, and is eternal only by virtue of the fact that it does know the whole of time.

Or again, some doctrines often speak of an eternal insight as something wholly and inexplicably *different* from any temporal type of consciousness, so that *how* God views His truth as eternal truth, no man can say. But our theory regards the essential relation of an eternal to a temporal type of consciousness as one of the simplest of the relations that are of primal importance for the definition of the Absolute. Listen to any musical phrase or rhythm, and grasp it as a whole, and you thereupon have present in you the image, so to speak, of the divine knowledge of the temporal order. To view all the course of time just as you then and there view the whole of that sequence,—this is to be possessed of an eternal type of insight.

"But," so many hereupon object,—"it appears impossible to see how this sort of eternal insight is possible, since just now, in time, the infinite past,—including, say, the geological periods and the Persian invasion of Greece, is *no longer*, while the future is *not yet*. How then for God shall this difference of past and future be transcended, and all be seen at once?" I reply, In precisely the same sense all the notes of the melody except this note are not *when* this note sounds, but are either *no longer* or *not yet*. Yet you may know a series of these notes at once. Now precisely so God knows the whole time-sequence of the world at once. The difference is merely one of span. You now exemplify the eternal type of knowledge, even as you listen to any briefest sequence of my words. For you, too, know time even by sharing the image of the Eternal.

Or again, a common wonder appears regarding how the divine knowledge can be in such wise eternal as to suffer no change to occur in it. How God should be unchangeable, yet express His will in a changing world, is an ancient problem. Our doctrine answers the question at a stroke. The knowledge of all change is itself indeed unchangeable, just because any change that occurs or that can occur to any being is already included amongst the objects known to the eternal point of view. The knowledge of this melody as one whole does not itself consist in an adding of other notes to the melody. The knowledge of all sequences does not itself follow as another sequence. Hence it is indeed not subject to the fate of sequence.

And finally, a mystery is very generally made of the fact that since time appears to us as inevitably infinite, and as therefore not, like the melody or the rhythm, capable of completion, an eternal knowledge, if it involves a knowledge of the whole of time, must be something that has to appear to us self-contradictory and impossible. Any complete answer to this objection involves, of course, a theory of the infinite. Such a theory I have set forth in the Supplementary Essay, published with the First Series of these lectures. The issue involved, that of the positive concept of an infinite whole, is indeed no simple one, and is not capable of any brief presentation. I can here only report that the considerations set forth in that Supplementary Essay have led me to the thesis that a Well-

Ordered Infinite Series, under the sole condition that it embodies a single plan, may be rightly viewed as forming a totality, and as an individual whole, precisely as a musical theme or a rhythm is viewed by our experience as such a whole. That the universe itself is such an infinite series, I have endeavored, in that paper, to show in great detail. If you view the temporal order of the world as also forming such an endless whole, expressing a single plan and Will (as I think you have a right to do), then the argument of the Supplementary Essay in question will apply to our present problem. The whole of time will contain a single expression of the divine Will, and therefore, despite its endlessness, the time-world will be present as such a single whole to the Absolute whose Will this is, and whose life all this sequence embodies.

V

In order to refer, as I close, to the practical interest which has guided me through all the abstract considerations even of this present lecture, I may be permitted to anticipate some of our later results about the Self, and, for the sake of illustration, to point out that from our point of view, as we shall later explain it more fully, your life, your Self, your will, your individuality, your deeds, can be and are present at once to the eternal insight of God; while, nevertheless, it is equally true that not only for you, but for God, your life is a genuine temporal sequence of deeds and strivings, whereof, when you view this life at the present temporal instant, the past is just now *no longer*, while the future is *not yet*. This twofold view of your nature, as a temporal process and as an eternal system of fact, is precisely as valid and as obvious as the twofold view of the melody or of the rhythm. Your temporal present looks back, as Will, upon your now irrevocable past. That past is irrevocable because it is the basis of your seeking for the future, and is the so far finished expression of your unique individual Will. Your future is the *not yet* temporally expressed region wherein you, as finite being, seek your own further expression. That future is still, in one aspect, as we shall see, causally undetermined, precisely in so far as therein something unique, that is yours and yours only, is to appear in the form of various individually designed expressions of your life-purpose,—various individual deeds. Therefore, as we shall be able to maintain, despite all your unquestionable causal and moral determinations, there will be an aspect of your future life that will be free, and yours, and such as no causation can predetermine, and such as even God possesses only in so far as your unique individuality furnishes it as a fact in His world.

And nevertheless, your future and your past, your aspect of individuality, and of freedom, and the various aspects wherein you are dependent upon the rest of the world, your whole life of deeds, and your attainment of your individual goal through your deeds,—all these manifold facts that are yours and that constitute you, are present at once to the Absolute,—as facts in the world, as temporal contents eternally viewed,—as a process eternally finished,—but eternally finished precisely by virtue of the temporal sequence of your deeds. And when you wonder how these aspects can be at once the aspects of your one life,—remember what is implied in the consciousness *at once* of the melody or the rhythm as a sequence,—and you will be in possession of the essential principle whereby the whole mystery is explained.

It is this view, once grasped in its various aspects, that will enable us to define in what sense man is one with God, and in what sense he is to be viewed as at present out of harmony with his own relation to God, and in that sense alienated from his true place in the eternal world. And so, in discussing this most elementary category, we are preparing the way for a most significant result as to the whole life of any man.

The temporal man, viewed just now in time, appears, at first, to be sundered even from his own past and future, and still more from God. He is a seeker even for to-morrow's bread,—still more for his salvation. He knows not just at this instant even his own individuality; still less should he immediately observe his relation to the Absolute in his present deed and in his fleeting experience. Only when he laboriously reflects upon his inmost meaning, or by faith anticipates the result of such reflection, does he become aware of how intimately his life is bound up with an Absolute life. This our finite isolation is, however, especially and characteristically a *temporal* isolation. That inattention of which we spoke in the last lecture, is especially an inattention to all but this act, as it now appears to me. I am not one with my own eternal individuality, especially and peculiarly because this passing temporal instant is not the whole of time, and because the rest of time is *no longer* or else *not yet when* this instant passes. Herein lies my peculiarly insurmountable human limitation. This is my present form of consciousness. To be sure, I am not wholly thus bound in the chains of my finitude. Within my present form and span of consciousness there is already exemplified an eternal type of insight, whereby the *totum simul* is in many cases and in brief span won. But beyond this my span of presentation, time escapes me as a past and future that is at once real and still either no longer or else not yet. From the eternal point of view, however, just this my life is *at once* present, in its Individuality and its wholeness. And because of this fact, just in so far as I am the eternal or true Individual, I stand in the presence of God, with all my life open before Him, and its meaning revealed to Him and to me. Yet this my whole meaning, while one with His meaning, remains, in the eternal world, still this unique and individual meaning, which the life of no other individual Self possesses. So that in my eternal expression I lose not my individuality, but rather win my only genuine individual expression, even while I find my oneness with God.

Now, in time, I seek, as if it were far beyond me, that goal of my Selfhood, that complete expression of my will, which in God, and for God, my whole life at once possesses. I seek this goal as a far-off divine event,—as my future fortune and success. I do well to seek. Seek and ye shall find. Yet the finding,—it does not occur merely as an event in time. It occurs as an eternal experience of this my whole striving. Every struggle, every tear, every misery, every failure, and repentance, and every rising again, every strenuous pursuit, every glimpse of God's truth,—all these are not mere incidents of the search for that which is beyond. They are all events in the life; they too are part of the fulfilment. In eternity all this is seen, and hereby,—even in and through these temporal failures, I win, in God's presence and by virtue of His fulfilment, the goal of life, which is the whole of life. What no temporal instant ever brings,—what all temporal efforts fail to win, that my true Self in its eternity, and in its oneness with the divine, possesses.

❧

THE CONCEPTION OF IMMORTALITY (1900)

I

I may as well begin this discussion by pointing out where, to my mind, lies the most central problem concerning man's immortality. In the real world in which our common-sense metaphysic believes, some things are obviously transient, and others, as, for instance, matter and the laws of nature, are more enduring, and perhaps (so common sense would nowadays tell us), are absolutely permanent. But permanence is of two sorts. A *type* may be permanent,—a law, a relationship. Thus the Binomial Theorem remains always true; and water continues to run down hill just as it did during the earliest geological periods. Or that may be permanent which we usually call an *individual* being. This particle of matter, as, for instance, an individual atom, or again, the individual whole called the entire mass of matter of the universe, may be permanent. Now when we ask about the Immortality of Man, it is the permanence of the Individual Man concerning which we mean to inquire, and not primarily the permanence of the human type, as such, nor the permanence of any other system of laws or relationships. So far then, as to the mere statement of our issue, I suppose that we are all agreed.

But in philosophy we who study any of these fundamental problems are unwilling to assert anything about a given subject, unless we first understand what we mean by that subject. Philosophy turns altogether upon trying to find out what our various fundamental ideas mean. Thus, when in practical life, you act dutifully, you may not be wholly clear as to just what you mean by your duty; but when you study Moral Philosophy, your primal question is, What does the very Idea of Duty mean?

86

Now precisely so, in case of the Immortality of the Individual Man, the question arises, What do you mean when we talk of an individual man at all? But this question, to my mind, is not a mere preliminary to an inquiry concerning immortality, but it includes by far the larger part of just that inquiry itself. For unless we know what an individual man is, we have no business even to raise the question whether he is immortal. But, on the other hand, if we can discover what we mean by an individual man, the very answer to that question will take us so far into the heart of things, and will imply so much as to our views about God, the World, and Man's place in the world, that the question about the immortality of man will become, in great measure, a mere incident in the course of this deeper discussion.

Accordingly, I shall here raise, and for the larger part of this lecture shall pursue, an inquiry concerning what we mean by an Individual Man. Only towards the end of this discussion shall we come clearly to see that in defining the Individual Man, we have indeed been defining his Immortality.

The question as to the nature of an individual man is at once a problem of logic and an issue of life. I shall have to consider the matter in both aspects. In the first aspect our question becomes identical with the problem, What is it that makes *any* real being an individual? This question is a very ancient, and if you choose commonplace one, which has been studied from time to time ever since Aristotle. I can give you small insight, in my brief time, into its complications; and what I needs must say about it may appear very formal and dreary. But like all the central problems of Logic, this one really pulsates with all the mystery of life; and before I am done, I shall hope to give you a glimpse of the sense in which this is true. Such a glimpse will become possible as soon as I apply the logical question about individuals to the case of the individual man. That all men including yourself are more or less mysterious beings to you, you are already aware. What I want to show you is that the chief mystery about any man is precisely the mystery of his individual nature, i.e., of the nature whereby he is this man and no other man. I want to show you that the only solution of this mystery lies in conceiving every man as so related to the world and to the very life of God, that in order to be an individual at all a man has to be very much nearer to the Eternal than in our present life we are accustomed to observe. So much then for an outline of our enterprise. And now for its inevitably complicated details.

II

We all naturally believe that the real world about us contains individ-ual things. And if you ask what we naturally mean by believing this, I first reply, apart from any more formal definition of individuality, by saying that we believe our world to consist of facts, of realities, which are all ultimately different from one another, and unlike one another, by virtue of precisely what constitutes their very existence as facts or as realities. Things may resemble one another as much as you will. But deeper than their resemblance has to be, according to our common-sense view, the fact that they are still somehow individually or numerically different beings. Yonder lights, for instance, are in your present opinion all of them different from one another, despite their resemblances as lu-minous objects. You and your neighbors are different beings. And such individual difference, as you hold, enters very deeply into your inmost constitution, or into the constitution of any person or thing in the uni-verse. No matter how much two people, say twins, look alike, talk alike, think alike, or feel alike, we still hold that they are different beings; and we naturally hold that this difference lies somehow deeper than do all their resemblances, inner or outer. For that each one of them is, or that he is this being, depends upon and implies the fact that he is nobody else; and just as neither of the twins could have any appearance, or voice, or thoughts, or feelings at all unless he first existed; just so, too, neither of them, as the individual that he is, could exist at all unless he were *this* person, and *not* the other. So that to exist implies, as we usually hold, to be different from the rest of the world of existences. And since I must exist if I am to have any qualities whereby I can resemble another being, and must differ from all other beings if I am to exist, it naturally seems that my difference from all the rest of the world is, in a sense, the deepest truth about me. However little I may know about myself, common sense therefore supposes me to be at least very sure that I am nobody else, and so am different from anybody else.

By an individual, then, we mean an essentially unique being, or a be-ing such that there exists, and can exist, but one of the type constituted by this individual being.

An easy task it is then, although indeed a very dry and abstract task, to tell what in general constitutes *individuality*, if we take the term simply as an abstract noun. For the beings of the world are made individ-uals by whatever truly serves to distinguish each of them from all the rest, to keep them, as it were, seemingly apart in their Being. But now, if we leave this barely abstract statement, and come closer to the facts of life, I may next point out that, if individuality in general is easily defined, this *individual*, precisely in so far as it is an unique being, is from the nature of the case peculiarly hard to characterize, or to explain, or to conceive, or to define, or to observe, or in any other way to know. In fact, when we look closer we soon see that our human thought is able to define only types of beings, and never individuals, so that *this individual* is always for us indefinable. On the other hand our human sense experience shows us only *kinds* of sensory impressions, and never unique objects as unique.

For now there comes to our attention a very commonplace, but important fact, regarding the process of our knowledge. We have so far accepted the natural view that the differences of various existent things lie at the basis, so to speak, of all resemblances. But whenever we know anything, we are dependent upon taking account at once, and in one act, of both likenesses and differences. These two aspects of facts are somewhat differently related to our consciousness; but we never really come to know a difference without in some wise either reducing to or consciously relating it to a likeness. One of the lights that you see differs, to your mind, from another light in size, in brightness, or in place. Yet just because you see them thus differing, all of them for that very reason are seen as in the same larger place, viz., in this room, or as alike in all being bright, or as alike in all having size. Thus, whenever you clearly see wherein they are different, say in brightness, size, place, you also see how, in just this same respect in which they differ, they also have some resemblances to one another. This fact, that you always know likenesses and differences at once, or in one act, makes it impossible to sift out in your knowledge all the resemblances of your world, and to put them in one place by themselves, in your mind, while you put all the differences in another place. For the likenesses stick to the differences, and always come away with them, when you try to analyze your world, even in the most abstract thinking process. Just as some of the miner's gold washes away in the tailings, and just as some of the accompanying substances that a chemist tries to remove by a particular process of distillation may distill over with whatever was to be separated from them, so too, when, in your discriminating observation, or in your abstract thinking, you try, for the purposes of your analysis, to wash the resemblances out of the facts, and to keep the differences, or to distill off the individuality of the different things, you find that always resemblance stubbornly clings to difference, and *vice versa.* Nor do our figures of the tailings and the distillations give quite an adequate idea of the actual hopelessness of trying to separate in our consciousness, for purposes of analysis, the like and the different aspects of our observed world. For, in our knowledge, the consciousness of likeness and the consciousness of difference help each other; and therefore in a measure, it is true that the more we get of one of them, before our knowledge, the more we get of the other. So they decline altogether to be known separately. Thus, only pretty closely similar objects can seem to us to stand, from our point of view, in an observably sharp contrast to one another. We can see the contrast only when we also see the close similarity. For instance, it is much easier to be aware of a definite difference or contrast between two poets than it is to be conscious of the difference or contrast between a poet and a blackberry or a parabola. Whenever we clearly see what a difference is, there we also observe a likeness, and the difference and the likeness, as seen, always relate to the same aspect of the objects.

This being the fashion of our knowledge, one sees at once how hard it must be for knowledge either to find the impressions of sense, or to define by thought, just wherein one thing ultimately differs from all other things. An individual being, as we have seen, is thought by our common sense to be, first of all, different from any other being. We try either to say or to see wherein it thus differs, or what constitutes its individuality. Forthwith we only the more clearly see and state and conceive points wherein it not only differs from all other objects, but also, and at the same time, resembles them. This is the fate of our knowing process, and therefore, whenever we observe closely, all individuality seems to be conceived and observed by us as merely relative. Individuality is known to us only as an aspect inseparable from what is not individuality. But just because a thing, according to our natural view, is to be an individual to the very heart and core of its existence, it seems that, if we are to be able to see or to express this individuality, we ought somewhere to be able to find or to conceive the individuality of each thing as a fact by itself,—as a difference, deeper than all resemblances, ideally separable from them, and not merely bound up in this inseparable way with them, or dependent upon them. Hence we always fail when we try to describe any individual exhaustively.

Moreover, still another aspect of our difficulty often occurs to our minds, and is especially baffling. Anything is an individual in so far as it genuinely differs not only from any other existent being, but from any other being that is genuinely possible or that is rightly conceivable. You, for instance, if you are a real individual, are such that nobody else, whether actual or possible, could ever share your individual nature, or be rightly confounded with you. Now, however closely we observe, and no matter how carefully we conceive a thing, we at best only observe or conceive actual likenesses and differences between this thing and the other present or remembered things. We can never either see or abstractly think just how or why it is that no other possible thing could possess the characters, whatever they are, which we have once noticed or have actually found this thing to possess. Suppose, for instance, that I see the color of an object. So far I in no sense see why other objects might not possess just that color. In general other objects do. So colors are not purely individual characteristics of things. Suppose, however, that I see a hundred autumn leaves, and sorting them, find indeed that no two of them are precisely alike in shading and in detail of coloring. In that case I at first seem to be finding what is individual in each leaf. But no. For so far I have only seen actual likenesses and differences; and so far only my present autumn leaves are indeed seen to be different. But I have not seen why there might not be in the world, unseen as yet by me, other autumn leaves precisely like any particular one of these leaves in every detail of coloring that I have noticed. Hence I have not yet taken note, in any leaf, of a coloring such as could not possibly be repeated somewhere else in the forest; and therefore I have not yet actually observed what it is that constitutes the truly individual existence of any one of the leaves. For whatever is a truly individual character of any existent thing is a character that simply could not be shared by another thing; and whatever makes you an existent individual being forbids anybody else, whether actual or possible, to be possessed of precisely your individual characteristics.

Historians and biographers try to tell us about individuals. Do they ever actually succeed in getting before us the adequate description of any one individual as such? No. *Man* you can define; but the true essence of any man, say, for instance, of Abraham Lincoln, remains the endlessly elusive and mysterious object of the biographer's interest, of the historian's comments, of popular legend, and of patriotic devotion. There is no adequate definition or description of Abraham Lincoln just in so far as he was the unique individual.

And why, I once more ask, is this so? Why can you not tell all that constitutes the individual what he is? One answer, I insist, lies just here. Suppose that you had overcome all the other limitations that hinder the biographer or the historian from knowing the facts about his hero. Suppose that you had a description or definition say of Abraham Lincoln, and suppose you assumed this definition or description to be an exact and exhaustive one. The definition would mention, perhaps, the physical appearance and bearing of Lincoln, the traits of his character, the secrets of his success, and whatever else you may choose to regard as characteristic of him. Well, suppose the definition finished. The question might be raised, at once, Is it possible, is it conceivable, that the world should contain another man who embodied just that now defined type,—who looked, spoke, thought, felt, commanded, and succeeded as Lincoln the War President did? If you answer, "No;" then we may at once retort, How can you know that only one man of this or of any once defined type can exist? Have you the secret of creation? Is every man's mould shattered (to use the familiar metaphor) when the man is made? And if so, how come you to be aware of the fact? But if you answer, "Yes; more than one man of this defined type is at least possible, or conceivable"; then equally well we may point out that hereby you merely admit that you have *not* yet defined what makes Abraham Lincoln different from any and from all other men, actual or possible. For if the possible men, fashioned after the likeness that your definition has expounded, were to come into existence, no one of these other men would be, in your opinion, Abraham Lincoln himself, or be entitled to his honors or his merits. They would differ from him by precisely the whole breadth of their individuality. They would have no right to his property, no share in his individual fame, and no hope, so to speak, of becoming worthy to take his place upon the Judgment Day. Yet, by hypothesis, they would conform to whatever definition of him you had once given as an adequate characterization of his type.

You may here interpose, if you will, by saying that all such idle suppositions about the possible reduplications of the type of Abraham Lincoln are worthless, since the practically interesting question is whether men whose identity runs any risk of being confounded with that of the great President exist or are to be found; and this question, according to our common view, is easily to be answered in the negative. But my present interest, in mentioning the possible cases of other representatives of Lincoln's once defined type, lies merely in showing that whatever the individuality of anything really is, we men never adequately come to know wherein it consists, and so I here point out that while you are doubtless somehow quite sure of Lincoln's individuality, or his unexampled uniqueness, you have not positively defined wherein that uniqueness and individuality consists, until your definition has actually expressed *why*, or at least *how* it is that there *can be no other* man of his type. So long as you merely appeal then to human experience to show that there *is* no other such man to be found, our present argument remains untouched.

But even if we passed back again to experience to help us, we should still find once more, as we found in case of the autumn leaves, that no experience can show us the unique. The facts of sense are essentially sorts of experience,—characters, types,—fashions of feelings. Uniqueness as such is thus precisely what I can never directly find present to my senses. When you first learn from the logic textbooks or from Aristotle that the individual is the indefinable, you are indeed fain with Aristotle to turn back to experience, as we just attempted to do in case of Abraham Lincoln. You are disposed to say that the individual is the proper object of sense. But Aristotle himself knew better than to rest content in this view. As he already saw, sense also, in its own way, brings to our consciousness only the more or less vaguely general, or at best the typical,—not the unique.

The very young children trust their senses for guidance, in the use of their earliest language at the time when they name every object by its vaguely observed type. So, perhaps, they name all men alike "papa," or for a while they call all animals "dogs," or identify cows as "cats," or use any other of the delightful confusions that characterize the first year of speech. Sense and feeling, taken as directly present experience, supply us only with general types, and, apart from other motives, guide us only to general ideas, never to a direct knowledge of individuals.

You see then, in sum, that our human type of knowledge never shows us existent individuals as being truly individual. Sense, taken by itself, shows us merely sense qualities,—colors, sounds, odors, tastes. These are general characters. Abstract thinking defines for us types. A discriminating comparison of many present objects of experience, such as autumn leaves, or human faces, or handwritings, shows us manifold differences, but always along with and subject to the presence of likenesses, so that we never find what common sense assumes to exist, namely, such a difference between any individual and all the rest of the world as lies deeper than every resemblance. And even if by comparisons and discriminations we had found how one being appears to differ from all other now existent beings, we should not yet have seen what it is that distinguishes each individual being from all possible beings. Yet such a difference from all possible beings is presupposed when you talk, for instance, of your own individuality.

III

Let us now, however, pass to a new aspect of the matter. If indeed it is true that you do not define in your thought, or empirically observe through any direct experience of your senses, that the world consists of unique individual beings, then we are next disposed to say that the dogma of common sense upon this subject is the result of some very recondite interpretation of your experience. But if we ask whence we came by this interpretation, I must call your attention to that region of your life where you are indeed surest of the individuality of the facts, and most familiar with its meaning. This region is that of your intimate human relationships. Your family and your nearest friends are indeed for your human faith and loyalty through and through individuals. You are sure of their uniqueness. You resist most decidedly the hypothesis that what for you constitutes the essence of their individuality could conceivably be shared, like the characters of a mere type, by other beings in the world. "There is no other child quite like my child,—no other love quite like my love,—no other friend wholly like this friend,—no other home the precise possible substitute for this home"—how familiar and human such assertions are. Now this affirmation of the uniqueness of our own, and of those to whom our hearts belong, has something about it that obviously goes beyond both sense and abstract thinking. It expresses itself in quite absolute terms. Meanwhile it is much warmer and more vital than the before-mentioned colorless assumption that all the real beings in the world are in some wise unique beings, or that the universe is made up of individuals. Yet this present and more vital assertion seems to express the very inmost spirit of intimacy of personal loyalty. And meanwhile it is, in its implications, quite as metaphysical as is the most general theory of any philosopher. For I must still insist,—not even in case of our most trusted friends,—not even after years of closest intimacy,—no, not even in the instance of Being that lies nearest to each one of us,—not even in the consciousness that each one of us has of his own

Self,—can we men as we now are either define in thought or find directly presented in our experience the individual beings whom we most of all love and trust, or most of all presuppose and regard, as somehow certainly real. For even within the circle of your closest intimacies our former rule holds true, that, if you attempt to define by your thought the unique, it transforms itself into an unsatisfactory abstraction,—a type and not a person,—a mere fashion of possible existence, that might as well be shared by a legion as confined to the case of a single being. And just so, too, the other previous result obtains, namely, that when you try to find the certainly unique even in your own household, it eludes your direct observation, for it is a form of Being that belongs to a far higher sphere than that of any merely immediate experience. It is just for this reason that the individual object of your oldest friendship is not merely a psychological problem to you, but also a metaphysical mystery. The real presence of your friend you may indeed love with an exclusive affection that forbids you to believe that any other could take his unique place anywhere in the whole realm of Being; but you meet this real presence of an individual never at any time as a fact of sense. Your doctrine about this real presence of your friend remains in common life a dogma just as truly as if it were a dogma of supernatural faith. It is with the individual of daily life as with the lady of Browning's lyric, for whom the lover searches through "room after room" of the house they "inhabit together:"—

"Yet the day wears,
     And door succeeds door;
   I try the fresh fortune—
     Range the wide house from the wing to the centre—
   Still the same chance! She goes out as I enter!"

And now, if you ask why this lady is thus elusive, I answer, because she is an individual. And an individual is a being that no finite search can find.

As for yourself, you notoriously are such that the Self is, and is a real individual. But who amongst us defines by his abstract statement of his own type, or finds by dwelling upon his familiar masses of mere organic sensation, what his own unique Self may be? Or who amongst us conceives himself in his uniqueness except as the remote goal of some ideal process of coming to himself and of awakening to the truth about his own life? Only an infinite process can show me who I am.

On the other hand, when we dwell upon these cases that lie nearest to our vital interests, we do indeed begin to find out the deeper meaning of something that in the instances formerly mentioned seemed to be a matter for cold and curious logical inquiry. We begin to find out, namely, the deeper meaning of this our so fixed, and yet at first sight so arbitrary assumption that our real world, despite the imperfections of our conception and the vague generality of our direct experience, does consist of individuals. For in case of the objects of our nearer and of our more consciously exclusive affections, we are often well aware how arbitrary our mere speech about the experienced or defined uniqueness of these objects of affection must seem to any external observer. We recognize this apparent arbitrariness of our description of the unique object; but we even glory therein. We confess that we cannot tell wherein our friend is so individual. We emphasize the confession. We make it a deliberate topic of portrayal in art. And what we feel, as we do this, is that this arbitrary speech of ours is a sign that we are pursuing a very precious secret, which nobody else has the right to share. Herein we find a hint also of a certain ideal view of the innermost nature of Being,—a view which simply cannot be translated into the language of abstract description, or adequately embodied in the materials of present sensation; but a view which is all the truer for that very reason. For this view the Real is indeed something beyond our present human sense and our descriptive science. The individuals are, as we are sure, the most real facts of our world. But yet there is for us, as for Browning's lover, something endlessly fascinating about our hopeless human inability to show to anybody else, or to verify by even our own immediate experience, just in what way they are thus so individual. This our finite situation has its own perplexing and beautiful irony. We rise above our helplessness even as we confess it; for this helplessness hints to us that our real world is behind the veil.

The inner nature, the true Being of these beloved individuals about us and of our own individuality within, thus constitutes, so to speak, the genuinely and wholesomely occult aspect of our most commonplace life. That we are really in the most intimate relations with this so familiar, and precious, and yet so occult world, where in truth our most intimate friends and our actual selves even now dwell, we are sure. But that the gates seem barred whenever we try to penetrate or to reveal the truth of this very world,—this is something so baffling, so stimulating, and yet in a way so absurd, that in our lighter moments we find our own incapacity to make our world manifest to our human vision endlessly amusing. And the play with these mysteries constitutes a great part of the poetic arts. It is, I must insist, merely a concrete instance of the fundamental logical and metaphysical problem as to how the world can consist of individuals. To mention a familiar instance. All the world loves a lover, and, in a sense, loves in sympathy with him. Yet nearly all the faithful lovers are certain profoundly to disagree with him as to the most central article of his faith. For he loves an individual, unique, without a peer,—one who is most lovable just because she occupies a place that no other could take. They,—the other faithful lovers, each one of them also loves a peerless individual. And therefore they all have to use indeed very nearly the same formulas whenever they try to tell why they love. But they all disagree, just because they apply their creeds to different objects. They all describe essentially the same type, namely, the perfect woman. They differ about her identity. Or if they do not thus disagree—then, to be sure, a tragedy is in the making. In the endless disagreement of the lovers lies their only hope of harmony.

Now the problem as to the worthy object of love is precisely, and, as I myself maintain, philosophically, identical with the logical problem as to what constitutes an individual being. Whom shall one love? The unique object. There shall be no other like the beloved. But for what characters shall one choose the beloved? For *mere* uniqueness, for *mere* oddities as such? No. For perfections, for excellencies, for ideally valuable qualities, is the beloved rightly chosen, and not otherwise. Be it so, then. The lover, if justified in his love, believes not only that his beloved is different from all other beings, but also that she is in some wise more excellent than all others. This great faith, if sincere, longs for expression. One must praise the beloved; or if one is no poet, one must look abroad to find the already written words with which to praise her. But in what language shall the praise be expressed? In human speech of general meaning, known and understood by all men. But the qualities that the lover finds in his own unique beloved, when once expressed in this common speech of men, become in large measure identical with the qualities that all the beloved women of the world have been said, by the poets and the lovers, to possess. Of course there are those well known differences in types of recognized perfection, which have to do with color of eyes, and with other features, but on the whole, the lover in expressing, in defining, if you will, the perfections of his love, has merely described with minor variations one type,—and, thank Heaven, an extremely general and universally well known type,—the type of all the beloved women. In other words, he has set forth every real or apparent noble quality of his beloved except precisely what makes her unique. Yet his loyalty still earnestly insists that he loves her for nothing so much as for that she *is* unique and is even thereby quite unlike all the other beloved women.

Hereupon the logician must become a little suspicious of the lover. The lover says that he loves but One. Yet when he tells about her he describes a type. Does he then really love only the type? For, alas, his poetic accounts are but general. Just when he describes his love—"So careful of the type he seems,—so careless of the single life." But no, this thought is an insult to loyal love. True love is indeed essentially careful of the single life. Yet is it then truly the unique being that one loves? Alas! if this is true, why then does the lover's halting speech, when it praises, describe absolutely nothing whatever but the type? The beloved, if logically disposed, may even notice this, the pathetic irony of our human loyalty. "You might have said all this," she may retort,—"you might have said all this to any other woman who merely happened to please you."

Now in vain would the lover attempt adequately to reply that the beloved is indeed, as a matter of mere experience, sufficiently different in face and carriage from all the other observable people to be capable of what we usually call identification, so that, for instance, the postman or the teller at the bank also no doubt recognizes her face when he sees it, and practically confuses her with nobody else. For the ground of loyal love is not meant to be simply the same as this practical ground that we use for purposes of ordinary identification. The lover does not mean that his beloved is merely capable of being identified. It is true that these facts of experience, these observed differences of face and manner, become, from the first, lighted up for the lover's appreciation with all the beauty of devotion, and so blend in his experience of affection with his sense of loyalty. That is so far as it should be. He loves indeed also the face and the voice, but for the sake of their unique owner. Yet the very question that before seemed to us a very formal matter of logic would become, if once raised, a very practical question for love. I do not advise anybody to raise it in any particular case. But, as a mere matter now of theory: If there were found in the world another with just such a face, voice, bearing, and other outward seeming and inward sentiment as the beloved, would the lover not merely by chance confuse the two, through his mortal ignorance, but actually and knowingly love both of them at once and equally? If he must answer, "Yes," then indeed, whatever his protestations, he loves not the real individual. There is then no true loyalty in his love. He is fond of a mere type.

But if he loves the individual, then indeed he could bear the easy test that, in the Hindu poem of Nala and Damayanti, the gods apply to the princess of the story. For when, in that story, the princess, by virtue of the privilege belonging to her rank, is about to choose her lover from amongst the suitors, assembled upon a solemn occasion to hear her decision, four of the gods, to please their high caprice, stand beside the real lover, whom the princess has already in her heart chosen. Each god assumes precisely the real lover's guise and seeming. The princess finds then before her five men, all absolutely alike, and all fashioned exactly as is the man of her heart. In her perplexity she wonders a brief moment; but then, perceiving in her mind the heavenly wiles, she lifts up her voice in humble prayer that those of the group who are *not* the right one may be pleased to behave a little more like gods, that she may see more clearly to choose her own. The gods relent, and obey. But the princess, as she thus finds her mortal lover, hereby shows us also somewhat more clearly what our loyal consciousness of the nature of an individual means. It means that for our Will, however sense deceives, and however ill thought defines, there *shall be* none precisely like the beloved. And just herein, namely, in this voluntary choice, in this active postulate, lies our essential consciousness of the true nature of individuality. Individuality is something that we demand of our world, but that, in this present realm of experience, we never find. It is the object of our purposes, but not now of our attainment; of our intentions, but not of their present fulfillment; of our will, but not of our sense nor yet of our abstract thought; of our rational appreciation, but not of our description; of our love, but not of our verbal confession. We pursue it with the instruments of a thought and of an art that can define only types, and of a form of experience that can show us only instances and generalities. The unique eludes us; yet we remain faithful to the ideal of it; and in spite of sense and of our merely abstract thinking, it becomes for us the most real thing in the actual world, although for us it is the elusive goal of an infinite quest.

And therefore it is that the lovers join in reporting the same things of all whom they love; yet in meaning, nevertheless, wholly different beings by their speech. Therefore it is that the soldiers in Bayard Taylor's Sebastopol lyric, as they sing in the trenches, before they storm the fort,

try to confess each the tearful secret of his own heart, as he thinks of
home, but they do so in words that are the same for all of them:—

> "Each heart recalled a different name,
> But all sang Annie Laurie."

The true individuals are thus not seen by us, not described by us. But in
our more intimate life we love individuals, we will to pursue them and
to be loyal to them. Love and loyalty never directly find their unique
objects, but remain faithful to them although unseen.

IV

We have so far dealt both with various negative aspects of this idea of
individuality and also with its positive significance for life. We must now
ask, Is there any truth in this idea of individuality? Are we in any sense
right in regarding our world as one where there are these unique individuals whom we mortals can define only in terms of our will to seek
them, and can conceive only as the goal of an essentially ideal process?

The adequate answer to this question as to the real Being of an individual would involve, as I have confessed from the very outset, an entire
system of philosophy. Shall I venture here merely to hint the grounds
upon which I think that we have a right at least to attempt just such
primal problems? This idea of the individuality of all things is, in my
own opinion, an idea not merely of the emotional interest now illustrated.
It is also an idea without which, in the end, all serious science is impossible. For science too, although not sentimental, is itself a loyal expression of an essentially practical interest in final, i.e., in individual truth.
Science, if unable to describe or to find the unique, everywhere postulates its existence as the goal of a process of inquiry. And this idea of the
individual is an idea that directs all conduct of our intellect in the presence of our experience. To believe anywhere in genuine reality is to believe in individuality. In every special science that deals with either
nature or man, you will find, then, if you look closer, that in some form
the concept and the problem of the individual enters in a fashion less
sentimental indeed than is the lover's problem, but quite as insistent,
quite as baffling, both for our empirical search and for our abstract definitions, and quite as suggestive that if our world has reality, this reality
is one which no finite process of finding and defining can exhaust. Quite

impossible is it, however, to decline to face this problem upon the supposed grounds that the ultimate nature of real things is once for all unknowable. The conception of reality itself is precisely as much an expression of our human needs and purposes, as is the conception of a steam
engine or of a political party; and if the conception so far baffles us, that
is because we have not yet looked deeply enough into the life out of
which this very conception of the real world of individuals springs. Let
us then inquire a little more searchingly. To be sure, for this inquiry
there is here no adequate space. I can give only a bare hint of an idealistic
interpretation of the real world. Elsewhere I have tried to state in explicit form the argument now to be barely indicated. Regard what follows, if you will, not as any attempt at proof, but as a mere summary.

We have up to this point spoken of the relation of the concept of the
individual to the direct experience of sense, and to the abstract definitions
of the intellect. We have found that neither of these could furnish to us
an adequate expression of the nature of an individual. We have also seen,
in speaking of the more vital aspects of our problem, that an individual,
if not describable, is still sincerely intended or willed as the object of a
devotion that, in us, can only express itself as the endless pursuit of a
goal. The natural statement of our problem becomes then this: Do these
endless pursuits of ideal goals, in terms of which we define our relation
to the undefinable individual beings whom we love, or whom in science
we seek to know,—do these ideal pursuits, I say, correspond to a truth
anywhere expressed beyond us? Is reality in its wholeness a realm of
Purpose, rather than merely of observable finite facts and of abstractly
definable characters?

As to the most general answer to this question, I must indeed first respond that, for the reasons now illustrated, I hold the concept of individuality to be not merely from our human point of view, but in itself,
essentially and altogether, a teleological concept,—a concept implying
that the facts of any world where there really are individuals express will
and purpose. Suppose a being not now a man, but a being as far above our
mere poverty of conscious life as you please, yet a being whose whole
life consists merely of sense contents, or of mere facts of immediate
feeling,—colors, forms, tastes, touches, pleasures, and pains. Such a being
could indeed observe. But he would never observe individuals as individuals. On the other hand, suppose any purely intelligent being, whose
mind was full of mere ideas, i.e., of patterns, types, schemes, class conceptions, definitions. Such a being, however wise in his own way, could

never know individual facts as such. He might know laws, orders of truth, systems of necessary validity; but if his world contained individual facts, he would never know this to be true. He would be, for instance, by our hypothesis, himself an individual, for we have just spoken of him as such; but he would never be able to know himself as this individual. With the proverbial absent-mindedness of the abstractly wise, this supposed pure intelligence would be quite unaware that he himself, or that anybody else, possessed individuality. He would be loyal to no individual objects. His world would be for him a collection of disembodied theorems, and of mere possibilities.

And now, even if you suppose the being of mere experience with whom we just began, to acquire all the wisdom of the other being, the supposed abstract thinker; still, even this resulting being, who would be an observer of ideal laws and of immediate experiences, in this combination would nevertheless not yet find true individuality in his world. His world would now be one where there were types and feelings; but still not one where unique beings were observed to be real.

But next suppose a being whose world not merely shows him contents of feeling and types of law, but also expresses his will, and not merely expresses this will, but satisfies it. Suppose that this being finds in his world, namely, all that his love and all that his wisdom seek. This being will observe his world as embodiment of his plans, as an exhaustive presentation of his will and purpose. Now this being can indeed say: "This world and *no other* is my world, for these facts and *no others* are what I want, just because in these facts my purposes are satisfied." For the satisfied will is precisely the will that seeks no other embodiment. Now such a being, and such a being only, would be aware of the uniqueness of his facts, and so would know individuals as individuals.

The very conception, then, of an individual as a real being, precisely because it is no abstract conception, but is rather the conception of a unique being, is one that no pure thought or experience can express, but is a conception expressible only in terms of a satisfied will. An individual is a being that adequately expresses a purpose. Or again, an individual so expresses a purpose that no other being can take the place of this individual as an expression of this purpose. And the sole test of this sort of uniqueness lies in the fact that in this individual being, just in so far as its type gets expression at all, the will or purpose which it expresses rests content with it, desires no other, will have no other.

I conclude then, so far, that if this world contains real individuals at all, it is a teleological world, and a world that not only expresses purpose, but completely and adequately expresses a purpose precisely in so far as it contains real individuals.

Nor need this result be interpreted merely with reference to the more sentimental illustrations used a moment since. The purposes which various individuals express may be those of science, or those of human love,—those of our warmer passions, or those of our calmer reason,—those of man, or those of God. Any of these various purposes, or all of them at once, may win a place in Being. My whole case so far is that whether you talk of angels or atoms, your individual beings, if real at all, are real only as unique embodiments of purpose. And their uniqueness can only depend upon the fact that in each of them some will is so satisfied that it seeks and will have no other. Therefore it is indeed that loyal human love is in us the best example of an individuating principle. The love that will have no other than this beloved is our best hint of the sense in which purpose must be fulfilled in the world, if individuals are to be real at all.

Our question then becomes this: Does the real world fulfill purposes? Does it express will? Does it embody ideals in unique and satisfactory fulfillment? But this question at once raises the most central issue of philosophy. In what sense is there any real world? What are its ultimate facts? What is Reality?

The answer to these questions must be, like the questions, founded upon a desire to deal with first principles for their own sake. For the issue upon which depends every philosophical problem about the general order of the world is raised when one asks the question, What is a fact? We have said that the most significant facts, even of the world of common sense and of science, have aspects that transcend the limits of our direct human consciousness. But we have not said that such facts have no relation whatever to our own experience, but only that our human type of experience is very inadequate to exhaust their meaning, or to present them in their wholeness. In truth, our whole search after facts, our whole belief in the reality of the world, depends upon a recognition that our experience is inadequate to express the conscious purposes that we have in mind even when we scrutinize this our experience itself, to see what it contains. And our own philosophical argument will hold that in consequence you must define the whole Reality of things in terms of Purpose.

At any thinking moment of your human life, you inquire, you find yourself ignorant, you doubt, you wonder, or you investigate. Now as you do this you have present to your consciousness what are called, in the narrower sense of that term, ideas,—that is, ideas of objects not now present to you, and of objects that, if present, would answer your questions, settle your doubts, accomplish the end of your investigations. Now your ideas, as such, mean precisely certain thoughtful processes that are more or less consciously present in your momentary state of mind as you inquire. But the objects concerning which you inquire are, by hypothesis, not wholly present to you at the instant of your doubt or wonder. For were they present, your inquiries would be answered. They are viewed as absent; and you also call them, taken, as it were, in themselves,—you call them, I say, the facts in the case. You conceive them, usually, as in large measure independent of your ideas. And yet the facts and your ideas cannot be in truth wholly independent of each other as ordinary Realism assumes; for were they without any mutual dependence whatever, how could the ideas really have the facts as their objects? Or how could it make any difference to the ideas, as conscious processes, with an intent or purpose of their own, whether the wholly independent facts agreed with them, or not? Or yet again, to put the same consideration in another form, the ideas, if they have any bearing upon facts at all, even if they simply express ignorance of the facts, or doubt about the facts, or error regarding facts, or blunder, or delusion,—yet still doubt, or error, or delusion about facts, which are really their objects,— the ideas, I say, must in any such case stand in that seemingly so mysterious relation to the facts beyond them which is implied when we say, *The ideas are such as genuinely to mean the facts.* Even in your conscious ignorance, in doubt, in error, in delusion, if you really doubt, or err, or are deluded, your ideas, however fragmentary, are thus linked by the tie of objectively genuine meaning to the outer facts, however lofty or remote, concerning which you think and are therefore in one Whole of Meaning with those facts.

Now what does this genuine tie, called the meaning of an idea, this link by which the idea is bound to its seemingly external object, called the outer fact,—what, I ask, does this link imply? What is the true union between any idea and its object? The question as stated is absolutely general, is involved in every inquiry, in any sort of fact, and is therefore at issue whenever you consider the relation of any of your ideas, and so of yourself as the person having these ideas, to facts whether physical or spiritual, to facts whether in a laboratory or in the eternal world, to facts whether in this room or in the remotest ages of time, to facts about your next friend, or to facts of God's mind or of immortality. If, for instance, I now have a genuine idea of your minds while I speak to you, or if you have any idea really referring to my own mind, then our minds are actually and metaphysically linked by the ties of mutual meaning. In other words, we are then not wholly sundered beings. We are somehow more whole of meaning. And if you now think of Sirius, or of the universe, then your idea, if it really means anything whatever that is objective, is in the same whole of meaning with your object. But what constitutes this whole of meaning?

The question has its especial difficulty in the fact that, in speaking of an idea and its object, just in so far as you sunder the two, and view them as mutually independent entities, you fail to see how the conscious idea can make any real reference to that entity yonder, beyond it, and different from it. For how should anybody, or how should anybody's ideas, consciously refer to an object that is still in no sense a part of the consciousness which possesses the idea? On the other hand, if the object to which our ideas refer is simply itself one of our own ideas, or is simply a fact present to our experience,—if, in other words, idea and object are in my own unity of consciousness together, then how should an idea be able to err, as we constantly find our own ideas erring, regarding their objects? How, in brief, should ignorance and error be at all possible?

To bring our whole problem then to a single focus: When I think of outer existence, I think of something as not wholly and just now consciously present to me; and yet I think of myself as meaning this something. My object is somehow here, in my consciousness,—genuinely here; and yet somehow not here, since I inquire and perhaps err about it. Now how can I thus mean to refer to more than my object now present to my consciousness, while still, in order thus to refer at all, I must fix my attention upon some fact now present in my mind?

To all these fundamental questions philosophy, as I hold, must answer: I can refer to any object beyond me solely by observing the inadequacy of my present and passing conscious idea to its own conscious purpose. I cannot directly look beyond my own consciousness; but I pass beyond my present solely by virtue of my will, my intent, my dissatisfaction. But this very will and dissatisfaction have my own present imperfection and inadequacy as their direct object. And consequently, by the object itself, by my real world, I can mean nothing but that which in the end, despite all my ignorance or error or finite misfortune, somehow adequately fulfills my whole will. Thus the very idea of a real being is the idea of something that fulfills a purpose. What is thus thought of is indeed conceived as the outer object of an idea, and so as a fact beyond the idea, and yet meant by the idea. This relation of being beyond an idea, and yet meant by that idea, is, however, a possible relation, a relation that has any sense whatever only in so far, first, as the idea is an inadequate expression in our present human consciousness of its own purpose, and in so far, secondly, as the object meant stands related to the idea as that which fulfills the whole intent which is now partially expressed in the idea. And so we can indeed say, as Schopenhauer said, although not wholly in his sense, The real world is my Will.

In other words, to be, to exist, to be a fact, to be real,—any one of these expressions simply means, to express in wholeness the meaning that imperfect conscious ideas, such as we mortals have, now only partially express. To be, or to be a fact, means then, not to be independent of finite ideas, but to accomplish fully and finally what they only intend, to present in wholeness what they only find in fragment, to be one with their purpose, but free from their inadequacy, to fulfill what they only propose, to attain what they only will. In saying this I in no sense mean that reality meets all your momentary wishes and caprices. For your momentary wishes and caprices are simply unconscious of their own whole meaning; and therefore they very generally have to be transformed in order to be satisfied. But what my doctrine does mean is that a world of ontological fragments, of facts that are not in one whole of meaning together, is never to be found. There are no ideas sundered from their objects. Ontologically speaking, where the idea is, there is the object also. Only the momentary human idea is the object imperfectly brought to a finite consciousness. The apparent sundering of idea and fact is therefore simply an illusion of our own finitude. Nor do the ideas mysteriously refer to objects that first exist beyond them and *then* are somehow the topics of this reference. No, the true relation of idea and object is not mysterious. It is merely the very relation so familiar to any of us, the relation which you have now in mind when you observe that you have not fully present to your momentary self the fulfillment of your own present conscious purposes, nor yet a full consciousness even of what those purposes themselves mean. In fact, just in so far as you lack anything, or in so far as you know not wholly what you mean, or have not now what you all the while consciously seek, just in so far you define your object as beyond you. The incompleteness of your present self-expression of your own meaning is then the sole warrant that you have for asserting that there is a world beyond you. And this incompleteness, so far as you are conscious of it, gives in its turn the only possible meaning to the externality ascribed to the complete expression of your present meaning. Thus while you indeed expect reality to defeat your caprices, and to refute your errors, you still rightly demand that reality should adequately express your whole true meaning.

In consequence, merely by reading this result in the reverse order you have at once a definition of the deepest essence of the existent world. What is real is simply, in its wholeness, that which consciously completes or finally expresses the very meaning that, in you, is at this instant of your human experience consciously incomplete. That meaning of yours, viz., the world, the reality, the whole, yes the absolute, is now in its very being really although inadequately present to your passing consciousness; but your finite defect is that you know not consciously, just now, the whole of what you even now genuinely mean. Or again: you have not now at once both wholly and consciously present the complete expression of your own will. But this complete expression, with you and in essence in you really, even now, but not consciously present to you now, this whole will and life of yours is the world. That complete expression, as the Hindoos said,—*that is the Reality, that is the Soul, that art Thou.* The real world then is teleological. It does express a purpose. It does express this purpose rationally, wholly, finally. And this purpose is the very purpose now hinted in your own passing thrill of hope and of longing.

V

But now, after listening to this mere sketch of the general idealistic theory of the ultimate reality, after hearing this interpretation of the essential nature of the world order in its wholeness, you may well ask how, in case there is this essential relation of every finite idea to the whole meaning of the world, there is any room left for finite individuality as any distinguishable fact. The doctrine that I have just sketched is indeed obviously a version of a doctrine about God as an Absolute Being, and about his relation to every finite conscious life just in so far as that life, seeing its own imperfections, is seeking for truth beyond itself. No one can seek for a truth beyond his present self, unless the seeker is already in his inmost purpose one with the Absolute Life in which all truth is expressed. But on the other hand, this oneness of divine and of finite purpose is in some sense sure to exist in case of every finite life; for all life is an expression of the one universal Will, and in its turn is in the most intimate relation to that one will. Ignorance and error as well as evil are, when viewed as such, and in their separation from the whole, imperfect self-expressions of the Absolute that can only appear within the limits of a finite fragment of the whole, such as any one of us now is. No finite idea can fail, even in the lowest depths of its finitude, to intend this oneness with the Absolute upon which, according to our account, all knowledge and all truth depend. But on the other hand, if all reality is one and for One, and is the expression of a single purpose, so that God is immanent, is everywhere nigh to the finite life, and is everywhere meant by us all,—then we seem indeed to have found that the world expresses one absolute purpose, and is real only as accomplishing that purpose. And we seem to have found also that at any instant what we consciously intend, in all our finite strivings, is oneness with God. But what, you may ask, has become of our individuality, in so far as we were to be just ourselves, and nobody else?

I reply, first, that in referring to reality in these idealistic terms, as the final fulfillment of a united purpose,—as the complete carrying out of what all finite purposes more or less blindly intend,—we have at least pointed out where there is attained something which no abstract description of finite facts could show us, namely, the uniqueness of the Divine Life, and of the real world in which this life is expressed. A will satisfied has in God's whole life found its goal, and seeks no other. I do not indeed conceive the Absolute as finding his goal at any one point in what we call time. Now we wait and suffer and seek. And all life, all striving, and all science are efforts to win ultimately this absolute meaning, which is our own will completely expressed. But it is the whole world of past, present, and future, it is that totality of life and of experience which our every moment of conscious life implies and seeks, which is fulfilled in the Absolute. Now neither abstract thought nor immediate experience, taken merely as we men find or define them, can describe or discover the unique. Only the complete fulfillment of purpose can leave no other fact beyond to be sought; and primarily, for this very reason, only the Absolute Life can be an entirely whole individual. God, then, is indeed the primary individual. His world, his life, his expression taken in its wholeness, is that individual fact which you and I are at all times trying to find, to win, to see, to describe, to attain. As finite beings we fail at every moment. It is our failure that we try to correct by our science or by our prudence. By no mystic vision can we win our union with him. We must toil. But he is our whole true life, in whom we live and move and have our being, and in him we triumph and attain,—not now, not here in time and amidst the blind strivings of this instant, but in that which our strivings always intend, and pursue, and love. For "restless are our souls," as Augustine in the familiar passage said, "until they rest, O God, in thee."

But now, on the other hand, consider the consequences of all this for ourselves. The two deepest facts about the real world are, from this idealistic point of view, that it is everywhere the expression, more or less partial and fragmentary, of meaning and of purpose. Therefore it makes our science and our practical work possible, and demands them of us. But if viewed as a whole it is an unique fulfillment of purpose,—the only begotten son of the Divine Will. It is such then, in its wholeness as a God's world, that nothing else could take its place consistently with the will which the whole freely expresses, carries out, and fulfills. But now of an unique whole, every fragment and aspect, just by virtue of its relation to the whole, is inevitably unique. Were the world essentially unfinished, and were it not the expression of a purpose, then the uniqueness or individuality of any of its parts or aspects would remain a fact nowhere present to anybody's insight. But if the absolute knowledge sees the whole as a complete fulfillment of purpose, then every fact in the world occupies its unique place in the world. Were just that fact changed, the meaning of the whole would be just in so far altered, and another world would take the place of the present one. Just as, in case a given cathedral is unique, and has not its equal in all the world of being, then every stone and every arch and every carving in that cathedral is unique, by having its one place in that whole, just so too, in the universe, if the whole is the expression of the single and absolute will, every fragment of life therein has its unique place in the divine life,—a place that no other fragment of life could fill.

And so, although you can never see, and can never abstractly define, your own unique or individual place in the world, or your character as this individual, you are unique and therefore individual in your life and meaning, just because you have your place in the divine life, and that life is one. And therefore it is true that in this same realm of the single divine life which loves and chooses this world as the fulfillment of its own purpose, and will have no other, your friend's life glows with just that unique portion of the divine will that no other life in all the world expresses. We finite beings then are unique and individual in our differences, from one another and from all possible beings, just because we share in the very uniqueness of God's individuality and purpose. We borrow our variety from our various relations to his unity.

And thus the claims of Knowledge and of Will are from the absolute point of view reconciled. For knowledge recognizes no diversity except upon the ground of an identity. And this is true of us all,—namely, that our very variety is based upon the fact that the absolute life and its world form one whole and are in their oneness unique. For just because the satisfied divine purpose permits no other to take the place of this world, in its wholeness, just so each one of us has his own distinct place in this unique whole. But on the other hand Will primarily seeks that which is different from all other objects,—namely, the individual, the finality, the single fulfillment of striving. And just such a fact is the whole world, and therefore is every part thereof unique in its own kind and degree of being.

VI

So far, then, as we live and strive at all, our lives are various, are needed for the whole, and are unique. No one of these lives can be substituted for another. No one of us finite beings can take another's place. And all this is true just because the Universe is one significant whole.

That follows from our general doctrine concerning our unique relation, as various finite expressions taking place within the single whole of the divine life. But now, with this result in mind, let us return again to the finite realms, and descend from our glimpse of the divine life to the dim shadows and to the wilderness of this world, and ask afresh: But *what* is the unique meaning of my life just now? What place do I fill in God's world that nobody else either fills or can fill?

How disheartening in one sense is still the inevitable answer. I state that answer again in all its negative harshness. I reply simply: For myself, I do not now know in any concrete human terms wherein my individuality consists. In my present human form of consciousness I simply cannot tell. If I look to see what I ever did that, for all I now know, some other man might have done, I am utterly unable to discover the certainly unique deed. When I was a child I learned by imitation as the rest did. I have gone on copying models in my poor way ever since. I never felt a feeling that I knew or could know to be unlike the feelings

of other people. I never consciously thought, except after patterns that
the world or my fellows set for me. Of myself, I seem in this life to be
nothing but a mere meeting-place in this stream of time where a mass of
the driftwood from the ages has collected. I only know that I have always tried to be myself and nobody else. This mere aim I indeed have
observed, but that is all. As for you, my beloved friend, I loyally believe
in your uniqueness; but whenever I try to tell you wherein it consists, I
helplessly describe only a type. That type may be uncommon. But it is
not you. For as soon as described, it might have other examples. But you
are alone. Yet I never tell you what you are. And if your face lights up
my world as no other can—well, this feeling too, when viewed as the
mere psychologist has to view it, appears to be simply what all the
other friends report about their friends. It is an old story, this life
of ours. There is nothing new under the sun. Nothing new, that is,
for us, as we now feel and think. When we imagine that we have
seen or defined uniqueness and novelty, we soon feel a little later the
illusion. We live thus, in one sense, so lonesomely here. For we love
individuals; we trust in them; we honor and pursue them; we glorify
them and hope to know them. But after we have once become keenly
critical and worldly wise, we know, if we are sufficiently thoughtful,
that we men can never either find them with our eyes, or define them
in our minds; and that hopelessness of finding what we most love
makes some of us cynical, and turns others of us into lovers of barren abstractions, and renders still others of us slaves to monotonous affairs that have lost for us the true individual meaning and novelty that
we had hoped to find in them. Ah, one of the deepest tragedies of this
human existence of ours lies in this very loneliness of the awakened critics of life. We seek true individuality and the true individuals. But we
find them not. For lo, we mortals see what our poor eyes can see; and
they, the true individuals,—they belong not to this world of our merely
human sense and thought.

They belong not to this world, in so far as our sense and our thought
now show us this world! Ah, therein,—just therein lies the very proof
that they even now belong to a higher and to a richer realm than ours.
Herein lies the very sign of their true immortality. For they are indeed
real, these individuals. We know this, first, because we mean them and
seek them. We know this, secondly, because, in this very longing of
ours, God too longs; and because the Absolute life itself, which dwells in
our life, and inspires these very longings, possesses the true world, and *is*

that world. For the Absolute, as we now know, all life is individual, but is individual as expressing a meaning. Precisely what is unexpressed here, then, in our world of mortal glimpses of truth, precisely what is sought and longed for, but never won in this our human form of consciousness, just that is interpreted, is developed into its true wholeness, is won in its fitting form, and is expressed, in all the rich variety of individual meaning that love here seeks, but cannot find, and is expressed too as a portion, unique, conscious, and individual, of an Absolute Life that even now pulsates in every one of our desires for the ideal and for the individual. We all even now really dwell in this realm of a reality that is not visible to human eyes. We dwell there as individuals. The oneness of the Absolute Will lives in and through all this variety of life and love and longing that now is ours, but cannot live in and through all without working out to the full precisely that individuality of purpose, that will to choose and to love the unique, which is in all of us the deepest expression of the ideal. Just because, then, God is One, all our lives have various and unique places in the harmony of the divine life. And just because God attains and wins and finds this uniqueness, all our lives win in our union with him the individuality which is essential to their true meaning. And just because individuals whose lives have uniqueness of meaning are here only objects of pursuit, the attainment of this very individuality, since it is indeed real, occurs not in our present form of consciousness, but in a life that now we see not, yet in a life whose genuine meaning is continuous with our own human life, however far from our present flickering form of disappointed human consciousness that life of the final individuality may be. Of this our true individual life, our present life is a glimpse, a fragment, a hint, and in its best moments a visible beginning. That this individual life of all of us is not something limited in its temporal expression to the life that now we experience, follows from the very fact that here nothing final or individual is found expressed.

VII

I have had time thus only to hint at what to my mind is the true basis of a rational conception of Immortality. I do not wish to have the concrete definiteness of the prophecies which can be based upon this conception in the least overrated. Individuality we mean and seek. That, in God, we win and consciously win, and in a life that is not this present mortal life. But we also seek pleasure, riches, joys. Those, so far as they are mere types of facts, we as individuals have no right to expect to win, either here or elsewhere, in the form in which we now seek them. How, when, where, in what particular higher form of finite consciousness our various individual meanings get their final and unique expression, I also in no wise pretend to know or to guess. The confidence of the student of philosophy when he speaks of the Absolute, arouses a curiously false impression in some minds that he supposes himself able to pierce further into all the other mysteries of the world than others do. But that is a mistake. I have had no time here to give even to my argument for my conception of the Absolute any sort of exact statement or defense. I well know how vague my hints of general idealism have been. I can only say that for that aspect of my argument I have tried to give, in a proper place, a fitting defense.

The case, however, for the present application of my argument to the problem of Human Immortality lies simply in these plain consider-ations: (1) The world is a rational whole, a life, wherein the divine Will is uniquely expressed. (2) Every aspect of the Absolute Life must there-fore be unique with the uniqueness of the whole, and must mean some-thing that can only get an individual expression. (3) But in this present life, while we constantly intend and mean to be and to love and know individuals, there are, for our present form of consciousness, no true individuals to be found or expressed with the conscious materials now at our disposal. (4) Yet our life, by virtue of its unity with the Divine Life, must receive in the end a genuinely individual and significant expression. (5) We men, therefore, to ourselves, as we feel our own strivings within us, and to one another as we strive to find one another, and to express our-selves to one another, are hints of a real and various individuality that is not now revealed to us, and that cannot be revealed in any life which merely assumes our present form of consciousness, or which is limited by what we observe between our birth and death. (6) And so, finally, the various and genuine individuality which we are now loyally meaning to express gets, from the Absolute point of view, its final and conscious ex-pression in a life that, like all life such as Idealism recognizes, is conscious, and that in its meaning, although not at all necessarily in time or in space, is continuous with the fragmentary and flickering existence wherein we now see through a glass darkly our relations to God and to the final truth.

I know not in the least, I pretend not to guess, by what processes this individuality of our human life is further expressed, whether through many tribulations as here, or whether by a more direct road to individual fulfillment and peace. I know only that our various meanings, through whatever vicissitudes of fortune, consciously come to what we individually, and God in whom alone we are individuals, shall together regard as the attainment of our unique place, and of our true relationships both to other individuals and to the all inclusive Individual, God himself. Further into the occult it is not the business of philosophy to go. My nearest friends are already, as we have seen, occult enough for me. I wait until this mortal shall put on—Individuality.

❧

THE PHILOSOPHY OF LOYALTY (1908)

LOYALTY AND RELIGION

I

Loyalty, so we said at the outset, is the willing and thoroughgoing devotion of a person to a cause. We defined a cause as something that unifies many human lives in one. Our intent in making these definitions was mainly practical. Our philosophy of loyalty was and is intended to be a practical philosophy. We used our definition first to help us to find out the purpose of life, and the supreme good which human beings can seek for themselves. We found this good to be, indeed, of a paradoxical seeming. It was a good found only by an act of sacrifice. We then developed the conception of loyalty to loyalty, and learned that, with this means of defining the one cause which is worthy of all men's devotion, we could unify and simplify the chaotic code of our conventional morality, could do full justice to the demands of a rational ethical individualism, and could leave to every man his right and his duty to choose some special personal cause of his own, while we could yet state the ideal of a harmony of all human causes in one all-embracing cause. Upon this basis we also could form a theory of conscience,—a theory which views conscience at once as rational and universal in its authority, and yet as individual in its expression in the life of each man, so that every man's conscience remains his own, and is, to himself, in many ways, mysterious; while the whole business of any man's conscience is, nevertheless, to direct that man to find his individual place in the one, universal, rational, moral order.

Hereupon we illustrated our theory of loyalty by applying it to a study of some of our own national problems. And next, our account of the practice of loyalty culminated in a doctrine of the nature of training for loyalty. Here we found the great paradox of loyalty afresh illustrated. Loyalty wins not only by sacrifice, but also by painful labor, and by the very agony of defeat. In this our human world the lost causes have proved themselves, in history, to be the most fruitful causes. In sum, loyalty is trained both through the presence of personal leaders, and through that idealization of our causes which adversity nourishes, which death illumines, and which the defeats of present time may render all the clearer and more ideally fascinating.

All these results showed us that loyalty has about it a character such as forbids us, after all, to interpret the true good of loyalty in terms of our merely individual human experiences. Man discovers, indeed, even within the limits of his own personal experience, that loyalty is his ethical destiny, and that without it he can win no peace; while, with loyalty once in possession of his active powers, he seems to himself to have solved the personal problem of the purpose of his life. But loyalty thus appears, after all, in the individual life, in a deeply mysterious form. It says to a man: "Your true good can never be won and verified by you in terms to which the present form and scope of our human experience is adequate. The best that you can get lies in self-surrender, and in your personal assurance that the cause to which you surrender yourself is indeed good. But your cause, if it is indeed a reality, has a good about it which no one man, and no mere collection of men, can ever verify. This good of the cause is essentially superhuman in its type, even while it is human in its embodiment. For it belongs to an union of men, to a whole of human life which transcends the individuality of any man, and which is not to be found as something belonging to any mere collection of men. Let your supreme good, then, be this, that you regard the cause as real, as good, and that, if the cause be lost to any merely human sight, you hold it to be nevertheless living in its own realm,—not apart, indeed, from human life, but in the form of the fulfilment of many human lives in one."

Now, this mysterious speech of loyalty implies something which is not only moral, but also metaphysical. Purely practical considerations, then, a study of our human needs, an ideal of the business of life,—these inevitably lead us into a region which is more than merely a realm of moral activities. This region is either one of delusions or else one of spiritual realities of a level higher than is that of our present individual human experience.

In the last lecture we undertook to consider this larger realm of spiritual unities which must be real in case our loyalty is not based upon illusion. And we attempted to sketch a general theory of truth which might show us that such spiritual unities are indeed realities, and are presupposed by our every effort to define truth. Thus our ethical theory has transformed itself into a general philosophical doctrine; and loyalty now appears to us not only as a guide of life but as a revelation of our relation to a realm which we have been obliged to define as one of an eternal and all-embracing unity of spiritual life.

We have called this realm of true life, and of genuine and united experience,—this realm which, if our argument at the last time was sound, includes our lives in that very whole which constitutes the real universe, —we have called this realm, I say, an eternal world,—eternal, simply because, according to our theory, it includes all temporal happenings and strivings in the conspectus of a single consciousness, and fulfils all our rational purposes together, and is all that we seek to be. For, as we argued, this realm of reality is conscious, is united, is self-possessed, and is perfected through the very wealth of the ideal sacrifices and of the loyal devotion which are united so as to constitute its fullness of being. In view of the philosophy that was thus sketched, I now propose a new definition of loyalty; and I say that this definition results from all of our previous study: *Loyalty is the will to manifest, so far as is possible, the Eternal, that is, the conscious and superhuman unity of life, in the form of the acts of an individual Self.* Or, if you prefer to take the point of view of an individual human self, if you persist in looking at the world just as we find it in our ordinary experience, and if you regard the metaphysical doctrine just sketched merely as an ideal theory of life, and *not* as a demonstrable philosophy, I can still hold to my definition of loyalty by borrowing a famous phrase from the dear friend and colleague some of whose views I at the last time opposed. I can, then, simply state my new definition of loyalty in plainer and more directly obvious terms thus: *Loyalty is the Will to Believe in something eternal, and to express that belief in the practical life of a human being.*

This, I say, is my new definition of loyalty, and in its metaphysical form, it is my final definition. Let me expound it further, and let me show a little more in detail how it results from the whole course of our inquiry.

II

However kindly you may have followed the discussion of my last lecture, some of you will feel doubts as to the theory of truth and of reality which I opposed to the doctrines of recent pragmatism, and which I now lay at the basis of my final definition of loyalty. I approached my own theory by the way of a polemic against my colleague's recently stated views regarding the nature of truth. But polemic often hinders our appreciation of some aspects of the questions at issue, even while it may help us to emphasize others. So let me now point out, apart from a polemic against other theories of truth, what is my main motive for viewing the real world as I do, and why I suppose that viewing the world as I do helps us to understand better the business of loyalty.

People who have faith in this or in that form of superhuman and significant reality often ask what they can do to turn their faith into something that more resembles clear insight. Shall they look into the evidences that are adduced in favor of this or of that miraculous story? Shall they themselves seek for the miraculous in their own personal experience? Will psychical research throw any light on the mysteries of being? Or, perhaps, will some sort of special mystical training reveal the higher truth? What is the way that leads towards the spiritual world? And thus those who doubt whether there are such higher realities to be found still sometimes try to get rid of these doubts by various appeals either to more or less magical arts, or to extraordinary personal experiences, or to mystical transformations of their personal life.

Now, whatever may be said of wonders, or of mystical revelations, our philosophy of loyalty is naturally interested in pointing out a road to the spiritual world, if, indeed, there be such a world,—a road, I say, which has a plain relation to our everyday moral life. And it seems to me, both that there is a genuinely spiritual world, and that there is a path of inquiry which can lead from such a practical faith in the higher world as loyalty embodies in its deeds, to a rational insight into the general constitution of this higher realm. I do not offer my opinions upon this subject as having any authority. I can see no farther through stone walls than can my fellow, and I enjoy no special revelations from any superhuman realm. But I ask you, as thoughtful people, to consider what your ordinary life, as rational beings, implies as its basis and as its truth.

What I was expounding at the close of my last lecture was a view of things which seems to me to be implied in any attempt to express, in a reasonable way, where we stand in our universe.

We all of us have to admit, I think, that our daily life depends upon believing in realities which are, in any case, just as truly beyond the scope of our ordinary individual experience as any spiritual realm could possibly be. We live by believing in one another's minds as realities. We give credit to countless reports, documents, and other evidences of present and past facts; and we do all this, knowing that such credit cannot be adequately verified by any experience such as an individual man can obtain. Now, the usual traditional account of all these beliefs of ours is that they are forced upon us, by some reality which is, as people say, wholly independent of our knowledge, which exists by itself apart from our experience, and which may be, therefore, entirely alien in its nature to any of our human interests and ideals.

But modern philosophy,—a philosophy in whose historical course of development our recent pragmatism is only a passing incident,—that philosophy which turns upon analyzing the bases of our knowledge, and upon reflectively considering what our human beliefs and ideas are intended to mean and to accomplish, has taught us to see that we can never deal with any wholly independent reality. The recent pragmatists, as I understand them, are here in full and conscious agreement with my own opinion. We can deal with no world which is out of relation to our experience. On the contrary, the real world is known to us in terms of *our* experience, is defined for us by *our* ideas, and is the object of *our* practical endeavors. Meanwhile, to declare anything real is to assert that it has its place in some realm of experience, be this experience human or superhuman. To declare that anything whatever is a fact, is simply to assert that some proposition, which you or I or some other thinking being can express in the form of intelligible ideas, is a true proposition. And the truth of propositions itself is nothing dead, is nothing independent of ideas and of experience, but is simply the successful fulfilment of some demand,—a demand which you can express in the form of an assertion, and which is fulfilled in so far, and only in so far, as some region of live experience contains what meets that demand. Meanwhile, every proposition, every assertion that anybody can make, is a deed; and every rational deed involves, in effect, an assertion of a fact. If the prodigal son says, "I will arise and go to my father," he even thereby asserts something to be true about himself, his father, and his father's house. If an astronomer or a chemist or a statistician or a man of business reports "this or this is a fact," he even thereby performs a deed,—an act having an ideal meaning, and embodying a live purpose; and he further declares that the constitution of experience is such as to make this deed essentially reasonable, successful, and worthy to be accepted by every man.

The real world is therefore *not* something independent of us. It is a world whose stuff, so to speak,—whose content,—is of the nature of experience, whose structure meets, validates, and gives warrant to our active deeds, and whose whole nature is such that it can be interpreted in terms of ideas, propositions, and conscious meanings, while in turn it gives to our fragmentary ideas and to our conscious life whatever connected meaning they possess. Whenever I have purposes and fail, so far, to carry them out, that is because I have not yet found the true way of expressing my own relation to reality. On the other hand, precisely in so far as I have understood some whole of reality, I have carried out successfully some purpose of mine.

There is, then, no merely theoretical truth, and there is no reality foreign, in its nature, to experience. Whoever actually lives the whole conscious life such as *can* be lived out with a definitely reasonable meaning,—such a being, obviously superhuman in his grade of consciousness, not only knows the real world, but *is* the real world. Whoever is conscious of the whole content of experience possesses all reality. And our search for reality is simply an effort to discover what the whole fabric of experience is into which our human experience is woven, what the system of truth is in which our partial truths have their place, what the ideally significant life is for the sake of which every deed of ours is undertaken. When we try to find out what the real world is, we are simply trying to discover the sense of our own individual lives. And we can define that sense of our lives only in terms of a conscious life in which ours is included, in which our ideas get their full meaning expressed, and in which what we fail to carry out to the full is carried out to the full.

III

Otherwise stated, when I think of the whole world of facts,—the "real world,"—I inevitably think of something that is *my own* world, precisely in so far as that world is any object of any reasonable idea of mine. It is true, of course, that, in forming an idea of my world of facts, I do not thereby give myself, at this instant, the least right to spin out of my inner consciousness any adequate present ideas of the detail of the contents of my real world. In thinking of the real world, I am indeed thinking of the whole of that very system of experience in which my experience is bound up, and in which I, as an individual, have my very limited and narrow place. But just now I am not in possession of that whole. I have to work for it and wait for it, and faithfully to be true to it. As a creature living along, from moment to moment, in time, I therefore indeed have to wait ignorantly enough for coming experience. I have to use as I can my fallible memory in trying to find out about my own past experience. I have no way of verifying what your experience is, except by using tests—and again the extremely fallible tests—which we all employ in our social life. I need the methods of the sciences of experience to guide me in the study of whatever facts fall within their scope. I use those practical and momentary successes upon which recent pragmatism insists, whenever I try to get a concrete verification of my opinions. And so far I stand, and must rightly stand, exactly where any man of common sense, any student of a science, any plain man, or any learned man stands. I am a fallible mortal, simply trying to find my way as I can in the thickets of experience.

And yet all this my daily life, my poor efforts to remember and to predict, my fragmentary inquiries into this or that matter of science or of business, my practical acknowledgment of your presence as real facts in the real world of experience, my personal definition of the causes to which I devote myself,—these are all undertakings that are overruled, and that are rendered significant, simply in so far as they are reasonable parts of one all-embracing enterprise. This enterprise is my active attempt to find out my true place in the real world. But now I can only define my real world by conceiving it in terms of experience. I can find my place in the world only by discovering where I stand in the whole system of experience. For what I mean by a fact is something that somebody finds. Even a merely possible fact is something only in so far as somebody actually *could* find it. And the sense in which it *is* an actual fact that somebody *could* find in his experience a determinate fact, is a sense which again can only be defined in terms of concrete, living, and not merely possible experience, and in terms of some will or purpose expressed in a conscious life. Even possible facts, then, are *really* possible only in so far as something is actually experienced, or is found by somebody. Whatever is real, then, be it distant or near, past or future present to your mind or to mine, a physical fact or a moral fact, a fact of our possible human experience, or a fact of a superhuman type of experience, a purpose, a desire, a natural object or an ideal object, a mechanical system or a value,

—whatever, I say, is real, *is real as a content present to some conscious being.* Therefore, when I inquire about the real world, I am simply asking what contents of experience, human or superhuman are actually and consciously found by somebody. My inquiries regarding facts, of whatever grade the facts may be, are therefore inevitably an effort to find out *what the world's experience is.* In all my common sense, then, in all my science, in all my social life, I am trying to discover what the universal conscious life which constitutes the world contains as its contents, and views as its own.

But even this is not the entire story of my place in the real world. For I cannot inquire about facts without forming my own ideas of these facts. In so far as my ideas are true, my own personal ideas are therefore active processes that go on within the conscious life of the world. If my ideas are true, they succeed in agreeing with the very world consciousness that they define. But this agreement, this success, if itself it is a fact at all, is once more a fact of experience,—yet not merely of my private experience, since I myself never personally find, within the limits of my own individual experience, the success that every act of truth seeking demands. If I get the truth, then, at any point of my life, my success if real only in so far as some conscious life, which includes my ideas and my efforts, and which also includes the very facts of the world whereof I am thinking, actually and observes my success, in the form of a conspectus of the world's facts, and of my own efforts to find and to define them.

In so far, then, as I get the truth about the world, I myself am a fragmentary conscious life that is included within the conscious conspectus of the world's experience, and that is in one self-conscious unity with that world consciousness. And it is in this unity with the world consciousness that I get my success, and am in concord with the truth.

But of course any particular idea of mine, regarding the world, or regarding any fact in the world, may be false. However, this possibility of my error is itself a real situation of mine, and involves essentially the same relation between the world and myself which obtains in case I have true ideas. For I can be in error about an object only in case I really mean to agree with that object, and to agree with it in a way which only my own purposes, in seeking this agreement, can possibly define. It is only by virtue of my own undertakings that I can fail in my undertakings. It is only because, after all, I am loyal to the world's whole truth that I can so express myself in fallible ideas, and in fragmentary opinions that, as a fact, I may, at any moment, undertake too much for my own momentary success to be assured, so that I can indeed in any one of my assertions fail justly to accord with that world consciousness which I am all the while trying to interpret in my own transient way. But when I thus fail, I momentarily fail *to interpret my place in the very world consciousness whose life I am trying to define.* But my failure, when and in so far as it occurs, is once more a fact,—and therefore a fact for the world's consciousness. If I blunder, but am sincere, if I think myself right, but am not right, then my error is a fact for a consciousness which includes my fallible attempts to be loyal to the truth, but which sees how they just now lose present touch with their true cause. Seeing this my momentary defeat, the world consciousness sees, however, my loyalty, and in its conspectus assigns, even to my fragmentary attempts at truth, their genuine place in the single unity of the world's consciousness. My very failure, then, like every loyal failure, is still a sort of success. It is an effort to define my place in the unity of the world's conspectus of all conscious life. I cannot fall out of that unity. I cannot flee from its presence. And I can err only as the loyal may give up their life for their cause. Whether I get truth, then, or whether I err in detail, *my loyal search for truth insures the fact that I am in a significant unity with the world's conscious life.*

The thesis that the world is one whole and a significant whole of conscious life is, for these reasons, a thesis which can only be viewed as an error, by reinstating this very assertion under a new form. For any error of mine concerning the world is possible only in so far as I really mean to assert the truth about the world; and this real meaning of mine can exist only as a fact within the conspectus of consciousness for which the real whole world exists, and within which I myself live.

This, then, in brief, is my own theory of truth. This is why I hold this theory to be no fantastic guess about what may be true, but a logically inevitable conclusion about how every one of us, wise or ignorant, is actually defining his own relation to truth, whether he knows the fact or not. I expressed my theory at the last time in terms of a polemic against the recent pragmatists; but as a fact their view, in its genuine and deeper meaning, is no more opposed to mine than my young Russian's vehement protest against loyalty, quoted in my second lecture, was, in its true spirit, opposed to my own view. My young Russian, you may remember, hated what he took to be loyalty, just because he was so loyal. And even so my friends, the recent pragmatists, reassert my theory of truth even in their every attempt to deny it. For, amongst other things, they assert that their own theory of truth is actually true. And that assertion implies just such a conspectus of all truth in one view,—just such a conspectus as I too assert.

IV

We first came in sight of this theory of truth, in these discussions, for a purely practical reason. Abstract and coldly intellectual as the doctrine, when stated as I have just stated it, may appear, we had our need to ask what truth is, because we wanted to know whether the loyal are right in supposing, as they inevitably do suppose, that their personal causes, and that their cause of causes, namely, universal loyalty, that any such causes, I say, possess genuine foundation in truth. Loyalty, as we found, is a practical service of superhuman objects. For our causes transcend expression in terms of our single lives. If the cause lives, then all conscious moral life—even our poor human life—is in unity with a superhuman conscious life, in which we ourselves dwell; and in this unity we win, in so far as we are loyal servants of our cause, a success which no transient human experience of ours, no joyous thrill of the flying moment, no bitterness of private defeat and loss, can do more or less than to illustrate, to illumine, or to idealize.

We asked: Is this faith of the loyal in their causes a pathetic fallacy? Our theory of truth has given us a general answer to this intensely practical question. The loyal try to live in the spirit. But, if thereupon they merely open their eyes to the nature of the reasonable truth, they see that it is in the spirit only that they do or can live. They would be living in this truth, as mere passing fragments of conscious life, as mere blind series of mental processes, even if they were not loyal. For all life, however dark and fragmentary, is either a blind striving for conscious unity with the universal life of which it is a fragment, or else, like the life of the loyal, is a deliberate effort to express such a striving in the form of a service of a superhuman cause. *And all lesser loyalties, and all serving of imperfect or of evil causes, are but fragmentary forms of the service of the cause of universal loyalty.* To serve universal loyalty is, however, to view the interests of all conscious life as one; and to do this is to regard all conscious life as constituting just such an unity as our theory of truth requires. Meanwhile, since truth seeking is indeed itself a practical activity, what we have stated in our theory of truth is itself but an aspect of the very life that the loyal are leading. Whoever seeks any truth is loyal, for he is determining his life by reference to a life which transcends his own. And he is loyal to loyalty; for whatever truth you try to discover is, if true, valid for everybody, and is therefore worthy of everybody's loyal recognition. The loyal, then, are truth seekers; and the truth seekers are loyal. And all of them live for the sake of the unity of all life. And this unity includes us all, but is superhuman.

Our view of truth, therefore, meets at once an ethical and a logical need. The real world is precisely that world in which the loyal are at home. Their loyalty is no pathetic fallacy. Their causes are real facts in the universe. The universe as a whole possesses that unity which loyalty to loyalty seeks to express in its service of the whole of life.

Herewith, however, it occurs to us to ask one final question. Is not this real world, whose true unity the loyal acknowledge by their every deed, and whose conscious unity every process of truth seeking presupposes,—is not this also the world which religion recognizes? If so, what is the relation of loyalty to religion?

The materials for answering this question are now in our hands. We have been so deliberate in preparing them for our present purpose, just for the sake of making our answer the simpler when it comes.

V

We have now defined loyalty as the will to manifest the eternal in and through the deeds of individual selves. As for religion,—in its highest historical forms (which here alone concern us),—religion, as I think, may be defined as follows. Religion (in these its highest forms) *is the interpretation both of the eternal and of the spirit of loyalty through emotion, and through a fitting activity of the imagination.*

Religion, in any form, has always been an effort to interpret and to make use of some superhuman world. The history, the genesis, the earlier and simpler forms of religion, the relations of religion and morality in the primitive life of mankind, do not here concern us. It is enough to say that, in history, there has often been a serious tension between the interests of religion and those of morality. For the higher powers have very generally seemed to man to be either non-moral or immoral. This very tension, only too frequently, still exists for many people today. One of the greatest and hardest discoveries of the human mind has been the discovery of how to reconcile, not religion and science, but religion and morality. Whoever knows even a small portion of the history of the cults of mankind is aware of the difficulties to which I refer. The superhuman has been conceived by men in terms that were often far enough from those which loyalty requires. Whoever will read over the recorded words of a writer nowadays too much neglected, the rugged and magnificently loyal Old Testament prophet Amos, can see for himself how bravely the difficulty of conceiving the superhuman as the righteous, was faced by one of the first who ever viewed the relation of religion and morality as our best teachers have since taught us to view them. And yet such a reader can also see how hard this very task of the prophet was. When we remember also that so great a mind as that of the originator of Buddhism, after all the long previous toil of Hindoo thought upon this great problem, could see no way to reconcile religion and morality, except by bringing them both to the shores of the mysterious and soundless ocean of Nirvana, and sinking them together in its depths (an undertaking which Buddha regarded as the salvation of the world), we get a further view of the nature of the problem. When we remember that St. Paul, after many years of lonely spiritual struggle, attempted in his teaching to reconcile morality and religion by an interpretation of Christianity which has ever since kept the Christian world in a most inspiring ferment of theological controversy and of practical conflict, we are again instructed as to the seriousness of the issue. But as a fact, the experience of the civilized man has gradually led him to see how to reconcile the moral life and the religious spirit. Since this reconciliation is one which our theory of truth, and of the constitution of the real world, substantially justifies, we are now ready for a brief review of the entire situation.

People often say that mere moraltiy is something very remote from true religion. Sometimes people say this in the interests of religion, meaning to point out that mere morality can at best make you only a more or less tolerable citizen, while only religion can reconcile you, as such people say, to that superhuman world whose existence and whose support alone make human life worth living. But sometimes almost the same assertion is made in the interest of pure morality, viewed as something independent of religion. Some people tell you, namely, that since, as they say, religion is a collection of doubtful beliefs, of superstitions, and of more or less exalted emotions, morality is all the better for keeping aloof from religion. Suffering man needs your help; your friends need as much happiness as you can give them; conventional morality is, on the whole a good thing. Learn righteousness, therefore, say they, and leave religion to the fantastic-minded who love to believe. The human is what we need. Let the superhuman alone.

Now, our philosophy of loyalty, aiming at something much larger and richer than the mere sum of human happiness in individual men, has taught us that there is no such sharp dividing line between the human and the superhuman as these attempts to sunder the provinces of religion and morality would imply. The loyal serve something more than individual lives. Even Nietzsche, individualist and ethical naturalist though he was, illustrates our present thesis. He began the later period of his teaching by asserting that "God is dead"; and (lest one might regard this as a mere attack upon monotheism, and might suppose Nietzsche to be an old-fashioned heathen polytheist) he added the famous remark that, in case any gods whatever existed, he could not possibly endure being himself no god. "*Therefore*," so he reasoned, "*there are no gods.*" All this seems to leave man very much to his own devices. Yet Nietzsche at once set up the cult of the ideal future being called the *Uebermensch* or Superman. And the *Uebermensch* is just as much of a god as anybody who ever throned upon Olympus or dwelt in the sky. And if the doctrine of the "Eternal Recurrence," as Nietzsche defined it, is true the *Uebermensch* belongs not only to the ideal future, but has existed an endless number of times already.

If our philosophy of loyalty is right, Nietzsche was not wrong in this appeal to the superhuman. The superhuman we indeed have always with us. Life has no sense without it. But the superhuman need not be the magical. It need not be the object of superstition. And if we are desirous of unifying the interests of morality and religion, it is well indeed to begin, as rugged old Amos began, by first appreciating what righteousness is, and then by interpreting righteousness, in a perfectly reasonable and non-superstitious way, in superhuman terms. Then we shall be ready to appreciate what religion, whose roots are indeed by no means wholly in our moral nature, nevertheless has to offer us as a supplement to our morality.

VI

Loyalty is a service of causes. But, as we saw, we do not, we cannot, wait until somebody clearly shows us how good the causes are in themselves, before we set about serving them. We first practically learn of the goodness of our causes through the very act of serving them. Loyalty begins, then, in all of us, in elemental forms. A cause fascinates us—we at first know not clearly why. We give ourselves willingly to that cause. Herewith our true life begins. The cause may indeed be a bad one. But at worst it is our way of interpreting the true cause. If we let our loyalty develop, it tends to turn into the service of the universal cause. Hence I deliberately declined, in this discussion, to *base* my theory of loyalty upon that metaphysical doctrine which I postponed to my latest lectures. It is a very imperfect view of the real world which most youth get before them before they begin to be loyal. Hosts of the loyal actually manifest the eternal in their deeds, and know not that they do so. They only know that they are given over to their cause. The first good of loyalty lies, then, in the fact which we emphasized in our earlier lectures. Reverberating all through you, stirring you to your depths, loyalty first unifies your plan of life, and thereby gives you what nothing else can give,—your self as a life lived in accordance with a plan, your conscience as your plan interpreted for you through your ideal, your cause expressed as your personal purpose in living.

In so far, then, one can indeed be loyal without being consciously and explicitly religious. One's cause, in its first intention, appears to him human, concrete, practical. It is *also* an ideal. It is *also* a superhuman entity. It also really *means* the service of the eternal. But this fact may be, to the hard-working, and especially to the unimaginative, and, in a worldly sense, fairly successful man, a latent fact. He then, to be sure, gradually idealizes his cause as he goes; but this idealizing in so far becomes no very explicitly emphasized process in his life, although, as we have seen, some tendency to deify the cause is inevitable.

Meanwhile, such an imperfectly developed but loyal man may also accept, upon traditional grounds, a religion. This religion will then tell him about a superhuman world. But in so far the religion need not be, to his mind, an essential factor in his practical loyalty. He may be superstitious; or he may be a religious formalist; or he may accept his creed and his church simply because of their social respectability and usefulness; or, finally, he may even have a rich and genuine religious experience, which still may remain rather a mysticism than a morality, or an aesthetic comfort rather than a love of his cause.

In such cases, loyalty and religion may long keep apart. But the fact remains that loyalty, if sincere, involves at least a latent belief in the superhuman reality of the cause, and means at least an unconscious devotion to the one and eternal cause. But such a belief is also a latent union of morality and religion. Such a service is an unconscious piety. The time may come, then, when the morality will consciously need this union with the religious creed of the individual whose growth we are portraying.

This union must begin to become an explicit union whenever that process which, in our sixth lecture, we called the idealizing of the cause, reaches its higher levels. We saw that those higher levels are reached in the presence of what seems to be, to human vision, a lost cause. If we believe in the lost cause, we become directly aware that we are indeed seeking a city out of sight. If such a cause is real, it belongs to a superhuman world. Now, every cause worthy, as we said, of lifelong service, and capable of unifying our life plans, shows sooner or later that it is a cause *which we cannot successfully express in any set of human experiences of transient joys and of crumbling successes.* Human life taken merely as it flows, viewed merely as it passes by in time and is gone, is indeed a lost river of experience that plunges down the mountains of youth and sinks in the deserts of age. Its significance comes solely through it relations to the air and the ocean and the great deeps of universal experience. For by such poor figures I may, in passing, symbolize that really rational relation of our personal experience to universal conscious experience,—that relation to which I have devoted these last two lectures.

Everybody ought to serve the universal cause in his own individual way. For this, as we have seen, is what loyalty, when it comes to know its own mind, really means. But whoever thus serves inevitably *loses* his cause in our poor world of human sense-experience, because his cause is too good for this present temporal world to express it. And that is, after all, what the old theology meant when it called you and me, as we now naturally are, lost beings. Our deepest loyalty lies in devoting ourselves to causes that are just now lost to our poor human nature. One can express this, of course, by saying that the true cause is indeed real enough, in the higher world, while it is our poor human nature which is lost. Both ways of viewing the case have their truth. Loyalty means a transformation of our nature.

Lost causes, then, we must serve. But as we have seen, in our sixth lecture, loyalty to a lost cause has two companions, grief and imagination. Now, these two are the parents of all the higher forms of genuinely ethical religion. If you doubt the fact, read the scriptures of any of the great ethical faiths. Consult the psalter, the hymns, the devotional books, or the prayers of the church. Such religion interprets the superhuman in forms that our longing, our grief, and our imagination invent, but also in terms that are intended to meet the demands of our highest loyalty. For we are loyal to that unity of life which, as our truer moral consciousness learns to believe, owns the whole real world, and constitutes the cause of causes. In being loyal to universal loyalty, we are serving the unity of life.

This true unity of the world-life, however, is at once very near to us and very far from us. Very near it is; for we have our being in it, and depend upon it for whatever worth we have. Apart from it we are but the gurgling stream soon to be lost in the desert. In union with it we have individual significance in and for the whole. But we are very far from it also, because our human experience throws such fragmentary light upon the details of our relation to its activities. Hence in order to feel our relations to it as vital relations, we have to bring it near to our feelings and to our imaginations. And we long and suffer the loneliness of this life as we do so. But because we know of the details of the world only through our empirical sciences, while these give us rather materials for a rational life than a view of the unity of life, we are indeed left to our imagination to assuage grief and to help in the training of loyalty. For here, that is, precisely as to the *details* of the system of facts whereby our life is linked to the eternal, our science forsakes us. We can know *that* we are thus linked. *How* we are linked, our sciences do not make manifest to us.

Hence the actual content of the higher ethical religions is endlessly rich in legend and in other symbolic portrayal. This portrayal is rich in emotional meaning and in vivid detail. What this portrayal attempts to characterize is, in its general outline, an absolute truth. This truth consists in the following facts: *First, the rational unity and goodness of the world-life; next, its true but invisible nearness to us, despite our ignorance; further, its fulness of meaning despite our barrenness of present experience; and yet more, its interest in our personal destiny as moral beings; and finally the certainty that, through our actual human loyalty, we come, like Moses, face to face with the true will of the world, as a man speaks to his friend.* In recognizing these facts, we have before us what may be called the creed of the Absolute Religion.

You may well ask, of course, whether our theory of truth, as heretofore expounded, gives any warrant to such religious convictions. I hold that it does give warrant to them. The symbols in which these truths are expressed by one or another religion are indeed due to all sorts of historical accidents, and to the most varied play of the imaginations both of

the peoples and of the religious geniuses of our race. But that our relations to the world-life are relations wherein we are consciously met,
from the other side, by a superhuman and yet strictly personal conscious
life, in which our own personalities are themselves bound up, but which
also is not only richer but is more concrete and definitely conscious and
real than we are,—this seems to me to be an inevitable corollary of my
theory of truth.

VII

And now, finally, to sum up our whole doctrine of loyalty and religion. Two things belonging to the world-life we know—two at least, if
my theory is true: *it is defined in terms of our own needs; and it includes
and completes our experience.* Hence, in any case, it is precisely as live
and elemental and concrete as we are; and there is not a need of ours
which is not its own. If you ask why I call it good—well, the very arguments which recent pragmatism has used are, as you remember, here my
warrant. A truth cannot be a merely theoretical truth. True is that which
successfully fulfils an idea. Whoever again, is not succeeding, or is facing
an evil, or is dissatisfied, is inevitably demanding and defining facts that
are far beyond him, and that are not yet consciously his own. A knower
of the totality of truth is therefore, of necessity, in possession of the
fulfilment of all rational purposes. If, however, you ask why this world-
life permits any evil whatever, or any finitude, or any imperfections, I
must indeed reply that here is no place for a general discussion of the
whole problem of evil, which I have repeatedly and wearisomely considered in other discussions of mine. But this observation does belong
here. Our theory of evil is indeed no "shallow optimism," but is founded
upon the deepest, the bitterest, and the dearest moral experience of the
human race. The *loyal*, and they alone, know the one great good of suffering, of ignorance, of finitude, of loss, of defeat—*and that is just the
good of loyalty*, so long as the cause itself can only be viewed as indeed
a living whole. Spiritual peace is surely no easy thing. We win that peace
only through stress and suffering and loss and labor. But when we find
the preciousness of the idealized cause emphasized through grief, we see
that, whatever evil is, it at least *may* have its place in an ideal order. What
would be the universe without loyalty; and what would loyalty be without trial? And when we remember that, from this point of view, our own
griefs are the griefs of the very world consciousness itself, in so far as

this world-life is expressed in our lives, it may well occur to us that the life of loyalty with all its griefs and burdens and cares may be the very foundation of the attainment of that spiritual triumph which we must conceive as realized by the world spirit.

Perhaps, however, one weakly says: "If the world will attains in its wholeness what we seek, why need we seek that good at all?" I answer at once that our whole philosophy of loyalty instantly shows the vanity of such speech. Of course, the world-life does *not* obtain the individual good that is involved in my willing loyalty unless indeed *I am loyal*. The cause may in some way triumph without me, but not as *my* cause. We have never defined our theory as meaning that the world-life is *first* eternally complete, but *then* asks us, in an indifferent way, to copy its perfections. Our view is that each of us who is loyal is doing his unique deed in that whole of life which we have called the eternal simply because it is the conspectus of the totality of life, past, present, and future. If my deed were not done, the world-life would miss my deed. Each of us can say that. The very basis of our theory of truth, which we found upon the deeds, the ideas, the practical needs, of each of us, gives every individual his unique place in the world order—his deed that nobody else can do, his will which is his own. "Our wills are ours to make them thine." The unity of the world is *not* an ocean in which we are lost, but a life which is and which needs all our lives in one. Our loyalty defines that unity for us as a living, active unity. We have come to the unity through the understanding of our loyalty. It is an eternal unity only in so far as it includes all time and change and life and deeds. And therefore, when we reach this view, since the view simply fulfils what loyalty demands, our loyalty remains as precious to us, and as practical, and as genuinely a service of a cause, as it was before. It is no sort of "moral holiday" that this whole world-life suggests to us. It is precisely as a whole life of ideal strivings in which we have our places as individual selves and are such selves only in so far as we strive to do our part in the whole,—it is thus, and thus only, that our philosophy of loyalty regards the universe.

Religion, therefore, precisely in so far as it attempts to conceive the universe as a conscious and personal life of superhuman meaning, and as a life that is in close touch with our own meaning, is eternally true. But now it is just this *general* view of the universe as a rational order that is indeed open to our rational knowledge. No part of such a doctrine gives us, however, the present right as human beings to determine with any certainty the details of the world-life, except in so far as they come within the scope of our scientific and of our social inquiries. Hence, when religion, in the service of loyalty, interprets the world-life to us with symbolic detail, it gives us indeed merely symbols of the eternal truth. That this truth is indeed eternal, that our loyalty brings us into personal relations with a personal world-life, which values our every loyal deed, and needs that deed, all this is true and rational. And just this is what religion rightly illustrates. But the parables, the symbols, the historical incidents that the religious imagination uses in its portrayals,—these are the more or less sacred and transient *accidents* in which the "real presence" of the divine at once shows itself to us, and hides the detail of its inner life from us. These accidents of the religious imagination endure through many ages; but they also vary from place to place and from one nation or race of men to another, and they ought to do so. Whoever sees the living truth of the personal and conscious and ethical unity of the world *through* these symbols is possessed of the absolute religion, whatever be his nominal creed or church. Whoever overemphasizes the empirical details of these symbols, and then asks us to accept these details as literally true, commits an error which seems to me simply to invert that error whereof, at the last time, I ventured to accuse my pragmatist friends. Such a literalist, who reads his symbols as revelations of the detailed structure of the divine life, seems to me, namely, to look for the eternal *within* the realm of the mere data of human sense and imagination. To do this, I think, is indeed to seek the risen Lord in the open sepulchre.

Concerning the living truth of the whole conscious universe, one can well say, as one observes the special facts of human sense and imagination: "He is not here; he is arisen." Yet equally from the whole circle of the heaven of that entire self-conscious life which *is* the truth, there comes always, and to all the loyal, the word: "Lo, I am with you alway, even unto the end of the world."

THE PROBLEM OF CHRISTIANITY (1913)

THE IDEA OF THE UNIVERSAL COMMUNITY

In accordance with the plan set forth at the close of our first lecture, we begin our study of the Problem of Christianity by a discussion of the Christian idea of the Church, and of its universal mission.

I

The Kingdom of Heaven, as characterized in the Sermon on the Mount and in the parables, is something that promises to the individual man salvation, and that also possesses, in some sense which the Master left for the future to make clearer, a social meaning. To the individual the doctrine says, "The Kingdom of Heaven is within you." But when in the end the Kingdom shall come, the will of God, as we learn, is to be done on earth as it is in heaven. And therewith the kingdoms of this world—the social order as it now is and as it naturally is—will pass away. Then there will come to pass the union of the blessed with their Father, and also, as appears, with one another, in the heavenly realm which the Father has prepared for them.

This final union of all who love is not described at length in the recorded words of the Master. A religious imagery familiar to those who heard the parables that deal with the end of the world was freely used; and this imagery gives us to understand that the consummation of all things will unite in a heavenly community those who are saved. But the organization, the administration, the ranks and dignities, of the Kingdom of Heaven the Master does not describe.

When the Christian Church began, in the Apostolic Age, to take visible form, the idea of the mission of the Church expressed the meaning which the Christian community came to attach to the social implications of the founder's doctrine. What was merely hinted in the parables now became explicit. The Kingdom of Heaven was to be realized in and through and for the Church,—in the fellowship of the faithful who constituted the Church as it was on earth; through the divine Spirit that was believed to guide the life of the Church; and for the future experience of the Church, whenever the end should come, and whenever the purpose of God should finally be manifested and accomplished.

Such, in brief, was the teaching of the early Christian community. Unquestionably th's teaching added something new to the original doctrine of the Kingd m. But this addition, as we shall later see, was more characteristic of the new religion than was any portion of the sayings that tradition attributed to the Master, and was as inseparable from the essence of primitive Christianity as the belief of the disciples themselves was inseparable from their very earliest interpretations of the person and the mission of their leader.

It is useless, I think, for the most eager defender and expounder of primitive Christianity in its purity to ignore the fact that, whatever else the Christian religion involves, some sort of faith or doctrine regarding the office and the meaning of the Church was an essential part of the earliest Christianity that existed after the founder had passed from earth.

Since our problem of Christianity involves the study of the most vital Christian ideas, how can we better begin our task than by asking what this idea of the Church really means, and what value and truth it possesses? Not only is such a beginning indeed advisable, but, at first sight, it seems especially adapted to enable us to use the manifold and abundant aids which, as we might suppose, the aspirations of all Christian ages would furnish for our guidance.

For, as you may naturally ask, is not the history of Christianity, viewed in at least one very significant way, simply the history of the Christian Church? Is not the idea of the Church, then, not only essential and potent, but one of the most familiar of the religious ideas of Christendom? Must not the consciousness of all really awakened Christian communities whose creeds are recorded stand ready to help the inquirer who wants to interpret this idea? May we not then begin this part of our enterprise with high hope, sure that, as we attempt to grasp and to estimate this first of our three essential Christian ideas, we shall have the ages of

Christian development as our helpers? So, I repeat, you may very naturally ask. But the answer to this question is not such as quite fulfils the hope just suggested.

II

As a fact, the idea and the doctrine of the Christian Church constitute indeed a vital and permanent part of Christianity; and a study of this idea is a necessary, and may properly be the first, part of our inquiry into the Problem of Christianity.

But we must not begin this inquiry without a due sense of its difficulty. We must remember at the very outset the fact that all the Christian ages, up to the present one, unite, not to present to us any finished interpretation of the idea of the Church, but rather to prove that this idea is as fluent in its expression as it is universal in its aim; and is as baffling, by reason of the conflicts of its interpreters, as it is precious in the longings that constitute its very heart.

If this idea comforts the faithful, it is also a stern idea; for it demands of those who accept it the resolute will to face and to contend against the greatest of spiritual obstacles, namely, the combined waywardness of the religious caprices of all Christian mankind. For the true Church, as we shall see, is still a sort of ideal challenge to the faithful, rather than an already finished institution,—a call upon men for a heavenly quest, rather than a present possession of humanity. "Create me,"—this is the word that the Church, viewed as an idea, addresses to mankind.

Meanwhile the contrast between the letter and the spirit of a fundamental doctrine is nowhere more momentous and more tragic than in case of the doctrine of the nature and the office of the Christian Church. The spirit of this doctrine consists, as we have already seen, in the assertion that there is a certain divinely ordained and divinely significant spiritual community, to which all must belong who are to attain the true goal of life; that is, all who, to use the distinctly religious phraseology, are to be saved.

How profoundly reasonable are the considerations upon which this doctrine is based we have yet to see, and can only estimate in the light of a due study of all the essential Christian ideas. To my own mind these considerations are such as can be interpreted and defended without our needing, for the purposes of such interpretation and defence, any acceptance of traditional dogmas. For these considerations are based upon human nature. They have to do with interests which all reasonable men, whether Christian or non-Christian, more or less clearly recognize, in proportion as men advance to the higher stages of the art of life.

The spirit, then, of the doctrine of the Church is as reasonable as it is universal. It is Christian by virtue of features which, when once understood, also render it simply and impressively human. This, I say, is what our entire study of the three Christian ideas will, in the end, if I am right, bring to our attention.

III

But the letter of the doctrine of the Church has been subject to fortunes such as, in various ways and degrees, attend the visible embodiment of all the great ideals of humanity; only that, as I have just said, the resulting tragedy is, in no other case in which spirit and letter are in conflict, greater than in this case.

In general the risks of temporary disaster which great ideals run appear to be directly proportioned to the value of the ideals. The disasters may be destined to give place to victory; but great truths bear long sorrows. What humanity most needs, it most persistently misunderstands. The spirit of a great ideal may be immortal; its ultimate victory, as we may venture to maintain, may be predetermined by the very nature of things; but that fact does not save such an ideal from the fires of the purgatory of time. Its very preciousness often seems to insure its repeated, its long-enduring, effacement. The comfort that it would bring if it were fully understood and accepted may make all the greater the sorrow of a world that still waits for the light.

In case of the history of the essential idea of the Church, the complications of dogma, the strifes of the sects, the horrors of the religious wars in former centuries, the confusions of controversy in our own day, must not make us despair. Such is the warfare of ideals. Such is this present world.

Least of all may we attempt, as many do, to accuse this or that special tendency or power in the actual Church, past or present, of being mainly responsible for this failure to appreciate the ideal Church. The defect lies deeper than students of such problems usually suppose. Human nature,— not any one party,—yes, the very nature of the processes of growth themselves, and not any particular form of religious or of moral error, must be viewed as the source of the principal tragedies of the history of all the Christian ideals.

In fact, the true idea of the Church has not been forsaken; it is, in a very real sense, still to be found, or rather, to be created. We have to do, in this case, not so much with apostasy as with evolution. To be sure, at the very outset, the ideal of the Church was seen afar off through a glass, darkly. The well-known apocalyptic vision revealed the true Church as the New Jerusalem that was yet to come down from heaven. The expression of the idea was left, by the early Church, as a task for the ages. The spirit of that idea was felt rather than ever adequately formulated, and the vision still remains one of the principal grounds and sources of the hope of humanity.

IV

Such doctrines, and such conflicts of spirit and letter, cannot be understood unless our historical sense is well awakened. On the other hand, they cannot be understood *merely* through a study of history. The values of ideals must be ideally discerned. If viewed without a careful and critical reflection, the history of such processes as the development of the idea of the Church presents a chaos of contending motives and actions. Apart from some understanding of history, all critical reflection upon this idea remains an unfruitful exercise in dialectics. We must therefore first divide our task, and then reunite the results, hoping thereby to win a connected view of the ideal that constitutes our present problem.

Let us, then, first point out certain motives which, when considered quite apart from any specifically Christian ideas or doctrines, may serve to make intelligible the ideal which is here in question. Then let us sketch the way in which the idea of the Christian Church first received expression.

This first expression of the idea of the Church, as we shall find, transformed the very teaching which it most eloquently reënforced and explained, namely, the teaching which the parables of the founder had left for the faith of the Christian community to interpret. This was the teaching about the office and the saving power of Christian love. For such, as we shall see, was the first result of the appearance of the idea of the Church in Christian history.

By sketching, then, some non-Christian developments and then a stage of early Christian life, we shall get two aspects of the ideal of the universal community before us. Hereby we shall not have reached any solution of our problem of Christianity; but we shall have brought together in our minds certain Christian and certain non-Christian ideas whose interrelations will hereafter prove to be of the utmost importance for our whole enterprise.

Next in order, then, comes a brief review of some of those motives which, apart from Christian history and Christian doctrine, make the ideal of the universal community a rationally significant ideal. These motives, in their turn, are of two kinds. Some of them are motives derived from the natural history of mankind. Some of them are distinctively ethical motives. We must become acquainted, through a very general summary, with both of these sorts of motives. Both sorts have interacted. The nature of man as a social being suggests certain ethical ideals. These ideals, in their turn, have modified the natural history of society.

V

As an essentially social being, man lives in communities, and depends upon his communities for all that makes his civilization articulate. His communities, as both Plato and Aristotle already observed, have a sort of organic life of their own, so that we can compare a highly developed community, such as a state, either to the soul of a man or to a living animal. A community is not a mere collection of individuals. It is a sort of live unit, that has organs, as the body of an individual has organs. A community grows or decays, is healthy or diseased, is young or aged, much as any individual member of the community possesses such characters. Each of the two, the community or the individual member, is as much a live creature as is the other. Not only does the community live, it has a mind of its own,—a mind whose psychology is not the same as the psychology of an individual human being. The social mind displays its psychological traits in its characteristic products,—in languages, in customs, in religions,—products which an individual human mind, or even a collection of such minds, when they are not somehow organized into a genuine community, cannot produce. Yet language, custom, religion are all of them genuinely mental products.

Communities, in their turn, tend, under certain conditions, to be organized into composite communities of still higher and higher grades. States are united in empires; languages coöperate in the production of universal literature; the corporate entities of many communities tend to organize that still very incomplete community which, if ever it comes into existence, will be the world-state, the community possessing the whole world's civilization.

So far, I have spoken only of the natural history of the social organization, and not of its value. But the history of thought shows how manifold are the ways in which, if once you grant that a community is or can be a living organic being, with a mind of its own, this doctrine about the natural facts can be used for ideal, for ethical, purposes. Few ideas have been, in fact, more fruitful than this one in their indirect consequences for ethical doctrines as well as for religion.

It is no wonder, then, that many object to every such interpretation of the nature of a community by declaring that, whatever our ethical ideals may demand, a community really has no mind of its own at all, and is no living organism. All the foregoing statements about the mind of a community (as such objectors insist) are metaphorical. A community is a collection of individuals. And the comparison of a community to an animal, or to a soul, is at best a convenient fiction.

Other critics, not so much simply rejecting the foregoing doctrine as hesitating, remark that to call a community an organism, and to speak of its possession of a mind, is to use some form of philosophical mysticism. And such mysticism, they say, stands, in any case, in need of further interpretations.

To such objectors I shall here only reply that one can maintain all the foregoing views regarding the real organic life and regarding the genuine mind of a community, without committing one's self to any form of philosophical mysticism, and without depending upon mere metaphors. For instance, Wundt, in his great book entitled "Volkerpsychologie," treats organized communities as psychical entities. He does so deliberately, and states his reasons. But he does all this purely as a psychologist. Communities, as he insists, behave as if they were wholes, and exhibit psychological laws of their own. Following Wundt, I have already said that it is the community which produces languages, customs, religions. These are, all of them, intelligent mental products, which can be psychologically analyzed, which follow psychological laws, and which exhibit characteristic processes of mental evolution,—processes that belong solely to organized groups of men. So Wundt speaks unhesitatingly of the *Gesammtbewusstsein*, or *Gesammtwille*, of a community; and he finds this mental life of the community to be as much an object for the student of the natural history of mind, as is the consciousness of any being whose life a psychologist can examine. His grounds are not mystical, but empirical,—if you will, pragmatic. A community behaves like an entity with a mind of its own. Therefore it is a fair "working hypothesis" for the psychologist to declare that it is such an entity, and that a community has, or is, a mind.

VI

So far, then, I have merely sketched what, in another context, will hereafter concern us much more at length. For in later lectures we shall have to study the metaphysical problems which we here first touch. A community can be viewed as a real unit. So we have seen, and so far only we have yet gone.

But we have now to indicate why this conception, whether metaphysically sound or not, is a conception that can be ethical in its purposes. And here again only the most elementary and fundamental aspects of our topic can be, in this wholly preparatory statement, mentioned. To all these problems we shall have later to return.

We have said that a community can behave like an unit; we have now to point out that an individual member of a community can find numerous very human motives for behaving towards his community as if it not only were an unit, but a very precious and worthy being. In particular he—the individual member—may love his community as if it were a person, may be devoted to it as if it were his friend or father, may serve it, may live and die for it, and may do all this, not because the philosophers tell him to do so, but because it is his own heart's desire to act thus.

Of such active attitudes of love and devotion towards a community, on the part of an individual member of that community, history and daily life present countless instances. One's family, one's circle of personal friends, one's home, one's village community, one's clan, or one's country may be the object of such an active disposition to love and to serve the community as an unit, to treat the community as if it were a sort of super-personal being, and as if it could, in its turn, possess the value of a person on some higher level. One who thus loves a community, regards its type of life, its form of being, as essentially more worthy than his own. He becomes devoted to its interests as to something that by its very nature is nobler than himself. In such a case he may find, in his devotion to his community, his fulfilment and his moral destiny. In order to view a community in this way it is, I again insist, not necessary to be a mystic. It is only necessary to be a hearty friend, or a good citizen, or a home-loving being.

Countless faithful and dutifully disposed souls, belonging to most various civilizations,—people active rather than fanciful, and earnest rather than speculative,—have in fact viewed their various communities in this way. I know of no better name for such a spirit of active devotion to the community to which the devoted individual belongs, than the excellent old word "Loyalty,"—a word to whose deeper meaning some Japanese thinkers have of late years recalled our attention.

Loyalty, as I have elsewhere defined it, is the willing and thoroughgoing devotion of a self to a cause, when the cause is something which unites many selves in one, and which is therefore the interest of a community. For a loyal human being the interest of the community to which he belongs is superior to every merely individual interest of his own. He actively devotes himself to this cause.

Loyalty exists in very manifold shapes, and belongs to no one time, or country, or people. Warlike tribes and nations, during the stages of their life which are intermediate between savagery and civilization, have often developed a high type of the loyal consciousness, and hence have defined their virtues in terms of loyalty. Such loyalty may last over into peaceful stages of social life; and the warlike life is not the exclusive originator of the loyal spirit. Loyalty often enters into a close alliance with religion, and from its very nature is disposed to religious interpretations. To the individual the loyal spirit appeals by fixing his attention upon a life incomparably vaster than his own individual life,—a life which, when his love for his community is once aroused, dominates and fascinates him by the relative steadiness, the strength and fixity and stately dignity, of its motives and demands.

The individual is naturally wayward and capricious. This waywardness is a constant source of entanglement and failure. But the community which he loves is rendered relatively constant in its will by its customs; yet these customs no longer seem, to the loyal individual, mere conventions or commands. For his social enthusiasm is awakened by the love of his kind; and he glories in his service, as the player in his team, or the soldier in his flag, or the martyr in his church. If his religion comes into touch with his loyalty, then his gods are the leaders of his community, and both the majesty and the harmony of the loyal life are thus increased. The loyal motives are thus not only moral, but also æsthetic. The community may be to the individual both beautiful and sublime.

Deep-seated, then, in human nature are the reasons that make loyalty appear to the individual as a solution for the problem of his personal life. Yet these motives tend to still higher and vaster conquests than we have here yet mentioned. Warlike tribes and nations fight together; and in so far loyalty contends with loyalty. But on a more highly selfconscious level the loyal spirit tends to assume the form of chivalry. The really devoted and considerate warrior learns to admire the loyalty of his foe; yes, even to depend upon it for some of his own best inspiration. Knighthood prizes the knightly spirit. The loyalty of the clansmen breeds by contagion a more intense loyalty in other clans; but at the same time it breeds a love for just such loyalty. Kindred clans learn to respect and, ere long, to share one another's loyalty. The result is an ethical motive that renders the alliance and, on occasion, the union of various clans and nationalities not only a possibility, but a conscious ideal.

The loyal are, in ideal, essentially kin. If they grow really wise, they observe this fact. The spirit that loves the community learns to prize itself as a spirit that, in all who are dominated by it, is essentially one, despite the variety of special causes, of nationalities, or of customs. The logical development of the loyal spirit is therefore the rise of a consciousness of the ideal of an universal community of the loyal,—a community which, despite all warfare and jealousy, and despite all varieties of gods and of laws, is supreme in its value, however remote from the present life of civilization.

The tendency towards the formation of such an ideal of an universal community can be traced both in the purely secular forms of loyalty, and in the history of the relations between loyalty and religion in the most varied civilizations. In brief, loyalty is, from the first, a practical faith that communities, viewed as units, have a value which is superior to all the values and interests of detached individuals. And the sort of loyalty which reaches the level of true chivalry and which loves the honor and the loyalty of the stranger or even of the foe, tends, either in company with or apart from any further religious motive, to lead men towards a conception of the brotherhood of all the loyal, and towards an estimation of all the values of life in terms of their relation to the service of one ideally universal community. To this community in ideal all men belong; and to act as if one were a member of such a community is to win in the highest measure the goal of individual life. It is to win what religion calls salvation.

When thus abstractly stated, the ideal of an universal community may appear far away from the ordinary practical interests of the plain man. But the history of the spirit of loyalty shows that there is a strong tendency of loyalty towards such universal ideals. Some such conception of the ideal community of all mankind, actually resulting from reflection upon the spirit of loyalty, received an occasional and imperfect formulation in Roman Stoicism. In this more speculative shape the Stoic conception of the universal community was indeed not fitted to win over the Roman world as a whole to an active loyalty to the cause of mankind.

Yet the conception of universal loyalty, as devotion to the unity of an ideal community, a community whereof all loyal men should be members, has not been left merely to the Stoics, nor yet to any other philosophers to formulate. The conception of loyalty both springs from the practical interests and tends of itself, apart from speculation, towards the enlargement of the ideal community of the loyal in the direction of identifying that community with all mankind. The history of the ideals and of the religion of Israel, from the Song of Deborah to the prophets, is a classic instance of the process here in question.

VII

We have thus indicated some of the fundamentally human motives which the ideal of the universal community expresses. We have next to turn in a wholly different direction and to remind ourselves of the way in which this ideal found its place in the early history of the Christian Church.

I cannot better introduce this part of my discussion than by calling attention to a certain contrast between the reported teaching of the Master regarding the Kingdom of Heaven, and some of the best-known doctrines of the Apostle Paul. This contrast is as obvious and as familiar as it has been neglected by students of the philosophy of Christianity. Every word that I can say about it is old. Yet a survey of the whole matter is not common, and I believe that this contrast has never more demanded a clear restatement than it does to-day.

The particular contrast which I here have in mind is *not* the one which both the apologists and the critics of Pauline Christianity usually emphasize. It is a contrast which does not directly relate to Paul's doctrine of the person and mission of Christ; and nevertheless it is a contrast that bears upon the very core of the Gospel. For it is a contrast that has to do with the doctrine about the nature, the office, the saving power of Christian love itself. I say that just this contrast between Paul's docrine and the teachings of Jesus, although perfectly familiar, has been neglected by students of our problem. Let me briefly show what I have in mind.

The best-known and, for multitudes, the most directly moving of the words which tradition attributes to Jesus, describe the duty of the man, the essence of religion, and the Kingdom of Heaven itself, in terms of the conception of Christian love. I have not here either the time or the power adequately to expound this the chief amongst the doctrines which tradition ascribes directly to Jesus. I must pass over what countless loving and fit teachers have made so familiar. Yet I must remind you of two features of Christ's doctrine of love which at this point especially concern our own enterprise.

First, it is needful for me to point out that, despite certain stubborn and widespread misunderstandings, the Christian doctrine of love, as that doctrine appears in the parables and in the Sermon on the Mount, involves and emphasizes a very positive and active and heroic attitude towards life, and is not, as some have supposed, a negative doctrine of passive self-surrender. And secondly, I must also bring to your attention the fact that the Master's teaching about love leaves unsolved certain practical problems, problems which this very heroism and this positive tendency of the doctrine make by contrast all the more striking.

These unsolved problems of the reported teaching of Jesus about love seem to have been deliberately brought before us by the Master, and as deliberately left unsolved. The way was thus opened for a further development of what the Master chose to teach. And such further development was presumably a part of what the founder more or less consciously foresaw and intended.

The grain of mustard seed—so his faith assured him—must grow. To that end it was planted. Now a part of the new growth, a contribution to the treatment of the problems which the original teaching about love left unsolved, was, in the sequel, due to Paul. This sequel, whether the Master foresaw it or not, is as important for the further office of Christianity as the original teaching was an indispensable beginning of the process. Jesus awaited in trust a further revelation of the Father's mind. Such a new light came in due season.

Two features, then, of the doctrine of love as taught by Jesus,—its impressively positive and active character, and the mystery of its unsolved problems,—these two we must next emphasize. Then we shall be ready to take note of a further matter which also concerns us,—namely,

Paul's new contribution to the solution of the very problems concerning love which the parables and the sayings of Jesus had left unsolved. This new contribution,—Paul himself conceived not as his own personal invention. For he held that the new teaching was due to the spirit of his risen and ascended Lord. What concerns us is that Paul's additional thought was a critical influence in determining both the evolution and the permanent meaning of Christianity.

VIII

The love which Jesus preached has often been misunderstood. Critics, as well as mistaken friends of the Master's teachings, have supposed Christian love to be more or less completely identical with self-abnegation,—with the amiably negative virtue of one who, as the misleading modern phrase expresses the matter, "has no thought of self." Another modern expression, also misleading, is used by some who identify Christian love with so-called "pure altruism." The ideal Christian, as such people interpret his virtue, "lives wholly for others." That is what is meant by the spirit which resists not evil, which turns the other cheek to the smiter, which forgives, and pities, and which abandons all worldly goods.

Now, against such misunderstandings, many of the wiser expounders of Christian doctrine, both in former times and in our own, have taken pains to show that love, as the Jesus of the sayings and of the parables conceived it, does *not* consist in mere self-abnegation, and is not identical with pure altruism, and is both heroic and positive. The feature of the Master's doctrine of love which renders this more positive and heroic interpretation of the sayings inevitable, is the familiar reason which is laid at the basis of his whole teaching. One is to love one's neighbor because God himself, as Father, divinely loves and prizes each individual man. Hence the individual man has an essentially infinite value, although he has this value only in and through his relation to God, and because of God's love for him. Therefore mere self-abnegation cannot be the central virtue. For the Jesus of the sayings not only rejoices in the divine love whereof every man is the object, but also invites every man to rejoice in the consciousness of this very love, and to delight also in all men, since they are God's beloved. The man whom this love of God is to transform into a perfect lover cannot henceforth merely forget or abandon the self. The parable of the servant who, although himself forgiven by his

Lord, will not forgive his fellow-servant, shows indeed how worthless self-assertion is when separated from a sense that all are equally dependent upon God's love. But the parable of the talents shows with equal clearness how stern the demands of the divine love are in requiring the individual to find a perfectly positive expression of the unique value which it is his office, and his alone, to return to his Lord with usury. Every man, this self included, has just such an unique value, and must be so viewed. Hence the sayings are full of calls to self-expression, and so to heroism. Love is divine; and therefore it includes an assertion of its own divinity; and therefore it can never be mere self-abnegation. Christian altruism never takes the form of saying, "I myself ought to be or become nothing; while only the others are to be served and saved." For the God who loves me demands not that I should be nothing, but that I should be his own. Love is never merely an amiable tolerance of whatever form human frailty and folly may take. To be sure, the lover, as Jesus depicts him, resists not evil, and turns his cheek to the smiter. Yes, but he does this with full confidence that God sees all and will vindicate his servant. The lover vividly anticipates the positive triumph of all the righteous; and so his love for even the least of the little ones is, in anticipation, an active and strenuous sharing in the final victory of God's will. His very non-resistance is therefore inspired by a divine contempt for the powers of evil. Why should one resist who always has on his side and in his favor the power that is irresistible, that loves him, and that will triumph even through his weakness?

Such a spirit renders pity much more than a mere absorption in attempting to relieve the misery of others. Sympathy for the sufferer, as the sayings of Jesus depict it, is but an especially pathetic illustration of one's serene confidence that the Father who cares for all triumphs over all evil, so that when we feel pity and act pitifully, we take part in this divine triumph. Hence pity is no mere tenderness. It is a sharing in the victory that overcomes the world.

Such, then, in brief, is the doctrine of Christian love as the sayings and the parables contain it,—a doctrine as positive and strenuous as it is humane, and as it is sure of the Father's good will and overruling power. So far I indeed merely remind you of what all the wiser expounders of Christian doctrine, whatever their theology or their disagreements, have, on the whole, and despite popular misunderstandings, agreed in recognizing. And hereupon you might well be disposed to ask: Is not this, in spirit and in essence, the deepest meaning,—yes, is it not really the whole of Christianity? What did Paul do, what could he do, when he spoke of love, but repeat this, the Master's doctrine?

IX

In answer to this question, we must next note that, over against this clear and positive definition of the spiritual attitude that Jesus attributes to the Christian lover, there stand certain problems which come to mind when we ask for more precise directions regarding what the lover is to do for the object of his love. Love is concerned not only with the lover's inner inspiration, but with the services that he is to perform for the beloved. Now, in the world in which the teaching of Jesus places the Christian lover, love has two objects,—God and one's neighbor. What is one to do in order to express one's love for each of these objects?

So far as concerns the lover's relation to God, the answer is clear, and is stated wholly in religious terms. Purity of heart in loving, perfect sincerity and complete devotion, the heroism of spirit just described,— these, with complete trust in God, with utter submission to the Father's will,—these are the services that the lover can render to God. In these there is no merit; for they are as nothing in comparison with one's debt to the Father. But they are required. And in so far the doctrine of love is made explicit and the rule of righteousness is definite.

But now let us return to the relation of love to the services that one is to offer to one's neighbor. What can the lover,—in so far as Jesus describes his task,—what can he do for his fellow-man?

To this question it is, indeed, possible to give one answer which clearly defines a duty to the neighbor; and this duty is emphasized throughout the teaching of Jesus. This duty is the requirement to use all fitting means,—example, precept, kindliness, non-resistance, heroism, patience, courage, strenuousness,—all means that tend to make the neighbor himself one of the lovers. The first duty of love is to produce love, to nourish it, to extend the Kingdom of Heaven by teaching love to all men. And *this* service to one's neighbor is a clearly definable service. And so far the love of the neighbor involves no unsolved problems.

But in sharp contrast with this aspect of the doctrine of love stands another aspect, which is indeed problematic. In addition to the extension of the loving spirit through example and precept, the lover of his neighbor has on his hands the whole problem of humane and benevolent practical activity,—the problem of the positively philanthropic life.

The doctrine of love,—so positive, so active, so resolute in its inmost spirit,—might naturally be expected to give in detail counsel regarding what to do for the personal needs of the lover's fellow-man. But, at this point, we indeed meet the more baffling side of the doctrine of love. Jesus has no system of rules to expound for guiding the single acts of the philanthropic life. Apart from insisting upon the loving spirit, apart from the one rule to extend the Kingdom of Heaven and to propagate this spirit of love among men, the Master leaves the practical decisions of the lover to be guided by loving instinct rather than by a conscious doctrine regarding what sort of special good one can do to one's neighbor.

Thus the original doctrine of love, as taught in the parables, involves no definite programme for social reform, and leaves us in the presence of countless unsolved practical issues. This is plainly a deliberate limitation to which the Master chose to subject his explanations about love.

Jesus tells us of many conditions that appear necessary to the practical living of the life of love for one's neighbor. But when we ask: Are these conditions not only necessary but sufficient? we are often left in doubt. Love relieves manifest suffering, when it can; love feeds the hungry, clothes the naked;—in brief, love seems, at first sight, simply to offer to the beloved neighbor whatever that neighbor himself most desires. It is easy to interpret the golden rule in this simple way. Yet we know, and the author of the parables well knows and often tells us, that the natural man desires many things that he ought not to desire and that love ought not to give him. Since the life is more than meat, it also follows that feeding the hungry and clothing the naked are not acts which really supply what man most needs. The natural man does not know his own true needs. Hence the golden rule does not tell us in detail what to do for him, but simply expresses the spirit of love. What is sure about love is that it indeed unites the lover, in spirit, to God's will. What constitutes, in this present world, the pathos, the tragedy of love, is that, because our neighbor is so mysterious a being to our imperfect vision, we do not now know how to make him happy, to relieve his deepest distresses, to do him the highest good; so that most loving acts, such as giving the cup of cold water, and helping the sufferer who has fallen by the wayside, seem, to our more thoughtful moods, to be mere symbols of what love would do if it could,—mere hints of the active life that love would lead if it were directly and fully guided by the Father's wisdom.

Modern philanthropy has learned to develop a technically clearer consciousness about this problem of effective benevolence, and has made familiar the distinction between loving one's neighbor, and finding out how to be practically useful in meeting the neighbor's needs. Hence, sometimes, the modern mind wonders how to apply the spirit of the parables to our special problems of benevolence, and questions whether, and in what sense, the original Gospel furnishes guidance for our own modern social consciousness.

The problems thus barely suggested are indeed in a sense answered, so far as the originally reported teaching of Jesus is concerned, but are answered by a consideration which awakens a new call for further interpretation. The parables and the Sermon on the Mount emphasize, in the present connection, two things: First, that it is indeed the business of every lover of his neighbor to help other men by rendering them also lovers; and secondly that, as to other matters, one who tries to help his neighbor must leave to God, to the all-loving Father, the care for the true and final good of the neighbor whom one loves. Since the judgment day is near, in the belief of Jesus and of his hearers, since the final victory of the Kingdom will erelong be miraculously manifested, the lover, so Jesus seems to hold, can wait. It is his task to use his talent as he can, to be ready for his Lord's appearance, and to be strenuous in the spirit of love. But the God who cares for the sparrows will care for the success of love.

It is simply not the lover's task to set this present world right; it is his only to act in the spirit that is the Father's spirit, and that, when revealed and triumphant, at the judgment day, will set all things right. In this way the heroism of the ideal of the Kingdom is perfectly compatible, in the parables, with an attitude of resignation with regard to the means whereby the ideal is to be accomplished. Serene faith as to the result, strenuousness as to the act, whatever it is, which the loving spirit just now prompts: this is the teaching of the parables.

I have said that the world of the parables contains two beings to whom Christian love is owed: God and the neighbor. Both, as you now see, are mysterious. The serene faith of the Master sets one mystery side by side with the other, bids the disciple lay aside all curious peering into what is not yet revealed to the loving soul, and leaves to the near future,—to the coming end of the world,—the lifting of all veils and the reconciliation of all conflicts.

X

Such, then, are the problems of the doctrine of love which the Master brings to light, but does not answer. Our next question is: What does Paul contribute to this doctrine of love?

Paul indeed repeated many of his Master's words concerning love; and he everywhere is in full agreement with their spirit. And yet this agreement is accompanied by a perfectly inevitable further development of the doctrine of Christian love,—a development which is due to the fact that into the world of Paul's religious life and teaching there has entered, not only a new experience, but a new sort of being,—a real object whereof the Master had not made explicit mention.

God and the neighbor are beings whose general type religion and common sense had made familiar long before Jesus taught, mysterious though God and one's neighbor were to the founder's hearers, and still remain to ourselves. Both of them are conceived by the religious consciousness of the parables as personal beings, and as individuals. God is the supreme ruler who, as Christ conceives him, is also an individual person, and who loves and wills. The neighbor is the concrete human being of daily life.

But the new, the third being, in Paul's religious world, seems to the Apostle himself novel in its type, and seems to him to possess a nature involving what he more than once calls a "mystery." To express, so far as he may, this "mystery," he uses characteristic metaphors, which have become classic.

This new being is a corporate entity,—the body of Christ, or the body of which the now divinely exalted Christ is the head. Of this body the exalted Christ is also, for Paul, the spirit and also, in some new sense, the lover. This corporate entity is the Christian community itself.

Perfectly familiar is the fact that the existence and the idea of this community constitute a new beginning in the evolution of Christianity. But neglected, as I think and as I have just asserted, is the subtle and momentous transformation, the great development which this new motive brings to pass in the Pauline form of the doctrine of Christian love.

What most interests us here, and what is least generally understood, I think, by students of the problem of Christianity, is the fact that this new entity, this corporate sort of reality which Paul so emphasizes, this being which is not an individual man but a community, does not, as one might suppose, render the Apostle's doctrine of love more abstract, more remote from human life, less direct and less moving, than was the original doctrine of love in the parables. On the contrary, the new element makes the doctrine of love more concrete, and, as I must insist, really less mysterious. In speaking of this corporate entity, the Apostle uses metaphors, and knows that they are metaphors; but, despite what the Apostle calls the new "mystery," these metaphors explain much that the parables left doubtful. These metaphors do not hide, as the Master, in using the form of the parable, occasionally intended for the time to hide from those who were not yet ready for the full revelation, truths which the future was to make clearer to the disciples. No, Paul's metaphors regarding the community of the faithful in the Church bring the first readers of Paul's epistles into direct contact with the problems of their own daily religious life.

The corporate entity—the Christian community—proves to be, for Paul's religious consciousness, something more concrete than is the individual fellow-man. The question: Who is my neighbor? had been answered by the Master by means of the parable of the Good Samaritan. But that question itself had not been due merely to the hardness of heart of the lawyer who asked it. The problem of the neighbor actually involves mysteries which, as we have already seen and hereafter shall still further see, the parables deliberately leave, along with the conception of the Kingdom of Heaven itself, to be made clearer only when the new revelation, for which the parables are preparing the way, shall have been granted. Now Paul feels himself to be in possession of a very precious part of this further revelation. He has discovered, in his own experience as Apostle, a truth that he feels to be new. He believes this truth to be a revelation due to the spirit of his Lord.

In fact, the Apostle has discovered a special instance of one of the most significant of all moral and religious truths, the truth that a community, when unified by an active in-dwelling purpose, is an entity more concrete and, in fact, less mysterious than is any individual man, and that such a community can love and be loved as a husband and wife love; or as father or mother love.

Because the particular corporate entity whose cause Paul represents, namely, the Christian community, is in his own experience something new, whose origin he views as wholly miraculous, whose beginnings and whose daily life are bound up with the influence which he believes to be due to the spirit of his risen and ascended Lord, Paul indeed regards the Church as a "mystery." But, as a fact, his whole doctrine regarding the community has a practical concreteness, a clear common sense about it, such that he is able to restate the doctrine of Christian love so as to be fully just to all its active heroism, while interpreting much which the parables left problematic.

XI

What can I do for my neighbor's good? The parables had answered: "Love him, help him in his obvious and bitter needs, teach him the spirit of love, and leave the rest to God." Does Paul make light of this teaching? On the contrary, his hymn in honor of love, in the first epistle to the Corinthians, is one of Christianity's principal treasures. Nowhere is the real consequence of the teaching of Jesus regarding love more completely stated. But notice this difference: For Paul the neighbor has now become a being who is primarily the fellow-member of the Christian community.

The Christian community is itself something visible; miraculously guided by the Master's spirit. It is at once for the Apostle a fact of present experience and a divine creation. And therefore every word about love for the neighbor is in the Apostle's teaching at once perfectly direct and human in its effectiveness and is nevertheless dominated by the spirit of a new and, as Paul believes, a divinely inspired love for the community.

Both the neighbor and the lover of the neighbor to whom the Apostle appeals are, to his mind, members of the body of Christ; and all the value of each man as an individual is bound up with his membership in this body, and with his love for the community.

Jesus had taught that God loves the neighbor,—yes, even the least of these little ones. Paul says to the Ephesians: "Christ loved the church, and gave himself up for it, that he might sanctify it; . . . that he might present the church to himself a glorious church, not having spot: . . . but that it should be holy and without blemish." One sees: The object of the divine love, as Paul conceives it, has been at once transformed and fulfilled.

In God's love for the neighbor, the parables find the proof of the infinite worth of the individual. In Christ's love for the Church Paul finds the proof that both the community, and the individual member, are the objects of an infinite concern, which glorifies them both, and thereby unites them. The member finds his salvation only in union with the Church. He, the member, would be dead without the divine spirit and without the community. But the Christ whose community this is, has given life to the members,—the life of the Church, and of Christ himself. "You hath he quickened, which were dead in trespasses and sins."

In sum: Christian love, as Paul conceives it, takes on the form of Loyalty. This is Paul's simple but vast transformation of Christian love.

Loyalty itself was, in the history of humanity, already, at that time, ancient. It had existed in all tribes and peoples that knew what it was for the individual so to love his community as to glory in living and dying for that community. To conceive virtue as faithfulness to one's community, was, in so far, no new thing. Loyalty, moreover, had long tended towards a disposition to enlarge both itself and its community. As the world had come together, it had gradually become possible for philosophers, such as the later Stoics, to conceive of all humanity as in ideal one community.

Although this was so far a too absract conception to conquer the world of contending powers, the spirit of loyalty was also not without its religious relationships, and tended, as religion tended, to make the moral realm appear, not only a world of human communities, but a world of divinely ordained unity. Meanwhile, upon every stage, long before the Christian virtues were conceived, loyalty had inspired nations of warriors with the sternest of their ideals of heroism, and with their noblest visions of the destiny of the individual. And the prophets of Israel had indeed conceived the Israel of God's ultimate triumph as a community in and through which all men should know God and be blessed.

But in Paul's teaching, loyalty, quickened to new life, not merely by hope, but by the presence of a community in whose meetings the divine spirit seemed to be daily working fresh wonders, keeps indeed its natural relation to the militant virtues, is heroic and strenuous, and delights to use metaphors derived from the soldier's life. It appears also as the virtue of those who love order, and who prefer law to anarchy, and who respect worldly authority. And it derives its religious ideas from the prophets.

But it also becomes the fulfilment of what Jesus had taught in the parables concerning love. For the Apostle, this loyalty unites to all these stern and orderly and militant traits, and to all that the prophets had dreamed about Israel's triumph, the tenderness of a brother's love for the individual brother. Consequently, in Paul's mind, love for the individual human being, and loyalty to the divine community of all the faithful; graciousness of sentiment, and orderliness of discipline; are so directly interwoven that each interprets and glorifies the other.

If the Corinthians unlovingly contend, brother with brother, concerning their gifts, Paul tells them about the body of Christ, and about the divine unity of its spirit in all the diversity of its members and of their powers. On the other hand, if it is loyalty to the Church which is to be interpreted and revivified, Paul pictures the dignity of the spiritual community in terms of the direct beauty and sweetness and tenderness of the love of brother for brother,—that love which seeketh not her own. The perfect union of this inspired passion for the community, with this tender fondness for individuals, is at once the secret of the Apostle's power as a missionary and the heart of his new doctrine. Of loyalty to the spirit and to the body of Christ, he discourses in his most abstruse as well as in his most eloquent passages. But his letters close with the well-known winning and tender messages to and about individual members and about their intimate personal concerns.

As to the question: "What shall I do for my brother?" Paul has no occasion to answer that question *except* in terms of the brother's relations to the community. But just for that reason his counsels can be as concrete and definite as each individual case requires them to be. Because the community, as Paul conceives it,—the small community of a Pauline church, —keeps all its members in touch with one another; because its harmony is preserved through definite plans for setting aside the differences that arise amongst individuals; because, by reason of the social life of the whole, the physical needs, the perils, the work, the prosperity of the individual are all made obvious facts of the common experience of the church, and are all just as obviously and definitely related to the health of the whole body,—Paul's gospel of love has constant and concrete practical applications to the life of those whom he addresses. The ideal of the parables has become a visible life on earth. So live together that the Church may be worthy of Christ who loves it, so help the individual brother that he may be a fitting member of the Church. Such are now the counsels of love.

All this teaching of Paul was accompanied, of course, in the Apostle's own mind, by the unquestioning assurance that this community of the Christian faith, as he knew it and in his letters addressed its various representatives, was indeed a genuinely universal community. It was already, to his mind, what the prophets had predicted when they spoke of the redeemed Israel. By the grace of God, all men belonged to this community, or would soon belong to it, whom God was pleased to save at all.

For the end of the world was very soon to come, and would manifest its membership, its divine head, and its completed mission. According to Paul's expectation, there was to be no long striving towards an ideal that in time was remote. He dealt with the interest of all mankind. But his faith brought him into direct contact with the institution that represented this world-wide interest. What loyalty on its highest levels has repeatedly been privileged to imagine as the ideal brotherhood of all who are loyal, Paul found directly presented, in his religious experience, as his own knowledge of his Master's purpose, and of its imminent fulfilment.

This vision began to come to Paul when he was called to be an apostle; and later, when he was sent to the Gentiles, the ideal grew constantly nearer and clearer. The Church was, for Paul, the very presence of his Lord.

Such, then, was the first highly developed Christian conception of the universal community. That which the deepest and highest rational interests of humanity make most desirable for all men, and that which the prophets of Israel had predicted afar off, the religious experience of Paul brought before his eyes as the daily work of the spirit in the Church. Was not Christ present whenever the faithful were assembled? Was not the spirit living in their midst? Was not the day of the Lord at hand? Would not they all soon be changed, when the last trumpet should sound?

Our sketch, thus far, of the spirit of the ideal of the universal community, solves none of our problems. But it helps to define them. This, the first of our three essential ideas of Christianity, is the idea of a spiritual life in which universal love for all individuals shall be completely blended, practically harmonized, with an absolute loyalty for a real and universal community. God, the neighbor, and the one church: These three are for Paul the objects of Christian love and the inspiration of the life of love.

Paul's expectations of the coming judgment were not realized. Those little apostolic churches, where the spirit daily manifested itself, gave place to the historical church of the later centuries, whose possession of the spirit has often been a matter of dogma rather than of life, and whose unity has been so often lost to human view. The letter has hidden the spirit. The Lord has delayed his coming. The New Jerusalem, adorned as a bride for her husband, remains hidden behind the heavens. The vision has become the Problem of Christianity.

Our sketch has been meant merely to help us towards a further definition of this problem. To such a definition our later lectures must attempt still further to contribute. We have a hint of the sources of the first of our three essential ideas of Christianity. We have still to consider what is the truth of this idea.

THE PROBLEM OF CHRISTIANITY (1913)

THE MORAL BURDEN OF THE INDIVIDUAL

"All things excellent," says Spinoza, "are as difficult as they are rare;" and Spinoza's word here repeats a lesson that nearly all of the world's religious and moral teachers agree in emphasizing. Whether such a guide speaks simply of "excellence," or uses the distinctively religious phraseology and tells us about the way to "salvation," he is sure, if he is wise, to recognize, and on occasion to say, that whoever is to win the highest goal must first learn to bear a heavy burden. It also belongs to the common lore of the sages to teach that this burden is much more due to the defects of our human nature than to the hostility of fortune. "We ourselves make our time short for our task": such comments are as trite as they are well founded in the facts of life.

I

But among the essential ideas of Christianity, there is one which goes beyond this common doctrine of the serious-minded guides of humanity. For this idea defines the moral burden, to which the individual who seeks salvation is subject, in so grave a fashion that many lovers of mankind, and, in particular, many modern minds, have been led to declare that so much of Christian doctrine, at least in the forms in which it is usually stated, is an unreasonable and untrue feature of the faith. This idea I stated at the close of our first lecture, side by side with the two other ideas of Christianity which I propose, in these lectures, to discuss. The idea of the Church,—of the universal community,—which was our topic in the second lecture, is expressed by the assertion that there is a real and

157

divinely significant spiritual community to which all must belong who are to win the true goal of life. The idea of the moral burden of the individual is expressed by maintaining that (as I ventured to state this idea in my own words): "The individual human being is by nature subject to some overwhelming moral burden from which, if unaided, he cannot escape. Both because of what has technically been called original sin, and because of the sins that he himself has committed, the individual is doomed to a spiritual ruin from which only a divine intervention can save him."

This doctrine constitutes the second of the three Christian ideas that I propose to discuss. I must take it up in the present lecture.

II

To this mode of continuing our discussion you may object that our second lecture left the idea of the Church very incompletely stated, and, in many most important respects, also left that idea uninterpreted, uncriticised, and not yet brought into any clear relation with the creed of the modern man. Is it well, you may ask, to discuss a second one of the Christian ideas, when the first has not yet been sufficiently defined?

I answer that the three Christian ideas which we have chosen for our inquiry are so closely related that each throws light upon the others, and in turn receives light from them. Each of these ideas needs, in some convenient order, to be so stated and so illustrated, and then so made the topic of a thoughtful reflection, that we shall hereby learn: First, about the basis of this idea in human nature; secondly, about its value,—its ethical significance as an interpretation of life; and thirdly, about its truth, and about its relation to the real world. At the close of our survey of the three ideas, we shall bring them together, and thus form some general notion of what is essential to the Christian doctrine of life viewed as a whole. We shall at the same time be able to define the way in which this Christian doctrine of life expresses certain actual needs of men, and undertakes to meet these needs. We shall then have grounds for estimating the ethical and religious value of the connected whole of the doctrines in question.

There will then remain the hardest part of our task: the study of the relation of these Christian ideas to the real world. So far as we are concerned, this last part of our investigation will involve, in the main, metaphysical problems; and the closing lectures of our course will therefore contain an outline of the metaphysics of Christianity, culminating in a return to the problems of the modern man.

Such is our task. On the way toward our goal we must be content, for a time, with fragmentary views. They will, ere long, come into a certain unity with one another; but for that unity we must wait, until each idea has had its own partial and preliminary presentation.

Of the idea of the universal community we have learned, thus far, two things, and no more. First, we have seen that this idea has a broad psychological basis in the social nature of mankind, while it gets its ethical value from its relations to the interests and needs of all those of any time or nation who have learned what is the deeper meaning of loyalty. By loyalty, as you remember, I mean the thoroughgoing, practical, and loving devotion of a self to an united community.

Secondly, we have seen that, in addition to its general basis in human nature, this idea has its specifically Christian form. The significance of this form we have illustrated by the way in which the original doctrine of Christian love, as Jesus taught it in his sayings and parables, received not only an application, but also a new development in the consciousness of the apostolic churches, when the Apostle Paul experienced and moulded their life.

The synthesis of the Master's doctrine of love with the type of loyalty which the life of the spirit in the Church taught Paul to express, makes concrete and practical certain more mysterious aspects of the doctrine of love which the Master had taught in parables, but had left for a further revelation to define. And herewith the spirit of the Christian idea of the universal community entered, as a permanent possession, into the history of Christianity.

This preliminary study of the idea of the universal community leaves us with countless unsolved problems. But it at least shows us where some portion of our main problem lies. The dogmas of the historical Church concerning its own authority we have so far left, in our discussion, almost untouched. That the spirit and the letter of this first of our Christian ideas are still very far apart, all who love mankind, and who regard Christianity wisely, well know. We have not yet tried to show how spirit and letter are to be brought nearer together. It has not been my privilege to tell you where the true Church is to-day to be found. As a fact, I believe it still to be an invisible Church. And I readily admit that a disembodied idea does not meet all the interests of Christianity, and does not answer all the questions of the modern man.

But we have yet, in due time, to consider whether, and to what extent, the universal community is a reality. That is a problem, partly of dogma, partly of metaphysics. It is not my office to supply the modern man, or any one else, with a satisfactory system of dogmas. But I believe that philosophy has still something to say which is worth saying regarding the sense in which there really is an universal community such as expresses what the Christian idea means. I shall hereafter offer my little contribution to this problem.

III

Let us turn, then, to our new topic. The moralists, as we have already pointed out, are generally agreed that whoever is to win the highest things must indeed learn to bear a heavy moral burden. But the Christian idea now in question adds to the common lore of the moralists the sad word: "*The individual cannot bear this burden.* His tainted nature forbids; his guilt weighs him down. If by salvation one means a winning of the true goal of life, the individual, unaided, cannot be saved. And the help that he needs for bearing his burden must come from some source entirely above his own level,—from a source which is, in some genuine sense, divine."

The most familiar brief statement of the present idea is that of Paul in the passage in the seventh chapter of the epistle to the Romans, which culminates in this cry: "O wretched man that I am!" What the Apostle, in the context of this passage, expounds as his interpretation both of his own religious experience and of human nature in general, has been much more fully stated in the form of well-known doctrines, and has formed the subject-matter for ages of Christian controversy.

In working out his own theory of the facts which he reports, Paul was led to certain often cited statements about the significance and the effect of Adam's legendary transgression. And, as a consequence of these words and of a few other Pauline passages, technical problems regarding original sin, predestination, and related topics have come to occupy so large a place in the history of theology, that, to many minds, Paul's own report of personal experience, and his statements about plain facts of human nature, have been lost to sight (so far as concerns the idea of the moral burden of the individual) in a maze of controversial complications. To numerous modern minds the whole idea of the moral burden of the individual seems, therefore, to be an invention of theologians, and to possess little or no religious importance.

Yet I believe that such a view is profoundly mistaken. The idea of the moral burden of the individual is, as we shall see, not without its inherent complications, and not without its relation to very difficult problems, both ethical and metaphysical. Yet, of the three essential ideas of Christianity which constitute our list, it is, relatively speaking, the simplest, and the one which can be most easily interpreted to the enlightened common sense of the modern man. Its most familiar difficulties are due rather to the accidents of controversy than to the nature of the subject.

The fate which has beset those who have dealt with the technical efforts to express this idea is partly explicable by the general history of religion; but is also partly due to varying personal factors, such as those which determined Paul's own training. This fate may be summed up by saying that, regarding just this matter of the moral burden of the individual, those who, by virtue of their genius or of their experience, have most known what they meant, have least succeeded in making clear to others what they know.

Paul, for instance, grasped the essential meaning of the moral burden of the individual with a perfectly straightforward veracity of understanding. What he saw, as to this matter, he saw with tragic clearness, and upon the basis of a type of experience that, in our own day, we can verify, as we shall soon see, much more widely than was possible for him. But when he put his doctrine into words, both his Rabbinical lore, and his habits of interpreting tradition, troubled his speech; and the passages which embody his theory of the sinfulness of man remain as difficult and as remote from his facts, as his report of these facts of life themselves is eloquent and true.

Similar has been the fortune of nearly all subsequent theology regarding the technical treatment of this topic. Yet growing human experience, through all the Christian ages, has kept the topic near to life; and to-day it is in closer touch with life than ever. The idea of the moral burden of the individual seems, to many cheerful minds, austere; but, if it is grave and stern, it is grave with the gravity of life, and stern only as the call of life, to any awakened mind, out to be stern. If the traditional technicalities have obscured it, they have not been able to affect its deeper meaning or its practical significance. Rightly interpreted, it forms, I think, not only an essential feature of Christianity, but an indispensable part of every religious and moral view of life which considers man's business justly, and does so with a reasonable regard for the larger connections of our obligations and of our powers.

IV

If we ourselves are to see these larger connections, we must, for the time, disregard the theological complications of the history of doctrine concerning original sin, and must also disregard the metaphysical problems that lie behind these complications. We must do this; but not as if these theological theories were wholly arbitrary, or wholly insignificant. We must simply begin with those facts of human nature which here most deeply concern us.

These facts have a metaphysical basis. In the end, we ourselves shall seek to come into touch with so much of theology as most has to do with our problem of Christianity. We cannot tell, until our preliminary survey is completed, and our metaphysical treatment of our problem is reached, what form our sketch of a theology will assume. We must be patient with our fragmentary views until we see how to bring them together.

But, for the time being, our question relates not to legend of Adam's fall, nor to something technically called original sin, but to man as we empirically know him. We ask: How far is the typical individual man weighed down, in his efforts to win the goal of life, by a burden such as Paul describes in his epistle to the Romans? And what is the significance of this burden?

Here, at once, we meet with the obvious fact, often mentioned, not only in ancient, but also in many modern, discussions of our topic,—with the fact that there are, deep-seated in human nature, many tendencies that our mature moral consciousness views as evil. These tendencies have a basis in qualities that are transmitted by heredity.

Viewed as an observant naturalist,—as a disinterested student of the life-process views them, all our inherited instincts are, in one sense, upon a level. For no instincts are, at the outset of life, determined by any purpose,—either good or evil,—of which we are then conscious. But, when trained, through experience and action, our instincts become interwoven into complex habits, and thus are transformed into our voluntary activities. What at the beginning is an elemental predisposition to respond to a specific sensory stimulus in a more or less vigorous but incoherent and generalized way, becomes, in the context of the countless other predispositions upon which is based our later training, the source of a mode of conduct, —of conduct that, as we grow, tends to become more and more definite, and that may be valuable for good or for ill. And, as a fact, many of our instinctive predispositions actually appear, in the sequel, to be like noxious plants or animals. That is, to use a familiar phrase, they "turn out ill." They are expressed in our maturer life in maladjustments, in vices, or perhaps in crimes.

Now Paul, like a good many other moralists, was impressed by the number and by the vigor of those amongst our instinctive predispositions which, under the actual conditions of human training, "turn out ill," and are interwoven into habits that often lead the natural man into baseness and into a maze of evil deeds. Paul summarizes this aspect of the facts, as he saw them, in his familiar picture, first, of the Gentile world, and then of the moral state of the unregenerate who were Jews. This picture we find in the opening chapters of his epistle to the Romans.

The majority of readers appear to suppose that the essential basis of Paul's theory about the moral burden of the individual is to be found in these opening chapters, and in the assertion that the worst vices and crimes of mankind are the most accurate indications of how bad human nature is. For such readers, whether they agree with Paul or not, the whole problem reduces to the question: "Are men, and are human traits and tendencies naturally as mischievous; are we all as much predisposed to vices and to crimes as Paul's dark picture of the world in which he lived bids us believe that all human characters are? Is man,—viewed as a fair observer from another planet might view him,—is man by nature, or by heredity, predominantly like a noxious plant or animal? Unless some external power, such as the power that Paul conceives to be Divine Grace, miraculously saves him, is he bound to turn out ill,—to be the beast of prey, the victim of lust, the venomous creature, whom Paul portrays in these earlier chapters of his letters to the Romans?"

You well know that, as to the questions thus raised, there is much to be said, both for and against the predominantly mischievous character of the natural and instinctive predispositions of men; and both for and against the usual results of training, in case of the people who make up our social world. Paul's account of this aspect of the life of the natural man has both its apologists and its critics.

I must simply decline, however, to follow the usual controversies as to the natural predispositions of the human animal any further in this place. I have mentioned the familiar topic in order to say at once that none of the considerations which the opening chapters of the epistle to the Romans suggest to a modern reader regarding the noxious or the useful instinctive predispositions of ordinary men, or even of extraordinarily defective or of exceptionally gifted human beings, seem to be of any great importance for the understanding of the genuine Pauline doctrine of the moral burden of the individual.

Paul opened the epistle to the Romans by considerations which merely prepared the way for his main thesis. His argument in the earlier chapters is also chiefly preparatory. But his main doctrine concerning our moral burden depends upon other considerations than a mere enumeration of the vices and crimes of a corrupt society. It depends, in fact, upon considerations which, as I believe, are almost wholly overlooked in most of the technical controversies concerning original sin, and concerning the evil case of the unregenerate man.

I shall venture to translate these more significant considerations which Paul emphasizes into a relatively modern phraseology. I believe that I shall do so in a way that is just to Paul's spirit, and that will enable us soon to return to the text of the seventh chapter of his epistle with a clearer understanding of the main issue.

V

Whoever sets out to study, as psychologist, the moral side of human nature, with the intention of founding upon that study an estimate of the part which good and evil play in our life, must make clear to his mind a familiar, but important, and sometimes neglected distinction. This is the distinction between the conduct of men, upon the one hand, and the grade or sort of consciousness with which, upon the other hand, their conduct, whatever it is, is accompanied.

Conduct, as we have already mentioned, results from the training which our hereditary predispositions, our instinctive tendencies, get, when the environment has played upon them in a suitable way, and for a sufficient time. The environment which trains us to our conduct may be animate or inanimate; although in our case it is very largely a human environment. It is not necessary that we should be clearly aware of what our conduct in a given instance is or means, just as it is not necessary that one who speaks a language fluently should be consciously acquainted with the grammar of that language, or that one who can actually find the way over a path in the mountains should be able to give directions to a stranger such as would enable the latter to find the same way.

In general, it requires one sort of training to establish in us a given form of conduct, and a decidedly different sort of training to make us aware of what that form of conduct is, and of what, for us ourselves, it means.

The training of all the countless higher and more complex grades and types of knowledge about our own conduct which we can find present in the world of our self-knowledge, is subject to a general principle which I may as well state at once. Conduct, as I have just said, can be trained through the action of any sort of tolerable environment, animate or inanimate. But the higher and more complex types of our consciousness about our conduct, our knowledge about what we do, and about why we do it,—all this more complex sort of practical knowledge of ourselves, is trained by a specific sort of environment, namely, by a social environment.

And the social environment that most awakens our self-consciousness about our conduct does so by opposing us, by criticising us, or by otherwise standing in contrast with us. Our knowledge of our conduct, in all its higher grades, and our knowledge of ourselves as the authors or as the guides of our own conduct, our knowledge of how and why we do what we do,—all such more elaborate self-knowledge is, directly or indirectly, a social product, and a product of social contrasts and oppositions of one sort or another. Our fellows train us to all our higher grades of practical self-knowledge, and they do so by giving us certain sorts of social trouble.

If we were capable of training our conduct in solitude, we should not be nearly as conscious as we now are of the plans, of the ideals, of the meaning, of this conduct. A solitary animal, if well endowed with suitable instincts, and if trained through the sort of experimenting that any intelligent animal carries out as he tries to satisfy his wants, would gradually form some sort of conduct. This conduct might be highly skilful. But if this animal lived in a totally unsocial, in a wholly inanimate, environment, he would meet with no facts that could teach him to be aware of what his conduct was, in the sense and degree in which we are aware of our own conduct. *For he, as a solitary creature, would find no other instance of conduct with which to compare his own.* And all knowledge rests upon comparison. It is my knowledge of my fellows' doings, and of their behavior toward me,—it is this which gives me the basis for the sort of comparison that I use whenever I succeed in more thoughtfully observing myself or estimating myself.

If you want to grasp this principle, consider any instance that you please wherein you are actually and clearly aware of how you behave and of why you behave thus. Consider, namely, any instance of a higher sort of skill in an art, in a game, in business,—an instance, namely, wherein you not only *are* skilful, but are fully observant of what your skill is, and of why you consciously prefer this way of playing or of working. You will find that always your knowledge and your estimate of your skill and of your own way of doing, turn upon comparing your own conduct with that of some real or ideal comrade, or fellow, or rival, or opponent, or critic; or upon knowing how your social order in general carries on or estimates this sort of conduct; or, finally, upon remembering or using the results of former social comparisons of the types mentioned.

I walk as I happen to walk, and in general, if let alone, I have no consciousness as to what my manner of walking is; but let my fellow's gait or pace attract my attention, or let my fellow laugh at my gait, or let him otherwise show that he observes my gait; and forthwith, if my interest is stirred, I may have the ground for beginning to observe what my own gait is, and how it is to be estimated.

In brief, it is our fellows who first startle us out of our natural unconsciousness about our own conduct; and who then, by an endless series of processes of setting us attractive but difficult models, and of socially interfering with our own doings, train us to higher and higher grades and to more and more complex types of self-consciousness regarding what we do and why we do it. Play and conflict, rivalry and emulation, conscious imitation and conscious social contrasts between man and man,—these are the source of each man's consciousness about his own conduct.

Whatever occurs in our literal social life, and in company with our real fellows, can be, and often is, repeated with endless variations in our memory and imagination, and in a companionship with ideal fellow-beings of all grades of significance. And thus our thoughts and memories of all human beings who have aroused our interest, as well as our thoughts about God, enrich our social environment by means of a wealth of real and ideal fellow-beings, with whom we can and do compare and contrast ourselves and our own conduct.

And since all this is true, this whole process of our knowledge about our own doings, and about our plans, and about our estimates of ourselves, is a process capable of simply endless variation, growth, and idealization. Hence the variations of our moral self-consciousness have all the wealth of the entire spiritual world. Comparing our doings with the standards that the social will furnishes to us, in the form of customs and of rules, we become aware both of what Paul calls, in a special instance, "the law," and of ourselves either as in harmony with or opposed to this law. The comparison and the contrast make us view ourselves on the one side, and the social will,—that is, "the law,"—on the other side, as so related that, the more we know of the social will, the more highly conscious of ourselves we become; while the better we know ourselves, the more clearly we estimate the dignity and the authority of the social will.

So much, then, for a mere hint of the general ways in which our moral self-consciousness is a product of our social life. This self is known to each one of us through its social contrasts with other selves, and with the will of the community. If these contrasts displease us, we try to relieve the tension. If they fascinate, we form our ideals accordingly. But in either case we become conscious of some plan or ideal of our own. Our developed conscience, psychologically speaking, is the product of endless efforts to clear up, to simplify, to reduce to some sort of unity and harmony, the equally endless contrasts between the self, the fellow-man, and the social will in general,—contrasts which our social experience constantly reveals and renders fascinating or agonizing, according to the state of our sensitiveness or of our fortunes.

VI

These hints of the nature of a process which you can illustrate by every higher form and gradation of the moral consciousness of men have now prepared us for one more observation which, when properly understood, will bring us directly in contact with Paul's own comments upon the moral burden of any human being who reaches a high spiritual level.

Our conduct may be, according to our instincts and our training, whatever it happens to be. Since man is an animal that is hard to train, it will often be, from the point of view of the social will of our community, more or less defective conduct. But it might also be fairly good conduct; and, in normal people of good training, it often is so. In this respect, then, it seems unpsychological to assert that the conduct of all natural men is universally depraved,—however ill Paul thought of his Gentiles.

Let us turn, however, from men's conduct to their consciousness about their conduct; and then the simple and general principles just enunciated will give us a much graver view of our moral situation. Paul's main thesis about our moral burden relates not to our conduct, but to our consciousness about our conduct.

Our main result, so far, is that, from a purely psychological point of view, my consciousness about my conduct, and consequently my power to form ideals, and my power to develop any sort of conscience, are a product of my nature as a social being. And the product arises in this way: Contrasts, rivalries, difficult efforts to imitate some fascinating fellow-being, contests with my foes, emulation, social ambition, the desire to attract attention, the desire to find my place in my social order, my interest in what my fellows say and do, and especially in what they say and do with reference to me,—such are the more elemental social motives and the social situations which at first make me highly conscious of my own doings.

Upon the chaos of these social contrasts my whole later training in the knowledge of the good and the evil of my own conduct is founded. My conscience grows out of this chaos,—grows as my reason grows, through the effort to get harmony into this chaos. However reasonable I become, however high the grade of the conscientious ideals to which, through the struggle to win harmony, I finally attain, all of my own conscientious life is psychologically built upon the lowly foundations thus furnished by the troubled social life, that, together with my fellows, I must lead.

VII

But now it needs no great pessimism to observe that our ordinary social life is one in which there is a great deal of inevitable tension, or natural disharmony. Such tension, and such disharmony, are due not necessarily to the graver vices of men. The gravest disharmonies often result merely from the mutual misunderstandings of men. There are so many of us. We naturally differ so much from one another. We comprehend each other so ill, or, at best, with such difficulty. Hence social tension is, so to speak, the primary state of any new social enterprise, and can be relieved only through special and constantly renewed efforts.

But this simple observation leads to another. If our social life, owing to the number, the variety, and the ignorance of the individuals who make up our social world, is prevailingly or primarily one in which strained social situations,—forms of social tension,—social troubles, are present, and are constantly renewed, it follows that every individual who is to reach a high grade of self-consciousness as to his own doings, will be awakened to his observation of himself by one or another form or instance of social tension. As a fact, it is rivalry, or contest, or criticism that first, as we have seen, naturally brings to my notice what I am doing. And the obvious rule is that, within reasonable limits, the greater the social tension of the situation in which I am placed, the sharper and clearer does my social contrast with my fellows become to me. And thus, the greater the social tension is, the more do I become aware, through such situations, both about my own conduct, and about my plans and ideals, and about my will.

In brief, my moral self-consciousness is bred in me through social situations that involve,—not necessarily any physical conflict with my fellows,—but, in general, some form of social conflict,—conflict such as engenders mutual criticism. Man need not be, when civilized, at war with his fellows in the sense of using the sword against them. But he comes to self-consciousness as a moral being through the spiritual warfare of mutual observation, of mutual criticism, of rivalry,—yes, too often through the warfare of envy and of gossip and of scandal-mongering, and of whatever else belongs to the early training that many people give to their own consciences, through taking a more or less hostile account of the consciences of their neighbors. Such things result from the very conditions of high grades of self-consciousness about our conduct and our ideals.

The moral self, then, the natural conscience, is bred through situations that involve social tension. What follows?

VIII

It follows that such tension, in each special case, indeed seems evil to us, and calls for relief. And in seeking for such relief, the social will, in its corporate capacity, the will of the community, forms its codes, its customary laws; and attempts to teach each of us how he ought to deal with his neighbors so as to promote the general social harmony. But these codes,—these forms of customary morality,—they have to be taught to us as conscious rules of conduct. They can only be taught to us by first teaching us to be more considerate, more self-observant, more formally conscientious than we were before. But to accomplish this aim is to bring us to some higher level of our general self-consciousness concerning our own doings. And this can be done, as a rule, only by applying to us some new form of social discipline which, in general, introduces still new and more complex kinds of tension,—new social contrasts between the general will and our own will, new conflicts between the self and its world.

Our social training thus teaches us to know ourselves through a process which arouses our self-will; and this tendency grows with what it feeds upon. The higher the training and the more cultivated and elaborate is our socially trained conscience,—the more highly conscious our estimate of our own value becomes, and so, in general, the stronger grows our self-will.

This is a commonplace; but it is precisely upon this very commonplace that the moral burden of the typical individual, trained under natural social conditions, rests. If the individual is no defective or degenerate, but a fairly good member of his stock, his conduct may be trained by effective social discipline into a more or less admirable conformity to the standards of the general will. But his conduct is not the same as his own consciousness about his conduct; or, in other words, his deeds and his ideals are not necessarily in mutual agreement. Meanwhile, his consciousness about his conduct, his ideals, his conscience, are all trained, under ordinary conditions, by a social process that begins in social troubles, in tensions, in rivalries, in contests, and that naturally continues, the farther it goes, to become more and more a process which introduces new and more complex conflicts.

This evil constantly increases. The burden grows heavier. Society can, by its ordinary skill, train many to be its servants,—servants who, being under rigid discipline, submit because they must. But precisely in proportion as society becomes more skilled in the external forms of culture, it trains its servants by a process that breeds spiritual enemies. That is, it breeds men who, even when they keep the peace, are inwardly enemies one of another; because every man, in a highly cultivated social world, is trained to moral self-consciousness by his social conflicts. And these same men are inwardly enemies of the collective social will itself, because in a highly cultivated social order the social will is oppressively vast, and the individual is trained to self-consciousness by a process which shows him the contrast between his own will and this, which so far seems to him a vast impersonal social will. He may obey. That is conduct. But he will naturally revolt inwardly; and that is his inevitable form of spiritual self-assertion, so long as he is trained to self-consciousness in this way, and is still without the spiritual transformations that some higher form of love for the community,—some form of loyalty, and that alone,— can bring.

This revolt will tend to increase as culture advances. High social cultivation breeds spiritual enmities. For it trains what we in our day call individualism, and, upon precisely its most cultivated levels, glories in creating highly conscious individuals. But these individuals are brought to consciousness by their social contrasts and conflicts. Their very consciences are tainted by the original sin of social contentiousness. The higher the cultivation, the vaster and deeper are precisely the more spiritual and the more significant of these inward and outward conflicts. Cultivaton breeds civilized conduct; it also breeds conscious independence of spirit and deep inner opposition to all mere external authority.

Before this sort of moral evil the moral individual, thus cultivated, is, if viewed merely as a creature of cultivation, powerless. His very conscience is the product of spiritual warfare, and its knowledge of good and evil is tainted by its origin. The burden grows; and the moral individual cannot bear it, unless his whole type of self-consciousness is transformed by a new spiritual power which this type of cultivation can never of itself furnish.

For the moral cultivation just described is cultivation in "the law"; that is, in the rules of the social will. But such cultivation breeds individualism; that is, breeds consciousness of self-will. And the burden of this self-will increases with cultivation.

As we all know, individualism, viewed as a highly potent social tendency, is a product of high cultivation. It is also a relatively modern product of such cultivation. Savages appear to know little about individualism. Where tribal custom is almighty, the individual is trained to conduct, but not to a high grade of self-consciousness. Hence the individual, in a primitive community, submits; but also he has no very elaborate conscience. Among most ancient peoples, individualism was still nearly unknown.

Two ancient peoples, living under special conditions and possessing an extraordinary genius, developed very high grades of individualism. One of these peoples was Israel,—especially that fragment of later Israel to which Judaism was due. Paul well knew what was the nature and the meaning of just that high development of individuality which Judaism had in his day made possible.

The other one of these peoples was the Greek people. Their individualism, their high type of self-consciousness regarding conduct, showed what is meant by being, as every highly individualistic type of civilization since their day has been, characteristically merciless to individuals. Greek individualism devoured its own children. The consciousness of social opposition determined the high grade of self-consciousness of the

Greek genius. It also determined the course of Greek history and politics; and so the greatest example of national genius which the world has ever seen promptly destroyed its own life, just because its self-consciousness was due to social conflicts and intensified them. The original sin of its own cultivation was the doom of that cultivation.

In the modern world the habit of forming a high grade of individual consciousness has now become settled. We have learned the lesson that Israel and Greece taught. Hence we speak of personal moral independence as if it were our characteristic spiritual ideal. This ideal is now fostered still more highly than ever before,—is fostered by the vastness of our modern social forces, and by the way in which these forces are to-day used to train the individual consciousness which opposes itself to them, and which is trained to this sort of opposition.

The result is that the training of the cultivated individual, under modern conditions, uses, on the one hand, all the motives of what Paul calls "the flesh,"—all the natural endowment of man the social being,—but develops this fleshly nature so that it is trained to self-consciousness by emphasizing every sort and grade of more skilful opposition to the very social will that trains it. Our modern world is therefore peculiarly fitted to illustrate the thesis of Paul's seventh chapter of the epistle to the Romans. To that chapter let us now, for a moment, return.

IX

The difficulty of the argument of Paul's seventh chapter lies in the fact that in speaking of our sinful nature, he emphasizes three apparently conflicting considerations: First, he asserts that sinfulness belongs to our elemental nature, to our flesh as it is at birth; secondly, he insists that sin is not cured but increased by cultivation, unless the power of the Divine Spirit intervenes and transforms us into new creatures; thirdly, he declares that our sinfulness belongs not to especially defective or degenerate sinners, but to the race in its corporate capacity, so that no one is privileged to escape by any good deed of his own, since we are all naturally under the curse.

To the first consideration many modern men reply that at birth we have only untrained instinctive predispositions, which may, under training, turn out well or ill, but which, until training turns them into conduct, are innocent.

This comment is true, but does not touch Paul's main thesis, which is that, being as to the flesh what we are,—that is, being essentially social animals,—all our natural moral cultivation, if successful, can only make us aware of our sinfulness. "Howbeit, I had not known sin but for the law." It is precisely this thesis which the natural history of the training of our ordinary moral self-consciousness illustrates. This training usually takes place through impressing the social will upon the individual by means of discipline. The result must be judged not by the accidental fortunes of this or that formally virtuous or obviously vicious individual. The true problem lies deeper than we are accustomed to look. It is just that problem which Paul understands.

Train me to morality by the ordinary modes of discipline and you do two things: First, and especially under modern conditions, you teach me so-called independence, self-reliance. You teach me to know and to prize from the depths of my soul, my own individual will. The higher the civilization in which this mode of training is followed, the more I become an individualist among mutually hostile individualists, a citizen of a world where all are consciously free to think ill of one another, and to say, to every external authority: "My will, not thine, be done."

But this teaching of independence is also a teaching of distraction and inner despair. For, if I indeed am intelligent, I also learn that, in a highly cultivated civilization, the social will is mighty, and daily grows mightier, and must, ordinarily and outwardly, prevail unless chaos is to come. Hence you indeed may discipline me into obedience, but it is a distracted and wilful obedience, which constantly wars with the very dignity of spirit which my training teaches me to revere. On the one hand, as reasonable being, I say: "I ought to submit; for law is mighty; and I would not, if I could, bring anarchy." So much I say, if I am indeed successfully trained. But I will not obey with the inner man. For I am the being of inalienable individual rights, of unconquerable independence. I have my own law in my own members, which, however I seem to obey, is at war with the social will. I am the divided self. The more I struggle to escape through my moral cultivation, the more I discern my divided state. Oh, wretched man that I am!

Now this my divided state, this my distraction of will, is no mishap of my private fortune. It belongs to the human race, as a race capable of high moral cultivation. It is the misfortune, the doom of man the social animal, if you train him through the discipline of social tension, through troubles with his neighbors, through opposition and through social conflict, through what Whistler called "the gentle art of making enemies." This, apart from all legends, is Paul's thesis; and it is true to human nature. The more outer law there is in our cultivation, the more inner rebellion there is in the very individuals whom our cultivation creates. And this moral burden of the individual is also the burden of the race, precisely in so far as it is a race that is social in a human sense.

Possibly all this may still seem to you the mere construction of a theorist. And yet an age that, like our own, faces in new forms the conflicts between what we often name individualism and collectivism,— a time such as the present one, when every new enlargement of our vast corporations is followd by a new development of strikes and of industrial conflicts,—a time, I say, such as ours ought to know where the original sin of our social nature lies.

For our time shows us that *individualism and collectivism are tendencies, each of which, as our social order grows, intensifies the other.* The more the social will expresses itself in vast organizations of collective power, the more are individuals trained to be aware of their own personal wants and choices and ideals, and of the vast opportunities that would be theirs if they could but gain control of these social forces. The more, in sum, does their individual self-will become conscious, deliberate, cultivated, and therefore dangerously alert and ingenious.

Yet, if the individuals in question are highly intelligent, and normally orderly in their social habits, their self-will, thus forcibly kept awake and watchful through the very powers which the collective will has devised, is no longer, in our own times, a merely stupid attempt to destroy all social authority. It need not be childishly vicious or grossly depraved, like Paul's Gentiles in his earlier chapters of the epistle to the Romans. It is a sensitive self-will, which feels the importance of the social forces, and which wants them to grow more powerful, so that haply they may be used by the individual himself.

And so, when opportunity offers, the individual self-will casts its vote in favor of new devices to enrich or to intensify the expression of the collective will. For it desires social powers. It wants them for its own use. Hence, in its rebellion against authority, when such rebellion arises, it is a consciously divided self-will, which takes in our day no form more frequently than the general form of moral unrest, of discontent with its own most ardent desires. It needs only a little more emphasis upon moral or religious problems than, in worldly people, in our day, it displays, in order to be driven to utter from a full heart Paul's word: "O wretched man that I am!"

For the highly trained modern agitator, or the plastic disciple of agitators, if both intelligent and reasonably orderly in habits, is intensely *both* an individualist and a man who needs the collective will, who in countless ways and cases bows to that will, and votes for it, and increases its power. The individualism of such a man wars with his own collectivism; while each, as I insist, tends to inflame the other. As an agitator, the typically restless child of our age often insists upon heaping up new burdens of social control,—control that he indeed intends to have others feel rather than himself. As individualist, longing to escape, perhaps from his economic cares, perhaps from the marriage bond, such a highly intelligent agitator may speak rebelliously of all restrictions, declare Nietzsche to be his prophet, and set out to be a Superman as if he were no social animal at all. Wretched man, by reason of his divided will, he is; and he needs only a little reflection to observe the fact.

But note: These are no mere accidents of our modern world. The division of the self thus determined, and thus increasing in our modern cultivation, is not due to the chance defects of this or of that more or less degenerate individual. Nor is it due merely to a man's more noxious instincts. This division is due to the very conditions to which the development of self-consciousness is subject, not only in our present social order, but in every civilization which has reached as high a grade of self-consciousness as that which Paul observed in himself and in his own civilization.

X

The moral burden of the individual, as Paul conceives it, and as human nature makes it necessary, has now been characterized. The legend of Adam's transgression made the fall of man due to the sort of self-consciousness, to the knowledge of good and evil, which the crafty critical remarks of the wise serpent first suggested to man, and which the resulting transgression simply emphasized. What Paul's psychology, translated into more modern terms, teaches, is that the moral self-consciousness of every one of us gets its cultivation from our social order through a process which begins by craftily awakening us, as the serpent did Eve, through critical observations, and which then fascinates our divided will by giving us the serpent's counsels. "Ye shall be as gods." This is the lore of all individualism, and the vice of all our worldly social ambitions. The resulting diseases of self-consciousness are due to the inmost nature of our social race.

They belong to its very essence as a social race. They increase with cultivation. The individual cannot escape from the results of them through any deed of his own. For his will is trained by a process which taints his conscience with the original sin of self-will, of clever hostility to the very social order upon which he constantly grows more and more consciously dependent.

What is the remedy? What is the escape? Paul's answer is simple. To his mind a new revelation has been made, from a spiritual realm wholly above our social order and its conflicts. Yet this revelation is, in a new way, social. For it tells us: "There is a certain divinely instituted community. It is no mere collection of individuals, with laws and customs and quarrels. Nor is its unity merely that of a mighty but, to our own will, an alien power. Its indwelling spirit is concrete and living, but is also a loving spirit. It is the body of Christ. The risen Lord dwells in it, and is its life. It is as much a person as he was when he walked the earth. And he is as much the spirit of that community as he is a person. Love that community; let its spirit, through this love, become your own. Let its Lord be your Lord. Be one in him and with him and with his Church. And lo! the natural self is dead. The new life takes possession of you. You are a new creature. The law has no dominion over you. In the universal community you live in the spirit; and hence for the only self, the only self-consciousness, the only knowledge of your own deeds which you possess or tolerate: these are one with the spirit of the Lord and of the community."

Translated into the terms that I ventured to use in our last lecture, Paul's doctrine is that salvation comes through loyalty. Loyalty involves an essentially new type of self-consciousness,—the consciousness of one who loves a community as a person. Not social training, but the miracle of this love, creates the new type of self-consciousness.

Only (as Paul holds) you must find the universal community to which to be loyal; and you must learn to know its Lord, whose body it is, and whose spirit is its life.

Paul is assured that he knows this universal community and this Lord. But, apart from Paul's religious faith, the perfectly human truth remains that loyalty (which is the love of a community conceived as a person on a level superior to that of any human individual)—loyalty,—and the devotion of the self to the cause of the community,—loyalty, is the only cure for the natural warfare of the collective and of the individual will,—a warfare which no moral cultivation without loyalty can ever end, but which all cultivation, apart from such devoted and transforming love of the community, only inflames and increases.

Thus the second of the essential ideas of Christianity illustrates the first, and is in turn illumined by the first. This, I believe is the deeper sense and truth of the doctrine of the inherent moral taint of the social individual.

THE PROBLEM OF CHRISTIANITY (1913)

THE REALM OF GRACE

The Christian world has been still more deeply influenced by the apostle Paul's teaching concerning the divine grace that saves, than by his account of the moral burden of the individual. The traditional lore of salvation is more winning, and, in many respects, less technical, than is the Christian teaching regarding our lost state.

The present lecture is to be devoted to a study of some aspects of the doctrine of grace. Yet, since our moral burden, and our escape from that burden, are matters intimately connected, we shall find that both topics belong to the exposition of the same essential Christian idea, and that, at the same time, they throw new light upon the first of the three essential Christian ideas, the idea of the universal community. Our present task will therefore enable us to reach a new stage in our survey of the larger connections of the Christian doctrine of life.

I

Christianity is most familiarly known as a religion of love, and this view, as far as it extends, is a true view of Christianity. Our second lecture has shown us, however, that this characterization is inadequate, because it does not render justly clear the nature of the objects to which, in our human world, Christian love is most deeply and essentially devoted. A man is known by the company that he keeps. In its human relations, and apart from an explicit account of its faith concerning the realm of the gods, or concerning God, a religion can be justly estimated only when you understand what kinds and grades of human beings it bids you recognize, as well as what it counsels you to do in presence of the beings

178

of each grade. Now, as our second lecture endeavored to point out, there are in the human world two profoundly different grades, or levels, of mental beings,—namely, the beings that we usually call human individuals, and the beings that we call communities.

Of the first of these two grades, or levels, of human beings, any one man whom you may choose to mention is an example. His organism is, in the physical world, separate from the organisms of his fellows. The expressive movements of this organism, his behavior, his gestures, his voice, his coherent course of conduct, the traces that his deeds leave behind them,—these, in your opinion, make more or less manifest to you the life of his mind. And, in your usual opinion, his mind is, on the whole, at least as separate from the minds of other men, as his organism, and his expressive bodily movements, are physically sundered from theirs.

Of the second of these two levels of human beings, a well-trained chorus, or an orchestra at a concert; or an athletic team, or a rowing crew, during a contest; or a committee, or a board, sitting in deliberation upon some matter of business; or a high court consisting of several members, who at length reach what legally constitutes "the decision of the court,"—all these are good examples. Each one of these is, in its own way, a community. The vaster communities, real and ideal, which we mentioned, by way of illustration, in our second lecture, also serve as instances of real beings with minds, whose grade or level is not that of the ordinary human individuals.

Any highly organized community—so in our second lecture we argued—is as truly a human being as you and I are individually human. Only a community is not what we usually call an individual human being; because it has no one separate and internally well-knit physical organism of its own; and because its mind, if you attribute to it any one mind, is therefore not manifested through the expressive movements of such a single separate human organism.

Yet there are reasons for attributing to a community a mind of its own. Some of these reasons were briefly indicated in our second lecture; and they will call for a further scrutiny hereafter. Just here it concerns my purpose simply to call attention to the former argument, and to say, that the difference between the individual human beings of our ordinary social intercourse, and the communities, is a difference justly characterized, in my opinion, by speaking of these two as *grades* or *levels* of human life.

The communities are vastly more complex, and, in many ways, are also immeasurably more potent and enduring than are the individuals.

Their mental life possesses, an Wundt has pointed out, a psychology of its own, which can be systematically studied. Their mental existence is no mere creation of abstract thinking or of metaphor; and is no more a topic for mystical insight, or for fantastic speculation, than is the mental existence of an individual man. As empirical facts, communities are known to us by their deeds, by their workings, by their intelligent and coherent behavior, just as the minds of our individual neighbors are known to us through their expressions.

Considered as merely natural existences, communities, like individuals, may be either good or evil, beneficent or mischievous. The level of mental existence which belongs to communities insures their complexity; and renders them, in general, far more potent and, for certain purposes and in certain of their activities, much more intelligent than are the human individuals whose separate physical organisms we ordinarily regard as signs of so many separate minds.

But a community,—in so far like a fallen angel,—may be as base and depraved as any individual man can become, and may be far worse than a man. Communities may make unjust war, may enslave mankind, may deceive and betray and torment as basely as do individuals, only more dangerously. The question whether communities are or are not real human beings, with their own level of mental existence, is therefore quite distinct from the question as to what worth this or that community possesses in the spiritual world. And, in our study of the doctrine of grace, we shall find how intimately the Christian teaching concerning the salvation of the individual man is bound up with the Christian definition, both of the saving community and of the power which, according to the Christian tradition, has redeemed that community, and has infused divine life into the level of human existence which this community, and not any merely human individual, occupies.

II

To the two levels of human mental existence correspond two possible forms of love: love for human individuals; love for communities. In our second lecture we spoke of the natural fact that communities can be the object of love; and that this love may lead to the complete practical devotion of an individual to the community which he loves. Such vital and effective love of an individual for a community constitutes what we called, in that lecture, Loyalty. And when, in our second lecture, the conception of loyalty as the love of an individual for a being that is on the level of a community first entered our argument, we approached this conception by using, as illustrations, what might be called either the more natural or the more primitive types of loyalty,—types such as grow out of family life, and tribal solidarity, and war. As we pointed out in the second lecture, Christianity is essentially a religion of loyalty. We have learned in our third lecture that, for Christianity, the problem of loyalty is enriched, and meanwhile made more difficult, by the nature of that ideal or universal community to which Paul first invited his converts to be loyal.

Paul and his apostolic Christians were not content with family loyalty, or with clan loyalty, or with a love for any community that they conceived as merely natural in its origin. A miracle, as they held, had created the body of Christ. To this new spiritual being, whose level was that of a community, and whose membership was human, but whose origin was, in their opinion, divine, their love and their life were due. Christianity was the religion of loyalty to this new creation. The idea involved has since remained, with all its problems and tragedies, essential to Christianity.

Our study of the moral burden of the individual has now prepared us for a new insight into the special problem which, ever since Paul's time, Christian loyalty has had to solve. This is no longer anywhere nearly as free from complications as are the problems which family loyalty and clan loyalty present, manifold as those problems of natural loyalty actually are. Even the idea of the rational brotherhood of mankind, of the universal community as the Stoics conceived it, presents no problems nearly as complex as is the problem which the Pauline concept of charity, and of Christian loyalty, has to meet.

For Paul, as you now know, finds that the individual man has to be won over, not to a loyalty which at first seems, to the flesly mind, natural, but to an essentially new life. The natural man has to be delivered from a doom to which "the law" only binds him faster, the more he seeks to escape. And this escape involves finding, for the individual man, a community to which, when the new life comes, he is to be thenceforth loyal as no natural clan loyalty or family loyalty could make him.

The power that gives to the Christian convert the new loyalty is what Paul calls Grace. And the community to which, when grace saves him, the convert is thenceforth to be loyal, we may here venture to call by a name which we have not hitherto used. Let this name be "The Beloved

Community." This is another name for what we before called the Universal Community. Only now the universal community will appear to us in a new light, in view of its relations to the doctrine of grace. And the realm of this Beloved Community, whose relations Christianity conceives, for the most part, in supernatural terms, will constitute what, in our discussion, shall be meant by the term "The Realm of Grace."

III

If we suppose that the two levels of human mental existence have both of them been recognized as real, and that hereupon the problem of finding an ideally lovable community has been, for a given individual, solved, so that this individual is sure of his love and loyalty for the community which has won his service, then, from the point of view of that individual, the two levels of human life will indeed be no longer merely distinguished by their complexity, or by their might, or by their grade of intelligence. Henceforth, for the loyal soul, the distinction between the levels, so far as the object of his loyalty is concerned, will be a distinction in value, and a vast one.

The beloved community embodies, for its lover, values which no human individual, viewed as a detached being, could even remotely approach. And in a corresponding way, the love which inspires the loyal soul has been transformed; and is not such as could be given to a detached human individual.

The human beings whom we distinguish in our daily life, and recognize through the seeming and the doings of their separate organisms, are real indeed, and are genuinely distinct individuals. But when we love them, our love, however ideal or devoted, has its level and its value determined by their own. And if this love for human individuals is the only form of human love that we know, both our morality and our religion are limited accordingly, and remain on a correspondingly lower level.

Such human love knows its objects precisely as Paul declared that, henceforth, he would no longer know Christ,—namely, "after the flesh." Loyalty knows its object (if I may again adapt Paul's word) "after the Spirit." For Paul's expression here refers, in so far as he speaks of human objects at all, to the unity of the spirit which he conceived to be characteristic of the Christian community, whereof Christ was, to the Apostle's mind, both the head and the divine life. Hence you see how vastly

significant, for our view of Christianity, is a comprehension of what is
meant by religion of loyalty.

With this indication of the connections which link the thoughts of
our lecture on the universal community with the task which lies next in
our path, let us turn, first to Paul's own account of the doctrine of grace,
and then to the later development of Paul's teachings into those views
about the Realm of Grace which came to be classic for the later Christian
consciousness. Our own interest in all these matters is here still an interest, first in the foundation which the Christian ideas possess in human
nature, and secondly in the ethical and religious values which are here
in question. And we still postpone any effort to pass judgment upon
metaphysical problems, or to decide the truth as to traditional dogmas.

IV

Let us next summarily review the original and distinctively Pauline
doctrine, both of our fallen state and of the grace which saves.

The last lecture furnished the materials for such a review. The pith of
the matter can be expressed, in terms of purely human psychology, thus:
Man's fallen state is due to his nature as a social animal. This nature is
such that you can train his conscience only by awakening his self-will.
By self-will, I here mean, as Paul meant, man's conscious and active assertion of his own individual desires, worth, and undertakings, over
against the will of his fellow, and over against the social will. Another
name for this sort of conscious self-will is the modern term "individualism," when it is used to mean the tendency to prefer what the individual man demands to what the collective will requires. In general, and
upon high levels of human intelligence, when you train individualism,
you also train collectivism; that is, you train in the individual a respect
for the collective will. And it belongs to Paul's very deep and searching
insight to assert that these two tendencies—the tendency towards individualism, and that towards collectivism—do not exclude, but intensify
and inflame each other.

Training, if formally successful in producing the skilful member of
human society, breeds respect, although not love, for "the law," that is,
for the expression of the collective will. But training also makes the individual conscious of the "other law" in "his members," which "wars
against" the law of the social will. The result may be, for his outward

conduct, whatever the individual's wits and powers make it. But so far as this result is due to cultivation in intelligent conduct, it inevitably leads to an inner division of the self, a disease of self-consciousness, which Paul finds to be the curse of all merely natural human civilization.

This curse is rooted in the primal constitution which makes man social, and which adapts him to win his intelligence through social conflicts with his neighbors. Hence the curse belongs to the whole "flesh" of man; for by "flesh" Paul means whatever first expresses itself in our instincts and thus lies at the basis of our training, and so of our natural life. The curse afflicts equally the race and the individual. Man is by inheritance adapted for this training to self-will and to inner division.

The social order, in training individuals, therefore breeds conscious sinners; and sins both in them and against them. The natural community is, in its united collective will, a community of sin. Its state is made, by its vast powers, worse than that of the individual. But it trains the individual to be as great a sinner as his powers permit.

If you need illustrations, Paul teaches you to look for them in the whole social order, both of Jews and of Gentiles. But vices and crimes, frequent as they are, merely illustrate the principle. The disease lies much deeper than outward conduct can show; and respectability of behavior brings no relief. All are under the curse. Cultivation increases the curse. The individual is helpless to escape by any will or deed of his own.

The only escape lies in Loyalty. Loyalty, in the individual, is his love for an united community, expressed in a life of devotion to that community. But such love can be true love only if the united community both exists and is lovable. For training makes self-will fastidious, and abiding love for a community difficult.

In fact, no social training that a community can give to its members can train such love in those who have it not, or who do not win it through other aid than their training supplies. And no social will that men can intelligently devise, apart from previously active and effective loyalty, can make a community lovable. The creation of the truly lovable community, and the awakening of the highly trained individual to a true love for that community, are, to Paul's mind, spiritual triumphs beyond the wit of man to devise, and beyond the power of man to accomplish. That which actually accomplishes these triumphs is what Paul means by the divine grace.

V

One further principle as to the human workings of this grace must still be mentioned, in order to complete our sketch of the foundations which our actual nature, disordered though it be, furnishes, not for the comprehension of this miracle of saving love, but for an account of the conditions under which the miracle takes place, so far as these conditions can fall under our human observation.

Natural love of individuals for communities, as we saw in our second lecture, appears in case of family loyalty, and in case of patriotism; and seems to involve no miracle of grace. But such love of an individual for a community, in so far as such love is the product of our ordinary human nature, tends to be limited or hindered by the influences of cultivation, and is blindly strongest in those who have not yet reached high grades of cultivation. It arises as mother-love or as tribal solidarity arises, from the depths of our still unconscious social nature. The infant or the child loves its home; the mother, her babe; the primitive man, his group.

But loyalty of the type that is in question when our salvation, in Paul's sense of salvation, is to be won, is the loyalty which springs up *after* the individual self-will has been trained through the processes just characterized. It is the loyalty that conquers us, even when we have become enemies of the law. It finds us as such enemies, and transforms us. It is the love which leads the already alert and rebellious self-will to devote all that it has won to the cause which henceforth is to remain, by its own choice, its beloved.

Such loyalty is not the blind instinctive affection from which cultivation inevitably alienates us, by awakening our self-will. It is the love that overcomes the already fully awakened individual. We cannot choose to fall thus in love. Only when once thus in love, can we choose to remain lovers.

Now such love comes from some previous love which belongs to the same high and difficult grade. The origin of this higher form of loyalty is hard to trace, unless some leader is first there, to be the source of loyalty in other men. If such a leader there is, his own loyalty may become, through his example, the origin of a loyalty in which the men of many generations may find salvation. You are first made loyal through the power of someone else who is already loyal.

But the loyal man must also be, as we have just said, a member of a lovable community. How can such a community originate? The family, as we have also remarked, is lovable to the dependent child. Yet often the wayward youth is socially trained to a point where such dependence, just because he has come to clear self-consciousness, seems to him unintelligible; and herewith his father's house ceases to be, for him, any longer lovable.

Great loyalty—loyalty such as Paul himself had in mind when he talked of divine grace—must be awakened by a community sufficiently lovable to win the enduring devotion of one who, like Paul, has first been trained to possess and to keep an obstinately critical and independent attitude of spirit,—an attitude such as, in fact, Paul kept to the end of his life, side by side with his own loyalty, and in a wondrous harmony therewith.

Such a marvellous union of unconquerable and even wilful self-consciousness, with an absolute loyalty to the cause of his life, breathes in every word of Paul's more controversial outbursts, as well as in all of his more fervent exhortations. Such loyalty is no mere childhood love of home. It comes only as a rushing, mighty wind.

In order to be thus lovable to the critical and naturally rebellious soul, the Beloved Community must be, quite unlike a natural social group, whose life consists of laws and quarrels, of a collective will, and of individual rebellion This community must be an union of members who first love it. The unity of love must pervade it, before the individual member can find it lovable. Yet unless the individuals first love it, how can the unity of love come to pervade it?

The origin of loyalty, if it is to arise,—not as the childhood love of one's home arises, unconsciously and instinctively; but as Paul's love for the Church arises, consciously and with a saving power,—in the life of one who is first trained to all the conscious enmities of the natural social order,—the origin of loyalty seems thus to resemble, in a measure, the origin of life, as the modern man views that problem. A living being is the offspring of a living being. And, in a similar fashion, highly conscious loyalty presupposes a previous loyalty, only a loyalty of even higher level than its own, as its source. Loyalty needs for its beginnings the inspiring leader who teaches by the example of his spirit. But the leader, in order to inspire to loyalty, must himself be loyal. In order to be loyal, he must himself have found, or have founded, his lovable community. And this, in order to be lovable, and a community, must already consist of loyal and loving members. It cannot win the love of the lost soul who is to be saved, unless it already consists of those who have been saved by their love for it. One moves thus in a circle. Only some miracle of grace (as it would seem) can initiate the new life, either in the individuals who are to love communities, or in the communities that are to be worthy of their love.

VI

If the miracle occurs, and then works according to the rules which, in fact, the contagion of love usually seems to follow, the one who effects the first great transformation and initiates the high type of loyalty in the distracted social world must, it would seem, combine in himself, in some way, the nature which a highly trained social individual develops as he becomes self-conscious, with the nature which a community possesses when it becomes intimately united in the bonds of brotherly love, so that it is "one undivided soul of many a soul."

For the new life of loyalty, if it first appears at all, will arise as a bond linking many highly self-conscious and mutually estranged social individuals in one, but this bond can come to mean anything living and real to these individuals, only in case some potent and loyal individual, acting as leader, first declares that for him it is real. In such a leader, and in his spirit, the community will begin its own life, if the leader has the power to create what he loves.

The individual who initiates this process will then plausibly appear to an onlooker, such as Paul was when he was converted, to be at once an individual and the spirit—the very life—of a community. But his origin will be inexplicable in terms of the processes which he himself originates. His power will come from another level than our own. And of the workings of this grace, when it has appeared, we can chiefly say this: That such love is propagated by personal example, although how, we cannot explain.

We know how Paul conceives the beginning of the new life wherein Christian salvation is to be found. This beginning he refers to the work of Christ. The Master was an individual man. To Paul's mind, his mission was divine. He both knew and loved his community before it existed on earth; for his foreknowledge was one with that of the God whose will he came to accomplish. On earth he called into this community its first members. He suffered and died that it might have life. Through his death and in his life the community lives. *He is now identical with the spirit of this community*. This, according to Paul, was the divine grace which began the process of salvation for man. In the individual life of each Christian this same process appears as a new act of grace. Its outcome is the new life of loyalty to which the convert is henceforth devoted.

VII

With any criticism of the religious beliefs of Paul, and with their metaphysical bearings, we are not here concerned. What we have attempted, in this sketch, is an indication of the foundation which human nature furnishes for the Pauline doctrine of divine grace. The human problem, as you see, when it is viewed quite apart from the realm of the gods, is the problem of the value and the origin of loyalty.

The value of loyalty can readily be defined in simply human terms. Man, the social being, naturally, and in one sense helplessly, depends on his communities. Sundered from them, he has neither worth nor wit, but wanders in waste places, and, when he returns, finds the lonely house of his individual life empty, swept, and garnished.

But, on the other hand, his communities, to which he thus owes all his natural powers, train him by teaching him self-will, and so teach him the arts of spiritual hatred. The result is distraction,—spiritual death. Escape through any mere multitude of loves for other individuals is impossible. For such loves, unless they are united by some supreme loyalty, are capricious fondnesses for other individuals, who, by nature and by social training, are as lonely and as distracted as their lover himself. Mere altruism is no cure for the spiritual disease of cultivation.

No wonder, then, that early Buddhism, fully sensible of the disorders of self-will and of the natural consciousness, sees no escape but through the renunciation of all that is individual, and preaches the passionless calm of knowing only what is no longer a self at all. If birth and training mean only distraction, why not look for the cessation of all birth, and the extinction of desire?

Loyalty, if it comes at all, has the value of a love which does not so much renounce the individual self as devote the self, with all its consciousness and its powers, to an all-embracing unity of individuals in one realm of spiritual harmony. The object of such devotion is, in ideal, the community which is absolutely lovable, because absolutely united, conscious, but above all distractions of the separate self-will of its members.

Loyalty demands many members, but one body; many gifts, but one spirit.

The value of this ideal lies in its vision of an activity which is endless, but always at rest in its own harmony. Such a vision, as Mr. F. C. S. Schiller has well pointed out, Aristotle possessed when, in dealing with quite another problem than the one now directly before us, he defined the life of God,—the Energeia of the unmoved mover. Such a vision, but interpreted in terms which were quite as human as they were divine, Paul possessed when he wrote to the Corinthians concerning the spiritual gifts. This was Paul's beatific vision, granted him even while he was in the life of earthly tribulation, the vision of the Charity which never faileth,—the vision of Charity as still the greatest of the Christian graces in the world whereto the saved are to be translated.

The realm of absolute loyalty, of the Pauline charity, is what Christianity opposes to the Buddhistic Nirvana. In Nirvana the Buddha sees all, but is no longer an individual, and neither desires nor wills anything whatever. In Paul's vision of beatitude, when I shall know even as I am known, an endlessly restful spiritual activity, the activity of the glorified and triumphant Church, fills all the scene. It is an activity of individuals who still will, and perform the deeds of love, and endlessly aim to renew what they possess,—the life of the perfected and perfectly lovable community, where all are one in Christ.

Paul's vision unites, then, Aristotle's ideal of the divine beatitude, always active yet always at the goal, with his own perfectly practical and concrete ideal of what the united Church, as a community, should be, and in the perfect state, as he thinks, will be.

Thus the value of the loyal life, and of the love of the ideal community, is expressible in perfectly human terms. The problem of grace is the problem of the origin of loyalty; and is again a perfectly human problem. Paul's solution, in the opening of his letter to the Ephesians, "By grace are ye saved, and that not of yourselves; it is the gift of God," is for him the inevitable translation into religious speech of that comment upon the origin of loyalty which we have just, in summary form, stated. The origin of the power of grace is psychologically inexplicable, as all transforming love is. The object to which grace directs the convert's mind is above the level of any human individual.

The realm of grace is the realm of the powers and the gifts that save, by thus originating and sustaining and informing the loyal life. This realm contains, at the very least, three essentially necessary constituent members: First, the ideally lovable community of many individuals in one spiritual bond; secondly, the spirit of this community, which is present both as the human individual whose power originated and whose example, whose life and death, have led and still guide the community, and as the united spiritual activity of the whole community; thirdly, Charity itself, the love of the community by all its members, and of the members by the community.

To the religion of Paul, all these things must be divine. They all have their perfectly human correlate and foundation wherever the loyal life exists.

VIII

We now may see how the characterization of Christianity as not only a religion of love, but as also, in essence, a religion of loyalty, tends to throw light upon some of the otherwise most difficult aspects of the problem of Christianity. We can already predict how great this light, if it grows, promises to become.

Christianity is not the only religion in whose conceptions and experiences a community has been central. Loyalty has not left itself without a witness in many ages of human life, and in many peoples. And all the higher forms of loyalty are, in their spirit, religious; for they rest upon the discovery, or upon the faith, that, in all the darkness of our earthly existence, we individual human beings, separate as our organisms seem in their physical weakness, and sundered as our souls appear by their narrowness, and by their diverse loves and fortunes, are not as much alone, and not as helpless, in our chaos of divided will, as we seem.

For we are members one of another, and members, too, of a real life that, although human, is nevertheless, when it is lovable, also above the level upon which we, the separate individuals, live our existence. By our organisms and by our individual divisions of knowledge and of purpose, we are chained to an order of nature. By our loyalty, and by the real communities to which we are worthily loyal, we are linked with a level of mental existence such that, when compared with our individual existence, this higher level lies in the direction of the divine. Whatever the origin of men's ideals of their gods, there should be no doubt that these gods have often been conceived, by their worshippers, as the representatives of some human community, and as in some sense identical with that community.

But loyalty exists in countless forms and gradations. Christianity is characterized not only by the universality of the ideal community to which, in its greatest deeds and ages, it has, according to its intent, been loyal; but also by the depth and by the practical intensity and the efficacy of the love towards this community which has inspired its most representative leaders and reformers; and, finally, by the profoundly significant doctrines and customs to which it has been led in the course of its efforts to identify the being of its ideal community with the being of God.

Other religions have been inspired by loyalty. Other religions have identified a community with a divine being. And, occasionally,—yes, as the world has grown wiser and more united, increasingly,—non-Christian thinking and non-Christian religion have conceived an ideal community as inclusive as mankind, or as inclusive as the whole realm of beings with minds, however vast that realm may be.

But, historically speaking, Christianity has been distinguished by the concreteness and intensity with which, in the early stages of its growth, it grasped, loved, and served its own ideal of the visible community, supposed to be universal, which it called its Church. It has further been contrasted with other religions by the skill with which it gradually revised its views of the divine nature, in order to be able to identify the spirit that, as it believed, guided, inspired, and ruled this Church, with the spirit of the one whom it had come to worship as its risen Lord.

IX

If we bear these facts in mind, there is much in the otherwise so difficult history of Christian dogma which we can easily see in a new light. I myself am far from being a technical theologian, and, in coming to the few fragments of an understanding of the meaning of the history of dogma which I possess, I owe much to views such as, in England, Professor Percy Gardner has set forth, both in his earlier discussions, and notably in his recent book on "The Religious Experience of the Apostle Paul." I also owe new light to the remarkable conclusions which Professor Troeltsch of Heidelberg states, at the close of his recently published volume on "The Social Doctrines of the Christian Churches." I shall make no endeavor in this place to deal with those technical aspects of the history of dogma which lie beyond my province as a philosophical student of the Christian doctrine of life. But if I attempt to restate a very few of the results of others in terms of that view of the essence of Christian loyalty which does concern me, my word, at this stage of our discussion, must be as follows:—

Jesus unquestionably taught, in the best-attested, and in the best-known, of his sayings, love for all individual human beings. But he taught this as an organic part of his doctrine of the Kingdom of Heaven. The individual whom you are bidden to love as your brother and your neighbor is, even while Jesus depicts him, transformed before your eyes. For, first, he is no longer the separate organism with a separate mind and a detached being and destiny, whom you ordinarily loathe if he is your enemy, and resist if he endangers or oppresses you. No,—when he asks your aid,—though he be "the least of these my brethren"—he speaks with the voice of the judge of all men, with the voice that you hope to hear saying: "Come ye blessed of my Father, for I was hungered and ye gave me meat." In other words, the real man, whom your eyes only seem to see, but whom on the level of ordinary human intercourse you simply ignore, actually belongs to another level of spiritual existence, above the level of our present life of divisions. The mystery of the real being of this man is open only to the divine Love.

If you view your neighbor as your Father would have you view him, you view him not only as God's image, but also as God's will and God's love. If one asks for further light as to how the divine love views this man, the answer of Jesus, in the parables is, in substance, that this man is a member of the Kingdom of Heaven.

The Kingdom of Heaven is obviously a community. But this community is itself a mystery,—soon to be revealed,—but so far in the visible world, of which Jesus speaks, not yet to be discovered. This Kingdom is a treasure hid in a field. Its Master has gone into a far country. Watch and be ready. The Lord will soon return. The doctrine of Christian love, as thus taught by Jesus, so far as the records guide us, implies loyalty to the Kingdom; but it expresses itself in forms which demand further interpretation, and which the Master intended to have further interpreted.

Now the apostolic churches held that those visions of the risen Lord, upon the memory and report of which their life as communities was so largely based, had begun for them this further interpretation. For them Christian loyalty soon became explicit; because their community became visible. And they believed their community to be the realization of the Kingdom; because they were sure that their risen Lord, whom the reported and recorded visions had shown, was henceforth in their midst as the spirit of this community.

The realm of grace, thus present to the Christian consciousness, needed to be further explored. The explorers were those who helped to define dogmas. The later development of the principal dogmas of the post-apostolic Church was due to a process in which, as Professor Troeltsch persuasively insists, speculation and the use of the results of ancient philosophy (however skilful and learned such processes might be), were in all the great crises of the history of doctrine wholly subordinate to practical religious motives.

To use the phraseology that I myself am obliged to prefer: The common sense of the Christian Church had three problems to solve. First: It was loyal to the universal spiritual community; and upon this loyalty, according to its view, salvation depended. But this universal community must be something concrete and practically efficacious. Hence the visible Church had to be organized as the appearance on earth of God's Kingdom. For what the parables had left mysterious about the object and the life of love, an authoritative interpretation, valid for the believers of those times, must be found, and was found in the visible Church.

Secondly, The life, the unity, the spirit of the Church had meanwhile to be identified with the person and with the spirit of the risen and ascended Lord, whom the visions of the first disciples had made henceforth a central fact in the belief of the Church.

The supernatural being whose body was now the Church, whose spirit was thus identified with the will and with the mind of a community, had once, as man, walked the earth, had really suffered and died. But since he had risen and ascended, henceforth—precisely because he was as the spirit whose body was this community, the Church—he was divine. Such was the essential article of the new faith.

Paul had already taught this. This very doctrine, in its further development, must be kept by the Church as concrete as the recorded life of the Master had been, as close to real life as the work of the visible Church was, and as true to the faith in the divine unity and destiny of the universal community, as Christian loyalty in all those formative centuries remained.

And yet all this must be held in touch with that doctrine of the unity, the personality, and the ineffable transcendence of God,—that doctrine which was the heritage of the Church, both from the religion of Israel and from the wisdom of Greece. Speaking in a purely historical and human sense, the dogma of the Trinity was the psychologically inevitable effort at a solution of this complex but intensely practical problem.

Loyalty to the community inspired this solution. The problem of the two natures of Christ, divine and human, was also psychologically forced upon Christianity by the very problem of the two levels of our human existence which I have just sketched.

I speak still, not of the truth, but of the psychological motives of the dogma. The problem of the two levels of human existence is concrete, is practical, and exists for all of us. Every man who learns what the true goal of life is must live this twofold existence,—as separate individual, limited by the flesh of this maladjusted and dying organism,—yet also as member of a spiritual community which, if loyal, he loves, and in which, in so far as he is loyal, he knows that his only true life is hidden, and is lived.

But for Christianity this problem of the two levels was vital, not only for the individual Christian, but also for the interpretation of the person of Christ, and for the life of the Church. Since, for historical and psychological reasons, the solution of this problem could not be, for Christianity, either polytheistic or disloyal in its spirit, the only humanly natural course was, first, to distinguish the transcendent divine being from the concretely active spirit whose daily work was that of the Church, and then also to distinguish both of these from the human individuality of the Master who had taught the mystery of the Kingdom, and who had then suffered and died, and, as was believed, had risen to create his Church. One had, I say, clearly to distinguish all these; to declare them all to be perfectly real facts. And then one had to unite and, in form, to identify them all, by means of dogmas which were much less merely ingenious speculations than earnest resolutions to act and to believe whatever the loyal Christian life and the work of the Church demanded for the unity of humanity and for the salvation of the world.

The result may be estimated philosophically, as one may judge to be reasonable. I have said nothing about the metaphysical truth of these dogmas. But the result should not be judged as due to merely speculative subtleties, or as a practical degeneration of the spirit of the early Church.

The common sense of the Church was simply doing its best to express the meaning of its loyalty. This loyalty had its spiritual community and its human master. And its problems were the problems of all loyalty. And it was as a religion of loyalty, with a community, a Lord, and a Spirit to interpret, that Christianity was led to the doctrine of the two natures of Christ, and to the dogma of the Trinity.

X

The psychological motives and the historical background of the capital dogmas of the Church are therefore best to be understood in the light of the conception of the universal community, if only one recognizes the historical fact that the Christian consciousness was by purely human motives obliged to define its community as due to the work of the Master who once walked the earth.

It is not surprising, then, that the Fourth Gospel, wherein the Pauline conception of the Church as the body of Christ, and of Christ as the spirit of the Church, is perfectly united with the idea of the divine Word made flesh, is, of all the Gospels, the one which, although much the farthest from the literal history of the human Master's earthly words and deeds, has been, in its wholeness, the nearest to the heart of the Christian world during many centuries.

The Synoptic Gospels stir the spirits of men by the single word or saying of Jesus, by the recorded parable, or by the impressive incident, be this incident a legend, or a fragment of literally true portrayal (we often know not which).

But the Fourth Gospel impresses us most in its wholeness. This Gospel faces the central practical problem of Christianity,—the problem of grace, the transformation of the very essence of the individual man. This transformation is to save him by making him a dweller in the realm which is at once inaccessibly above his merely natural level as an individual, and yet daily near to whatever gives to his otherwise ruined natural existence its entire value. This realm is the realm of the level of the united and lovable community.

From this realm comes all saving grace. Wherever two or three are gathered together in a genuine unity of spirit,—this realm does indeed begin to display itself. Other religions besides Christianity have illustrated that fact. And whatever, apart from legend on the one hand, and speculative interpretation on the other, we human beings can appreciate, in a vital sense, concerning the meaning of what we call divine, we learn through such love for communities as arises from the companionships of those who are thus joined.

This truth humanity at large has long since possessed in countless expressions and disguises. But the fortune of Christianity led the Church to owe its foundation to teachings, to events, to visions, and, above all, to a practical devotion, which, from the first, required the faithful to identify a human individual with the saving spirit of a community, and with the spirit of a community which was also conceived as wholly divine.

The union of the concrete and the ineffable which hereupon resulted, —the union of what touches the human heart and stirs the soul as only the voice of a living individual leader can touch it,—the complete union of this with the greatest and most inspiring of human mysteries,—the mystery of loving membership in a community whose meaning seems divine,—this union became the central interest of Christianity.

Apart from what is specifically Christian in belief, such union of the two levels has its place in our daily lives wherever the loyalty of an individual leader shows to other men the way that leads them to the realm of the spirit. And whenever that union takes place, the divine and the human seem to come into touch with each other as elsewhere they never do.

The mystery of loyalty, as Paul well knew, is the typical mystery of grace. It is, in another guise, the mystery of the incarnation. According to the mind of the early Christian Church, one individual had solved that mystery for all men.

He had risen from the shameful death that, for Christianity, as for its greatest rival Buddhism, is not only the inevitable but the just doom of whoever is born on the natural level of the human individual;—he had ascended to the level of the Spirit, and had become, in the belief of the faithful, the spirit of a community whose boundaries were coextensive with the world, and of whose dominion there was to be no end.

The Fourth Gospel conceives this union of the two levels of spiritual existence with a perfect mastery at once of the exalted poetry and of the definitely practical concreteness of the idea, and of the experiences which make it known to us. That the conception of the Logos—a philosophical conception of Greek origin—is used as the vehicle of the portrayal is, for our present purpose, a fact of subordinate importance.

What is most significant is the direct and vital grasp of the new problem, as it appears in the Fourth Gospel. The spirit of the infant Church is here expressed with such unity and such pathos that all the complications of the new ideas vanish; and one sees only the symbol of the perfectly literal and perfectly human triumph of the Spirit,—a triumph which can appear only in this form of the uniting of the level of individuality with the level of perfect loyalty.

In the tale here presented, the dust of our natural divisions is stirred into new life. From the tomb of individual banishment into which the divine has freely descended, from the wreck to which every human individual is justly doomed, the Word made flesh arises.

But "Who is this King of Glory?" He is, in this portrayal, the one who says: "I am the vine. Ye are the branches." The Spirit of the Community speaks. The Pauline metaphor appears in a new expression. But it is uttered not by the believer, but by the being who has solved the mystery of the union of the self and the community. He speaks to individuals who have not yet reached that union. He comforts them:—

"Peace I leave with you; my peace I give unto you; not as the world giveth give I unto you." This is the voice of the saving community to the troubled soul of the lonely individual.

"Let not your heart be troubled, neither let it be fearful. Ye have heard how I said to you, I go away, and I come to you." "Abide in me, and I in you. As the branch cannot bear fruit of itself except it abide in the vine; so neither can ye, except ye abide in me."

"These things have I spoken unto you in proverbs: The hour cometh, when I shall no more speak unto you in proverbs, but shall tell you plainly of the Father." "In the world ye shall have tribulation; but be of good cheer; I have overcome the world."

The loyal alone know whose world this is, and for whom. In the prayer with which this farewell closes, the Jesus of the Fourth Gospel prays: "Holy Father, keep them in thy name which thou hast given me, that they may be one, even as we are one."

These are explicitly the words of the spirit of the universal community, whom mortal eyes no longer see, and whom, in a lonely world of tribulation, men doomed to die now miss with grief and expect with longing. But: "Hast thou been so long with me, and hast not known me?"

In such words the Fourth Gospel embodies the living spirit of the lovable community. This is what the loyal soul knows.

That is why I venture to say in my own words (though I am neither apologist, nor Christian preacher, nor theologian), that Christianity is a religion not only of love, but also of loyalty. And that is why the Fourth Gospel tells us the essential ideas both of Christianity, and of the Christian Realm of Grace, more fully than do the parables, unless you choose to read the parables as the voice of the Spirit of the Church.

In all this I have meant to say, and have said, nothing whatever about the truth, or about the metaphysical bases of Christian dogma.

I have been characterizing the human motives that lie at the basis of the doctrine of the realm of grace, and have been pointing out the ethical and religious value of these motives.

THE PROBLEM OF CHRISTIANITY (1913)

TIME AND GUILT

In Matthew Arnold's essay on "St. Paul and Protestantism," there is a well-known passage from which I may quote a few words to serve as a text for the present lecture. These words express what many would call a typical modern view of an ancient problem.

I

In this essay, just before the words which I shall quote, Matthew Arnold has been speaking of the relation between Paul's moral experiences and their religious interpretation, as the Apostle formulates it in the epistle to the Romans. Referring to a somewhat earlier stage of his own argument, Arnold here says: "We left Paul in collision with a fact of human nature, but in itself a sterile fact, a fact upon which it is possible to dwell too long, although Puritanism, thinking this impossible, has remained intensely absorbed in the contemplation of it, and indeed has never properly got beyond it,—the sense of sin." "Sin," continues Matthew Arnold, "is not a monster to be mused on, but an impotence to be got rid of. All thinking about it, beyond what is indispensable for the firm effort to get rid of it, is waste of energy and waste of time. We then enter that element of morbid and subjective brooding, in which so many have perished. This sense of sin, however, it is also possible to have not strongly enough to beget the firm effort to get rid of it; and the Greeks, with all their great gifts, had this sense not strongly enough; its strength in the Hebrew people is one of this people's mainsprings. And no Hebrew prophet or psalmist felt what sin was more powerfully than Paul." In the sequel, Arnold shows how Paul's experience of the spiritual influence of Jesus enabled the Apostle to solve his own problem of sin without falling into that dangerous brooding which Arnold attributes to the typical Puritan spirit. As a result, Arnold identifies his own view of sin with that of Paul and counsels us to judge the whole matter in the same way.

We have here nothing to do with the correctness of Matthew Arnold's criticism of Protestantism; and also nothing to say, at the present moment, about the adequacy of Arnold's interpretation, either of Paul or of Jesus. But we are concerned with that characteristically modern view of the problem of sin which Arnold so clearly states in the words just quoted.

What constitutes the moral burden of the individual man,—what holds him back from salvation,—may be described in terms of his natural heritage,—his inborn defect of character,—or in terms of his training,—or, finally, in terms of whatever he has voluntarily done which has been knowingly unrighteous. In the present lecture I am not intending to deal with man's original defects of moral nature, nor yet with the faults which his training, through its social vicissitudes, may have bred in him. I am to consider that which we call, in the stricter sense, sin.

Whether correctly or incorrectly, a man often views certain of his deeds as in some specially intimate sense his own, and may also believe that, amongst these his own deeds, some have been wilfully counter to what he believes to be right. Such wrongful deeds a man may regard as his own sins. He may decline to plead ignorance, or bad training, or uncontrollable defect of temper, or overwhelming temptation, as the ground and excuse for just these deeds. Before the forum of his own conscience he may say: "That deed was the result of my own moral choice, and was my sin." For the time being I shall not presuppose, for the purposes of this argument, any philosophical theory about free will. I shall not, in this lecture, assert that, as a fact, there is any genuinely free will whatever. At the moment, I shall provisionally accept only so much of the verdict of common sense as any man accepts when he says: "That was my own voluntary deed, and was knowingly and wilfully sinful." Hereupon I shall ask: Is Matthew Arnold's opinion correct with regard to the way in which the fact and the sense of sin ought to be viewed by a man who believes that he has, by what he calls his own "free act and deed," sinned? Is Arnold's opinion sound and adequate when he says: "Sin is not a monster to be mused on, but an impotence to be got rid of." Arnold praises Paul for having taken sin seriously enough to get rid of it, but also praises him for not having brooded over sin except to the degree that was "indispensable to the effort to get rid of it." Excessive brooding over sin is, in Arnold's opinion, an evil characteristic of Puritanism. Is Arnold right?

II

Most of us will readily agree that Arnold's words have a ring of sound modern sense when we first hear them spoken. Brooding over one's sins certainly appears to be not always,—yes, not frequently,—and surely not for most modern men, a convenient spiritual exercise. It tends not to the edification, either of the one who broods, or of his brethren. Brooding sinners are neither agreeable companions nor inspiring guides. Arnold is quite right in pointing out that Paul's greatest and most eloquent passages—those amongst his words which we best remember and love—are full of the sense of having somehow "got rid" of the very sin to which Paul most freely confesses when he speaks of his own past as a persecutor of the Church and as an unconverted Pharisee. It is, then, the escape from sin, and not the bondage to sin, which helps a man to help his fellows. Ought not, therefore, the thought of sin to be used only under the strict and, so to speak, artistic restraints to which Matthew Arnold advises us to keep it subject? You have fallen into a fault; you have given over your will to the enemy; you have wronged your fellow; or, as you believe, you have offended God in word and deed. What are you now to do about this fact? "Get rid of your sin," says Matthew Arnold. Paul did so. He did so through what he called a loving union with the spirit of Christ. As he expressed the matter, he "died" to sin. He "lived" henceforth to the righteousness of his Master and of the Christian community. And that was, for him, the end of brooding, unless you call it brooding when his task as missionary required him to repeat the simple confession of his earlier life,—the life that he had lived before the vision of the risen Christ transformed him. Matthew Arnold counsels a repetition of Paul's experience in modern fashion, and with the use of modern ideas rather than of whatever was narrow, and of whatever is now superseded, in Paul's religious opinions and imagery.

The modern version of Paulinism, as set forth by Arnold, would involve, first, a return to the primitive Christianity of the sayings of Jesus; next, a "falling in love" with the person and character of Jesus; and, finally, a "getting rid of sin" through a new life of love, lived in the spirit of Jesus. Matthew Arnold's version of the Gospel is, at the present moment, more familiar to general readers of the literature of the problem of Christianity than it was when he wrote his essays on religion. So far as sin is concerned, is not this version heartily acceptable to the modern mind? Is it not sensible, simple, and in spirit strictly normal, as well as moral and religious? Does it not dispose, once for all, both of the religious and of the practical aspect of the problem of sin?

I cannot better state the task of this lecture than by taking the opportunity which Arnold's clearness of speech gives me to begin the study of our question in the light of so favorite a modern opinion.

III

It would not be useful for us to consider any further, in this place, Paul's own actual doctrine about such sin as an individual thinks to have been due to his own voluntary and personal deed. Paul's view regarding the nature of original sin involves other questions than the one which is at present before us. We speak here not of original sin, but of knowing and voluntary evil doing. Paul's idea of salvation from original sin through grace, and through loving union with the spirit of the Master, is inseparable from his special opinions regarding the Church as the body of Christ, and regarding the supernatural existence of the risen Christ as the Spirit of the Church. These matters also are not now before us. The same may be said of Paul's views concerning the forgiveness of our voluntary sins. For, in Paul's mind, the whole doctrine of the sins which the individual has knowingly and wilfully committed, is further complicated by the Apostle's teachings about predestination. And for an inquiry into those teachings there is, in this lecture, neither space nor motive. Manifold and impressive though Paul's dealings with the problem of sin are, we shall therefore do well, upon this occasion, to approach the doctrine of the voluntary sins of the individual from another side than the one which Paul most emphasizes. Let us turn to aspects of the Christian tradition about wilful sin for which Paul is not mainly responsible.

We all know, in any case, that Arnold's own views about the sense and the thought of sin are not the views which have been prevalent in the past history of Christianity. And Arnold's hostility to the Puritan spirit carries him too far when he seems to attribute to Puritanism the principal responsibility for having made the fact and the sense of sin so prominent as it has been in Christian thought. Long before Puritanism, mediæval Christianity had its own meditations concerning sin. Others than Puritans have brooded too much over their sins. And not all Puritans have cultivated the thought of sin with a morbid intensity.

I have no space for a history of the Christian doctrine of wilful sin. But, by way of preparation for my principal argument, I shall next call to mind a few of the more familiar Christian beliefs concerning the perils and the results of voluntary sin, without caring, at the moment, whether these beliefs are mediæval, or Puritan, or not. Thereafter, I shall try to translate the sense of these traditional beliefs into terms which seem to me to be worthy of the serious consideration of the modern man. After this restatement and interpretation of the Christian doctrine,—not of original sin, but of the voluntary sin of the individual,—we shall have new means of seeing whether Arnold is justified in declaring that no thought about sin is wise except such thought as is indispensable for arousing the effort "to get rid of sin."

IV

The teaching of Jesus concerning wilful sin, as it is recorded in some of the best known of his sayings, is simple and searching, august in the severity of the tests which it uses for distinguishing sinful deeds from righteous deeds, and yet radiant with its familiar message of hope for the sincerely repentant sinner. I have no right to judge as to the authenticity of the individual sayings of Jesus which our Gospels record. But the body of the teachings of the Master concerning sin is not only one of the most frequently quoted portions of the Gospel tradition, but is also an essential part of that doctrine of Christian love which great numbers of Christian souls, both learned and unlearned, find to be the most obviously characteristic expression of what the founder had at heart when he came to seek and to save that which was lost. Searching is this teaching about sin, because of what Matthew Arnold called the *inwardness* of the spirit which Jesus everywhere emphasized in telling us what is the essence of righteousness. August is this teaching in the severity of the tests which it applies; because all seeming, all worldly repute, all outward conformity to rules, avail nothing in the eyes of the Master, unless the interior life of the doer of good works is such as fully meets the requirements of love, both towards God and towards man.

Countless efforts have been made to sum up in a few words the spirit of the ethical teaching of Jesus. I make no new effort, I contribute no novel word or insight, when I now venture to say, simply in passing, that the religion of the founder, as preserved in the sayings, is a religion of Whole-Heartedness. The voluntary good deed is one which, whatever its outward expression may be, carries with it the whole heart of love, both to God and to the neighbor. The special act—whether it be giving the cup of cold water, or whether it be the martyr's heroism in confessing the name of Jesus in presence of the persecutor—matters less than the inward spirit. The Master gives no elaborate code to be applied to each new situation. The whole heart devoted to the cause of the Kingdom of Heaven,—this is what is needed.

On the other hand, whatever wilful deed does not spring from love of God and man, and especially whatever deed breaks with the instinctive dictates of whole-hearted love, is sin. And sin means alienation from the Kingdom and from the Father; and hence, in the end, means destruction. Here again the august severity of the teaching is fully manifested. But from this destruction there is indeed an escape. It is the escape by the road of repentance. That is the only road which is emphatically and repeatedly insisted upon in the sayings of Jesus, as we have them. But this repentance must include a whole-hearted willingness to forgive those who trespass against us. Thus repentance means a return both to the Father and to the whole-hearted life of love. Another name for this whole-heartedness, in action as well as in repentance, is faith. For the true lover of God instinctively believes the word of the Son of Man who teaches these things, and is sure that the Kingdom of God will come.

But like the rest of the reported sayings of Jesus, this simple and august doctrine of the peril of sin, and of the way of escape through repentance, comes to us with many indications that some further and fuller revelation of its meaning is yet to follow. Jesus appears in the Gospel reports as himself formally announcing to individuals that their sins are forgiven. The escape from sin is therefore not always wholly due to the repentent sinner's own initiative. Assistance is needed. And Jesus appears in the records, as assisting. He assists, not only as the teacher who announces the Kingdom, but as the one who has "power to forgive sins." Here again I simply follow the well-known records. I am no judge as to what sayings are authentic.

I am sure, however, that it was but an inevitable development of the original teaching of the founder and of these early reports about his authority to forgive, when the Christian community later conceived that salvation from personal and voluntary sin had become possible through the work which the departed Lord had done while on earth. *How* Christ saved from sin became hereupon a problem. But *that* he saved from sin, and that he somehow did so through what he won for men by his death, became a central constituent of the later Christian tradition.

A corollary of this central teaching was a further opinion which tradition also emphasized, and, for centuries, emphasized the more, the further the apostolic age receded into the past. This further opinion was: That the wilful sinner is powerless to return to a whole-hearted union with God through any deed of his own. He could not "get rid of sin," either by means of repentance or otherwise, unless the work of Christ had prepared the way. This, in sum, was long the common tradition of the Christian world. How the saving work of Christ became or could be made efficacious for obtaining the forgiveness of the wilful sin of an individual,—this question, as we well know, received momentous and conflicting answers as the Christian church grew, differentiated, and went through its various experiences of heresy, of schism, and of the learned interpretation of its faith. Here, again, the details of the history of dogma, and the practice of the Church and of its sects in dealing with the forgiveness of sins, concern us not at all.

We need, however, to remind ourselves, at this point, of one further aspect of the tradition about wilful sin. That sin, if unforgiven, leads to "death," was a thought which Judaism had inherited from the religion of the prophets of Israel. It was a grave thought, essential to the ethical development of the faith of Israel, and capable of vast development in the light both of experience and of imagination.

Because of the later growth of the doctrine of the future life, the word "death" came to mean, for the Christian mind, what it could not yet have meant for the early prophets of Israel. And, in consequence, Christian tradition gradually developed a teaching that the divinely ordained penalty of unforgiven sin—the doom of the wilful sinner—is a "second death," an essentially endless penalty. The Apocalypse imaginatively pictures this doom. When the Church came to define its faith as to the future life, it developed a well-known group of opinions concerning this endless penalty of sin. In its outlines this group of opinions is familiar even to all children who have learned anything of the faith of the fathers.

An essentially analogous group of opinions is found in various religions that are not Christian. In its origin this group of opinions goes back to the very beginnings of those forms of ethical religion whose history is at all closely parallel to the history of Judaism or of Christianity. The motives which are here in question lie deeply rooted in human nature; but I have no right and no time to attempt to analyze them now. It is enough for my purpose to remind you that the idea of the endless penalty of unforgiven sin is by no means peculiar to Puritanism; and that it is certainly an idea which, for those who accept it with any hearty faith, very easily leads to many thoughts about sin which tend to exceed the strictly artistic measure which Matthew Arnold assigns as the only fitting one for all such thoughts.

To think of a supposed "endless penalty" as a certain doom for all unforgiven sin, may not lead to morbid brooding. For the man who begins such thoughts may be sedately sure that he is no sinner. Or again, although he confesses himself a sinner, he may be pleasantly convinced that forgiveness is readily and surely attainable, at least for himself. And, as we shall soon see, there are still other reasons why no morbid thought need be connected with the idea of endless penalty. But no doubt such a doctrine of endless penalty tends to awaken thoughts which have a less modern seeming, and which involve a less sure confidence in one's personal power to "get rid of sin" than Matthew Arnold's words, as we have cited them, convey. If, without any attempt to dwell further, either upon the history or the complications of the traditional Christian doctrine of the wilful sin of the individual, we reduce that doctrine to its simplest terms, it consists of two theses, both of which have had a vast and tragic influence upon the fortunes of Christian civilization. The theses are these: First: "By no deed of his own, unaided by the supernatural consequences of the work of Christ, can the wilful sinner win forgiveness." Second: "The penalty of unforgiven sin is the endless second death."

V

The contrast between these two traditional theses and the modern spirit seems manifest enough, even if we do not make use of Matthew Arnold's definition of the reasonable attitude towards sin. This contrast of the old faith and the modern view is one of the most frequently emphasized means of challenging the ethical significance of the Christian tradition.

It is indeed difficult to define just who the "modern man" is, and what views he has to hold in order to be modern. But very many people, I suppose, would be disposed to accept as a partial definition of the modern man, this formulation: "The modern man is one who does not believe in hell, and who is too busy to think about his own sins." If this definition is indeed too trivial to be just, it would still seem to many serious people that, at this point, if at no other, the modern man has parted company with Christian tradition.

And the parting would appear to be not accidental, nor yet due to superficial motives. The deepest ethical interests would be at stake, if the appearances here represent the facts as they are. For the old faith held that the very essence of its revelation concerning righteousness was bound up with its conception of the consequences of unforgiven sin. On the other hand, if the education of the human race has taught us any coherent lesson, it has taught us to respect the right of a rational being to be judged by moral standards that he himself can see to be reasonable.

Hence the moral dignity of the modern idea of man seems to depend upon declining to regard as just and righteous any penalty which is supposed to be inflicted by the merely arbitrary will of any supernatural power. The just penalty of sin, to the modern mind, must therefore be the penalty, whatever it is, which the enlightened sinner, if fully awake to the nature of his deed, and rational in his estimate of his deed, would voluntarily inflict upon himself. And how can one better express that penalty than by following the spirit of Matthew Arnold's advice: "Get rid of your sin"? This advice, to be sure, has its own deliberate sternness. For "the firm effort to get rid of sin" may involve long labor and deep grief. But "endless penalty," a "second death,"—what ethically tolerable meaning can a modern mind attach to these words?

Is not, then, the chasm between the modern ethical view and the ancient faith at this point simply impassable? Have the two not parted company altogether, both in letter and, still more, in their inmost spirit?

To this question some representatives of modern liberal Christianity would at once reply that, as I have already pointed out, the early Gospel tradtion does not attribute to Jesus himself the more hopeless aspects of the doctrine of sin, as the later tradition was led to define them. Jesus, according to the reports of his teaching in the Gospels, does indeed more than once use a doctrine of the endless penalty of unforgiven sin,—a doctrine with which a portion of the Judaism of his day was more or less familiar. In well-known parables he speaks of the torments of another world. And in general he deals with wilful sin unsparingly. But, so far as the present life is concerned, he seems to leave the door of repentance always open. The Father waits for the Prodigal Son's return. And the Prodigal Son returns of his own will. We hear nothing in the parables about his being unable effectively to repent unless some supernatural plan of salvation has first been worked out for him. Is it not possible, then, to reconcile the Christian spirit and the modern man by simply returning to the Christianity of the parables? So, in our day, many assert.

I do not believe that the parables, in the form in which we possess them, present to us any complete view of the essence of the Christian doctrine of sin, or of the sinner's way of escape. I do not believe that they were intended by the Master to do so. I have already pointed out how our reports of the founder's teachings about sin indicate that these teachings were intended to receive a further interpretation and supplement. Our real problem is whether the interpretation and supplement which later Christian tradition gave, through its doctrine of sin, and of the endless penalty of sin, was, despite its tragedy, its mythical setting, and its arbitrariness, a teaching whose ethical spirit we can still accept or, at least, understand. Is the later teaching, in any sense, a just development of the underlying meaning of the parables? Does any deeper idea inform the traditional doctrine that the wilful sinner is powerless to save himself from a just and endless penalty through any repentance, or through any new deed of his own?

As I undertake to answer these questions, let me ask you to bear in mind one general historical consideration. Christianity, even in its most imaginative and in its most tragic teachings, has always been under the influence of very profound ethical motives,—the motives which already inspired the prophets of Israel. The founder's doctrine of the Kingdom, as we now possess that doctrine, was an outline of an ethical religion. It was also a prologue to a religion that was yet to be more fully revealed, or at least explained. This, as I suppose, was the founder's personal intention. When the early Church sought to express its own spirit, it was never knowingly false; it was often most fluently, yet faithfully, true to the deeper meaning of the founder. Its expressions were borrowed from many sources. Its imagination was constructive of many novelties. Only its deeper spirit was marvellously steadfast. Even when, in its darker moods, its imagination dwelt upon the problem of sin, it saw far more than it was able to express in acceptable formulas. Its imagery was often of local, or of heathen, or even of primitive origin. But the truth which the imagery rendered edifying and teachable,—this often bears and invites an interpretation whose message is neither local nor primitive. Such an interpretation I believe to be possible in case of the doctrine of sin and of its penalty; and to my own interpretation I must now ask your attention.

VI

There is one not infrequent thought about sin upon which Matthew Arnold's rule would surely permit us to dwell; for it is a thought which helps us, if not wholly "to get rid of sin," still, in advance of decisive action, to forestall some temptations to sin which we might otherwise find too insistent for our safety. It is the thought which many a man expresses when he says, of some imagined act: "If I were to do that, I should be false to all that I hold most dear; I should throw away my honor; I should violate the fidelity that is to me the very essence of my moral interest in my existence." The thought thus expressed may be sometimes merely conventional; but it may also be very earnest and heartfelt.

Every man who has a moral code which he accepts, not merely as the customary and, to him, opaque or senseless verdict of his tribe or of his caste, but as his own chosen personal ideal of life, has his power to formulate what for him would seem (to borrow the religious phraseology) his "sin against the Holy Ghost,"—his own morally "impossible" choice, so far as he can now predetermine what he really means to do.

Different men, no doubt, have different exemplary sins in mind when they use such words. Their various codes may be expressions of quite different and largely accidental social traditions; their diverse examples of what, for each of them, would be his own instance of the unpardonable sin, may be the outcome of the *tabus* of whatever social order you please. I care for the moment not at all for the objective ethical correctness of any one man's definition of his own moral code. And I am certainly here formulating no ethical code of my own. I am simply pointing out that, when a man becomes conscious of his own rule of life, of his own ideal of what makes his voluntary life worth while, he tends to arrange his ideas of right and wrong acts so that, for him at least, *some* acts, when he contemplates the bare possibility of doing them himself, appear to him to be acts such that they would involve for him a kind of moral suicide,—a deliberate wrecking of what makes life, for himself, morally worth while.

One common-sense way of expressing such an individual judgment upon these extreme acts of wrong-doing, is to say: "If I were to do that of my own free will, I could thereafter never forgive myself."

Since I am here not undertaking any critical discussion of the idea of the "Ought," I do not now venture the thesis that every man who is a reasonable being at all, or who, as they say, "has a conscience," must needs be able to name instances of acts which, if he knowingly chose to do them, would make his life, in his own eyes, a moral chaos,—a failure, —so that he would "never forgive" himself for those acts. If a student of ethics asks me to prove that a man ought to view his own life and his own will in this way, I am not here concerned to offer such a proof in philosophical terms.

But this I can point out: In case a man thinks of his own possible actions in this way, he need not be morbidly brooding over sins of which it is well not to think too much. He *may* be simply surveying his plan of life in a resolute way, and deciding, as well as he can, where he stands; what his leading ideas are, and what makes his voluntary life, from his own point of view, worth living. To be resolute, is at all events no weakness; and nobody "perishes" merely because he has his mind clearly made up regarding what, for him, would be his own unpardonable sin. There is no loss for one's manhood in knowing how one's "sin against the Holy Ghost," one's possible act for which one is resolved never to ask one's own forgiveness, is defined. Such thoughts tend to clear our moral air, if only we think them in terms of our own personal ideals, and do not, as is too often the case, apply them solely to render more dramatic our judgments about our neighbors.

VII

In order to be able to formulate such thoughts, one must have an "ideal," even if one cannot state it in an abstract form. One must think of one's voluntary life in terms of fidelity to some such "ideal," or set of ideals. One must regard one's self as a creature with a purpose in living. One must have what they call a "mission" in one's own world. And so, whether one uses philosophical theories or religious beliefs, or does not use them, one must, when one speaks thus, actually have some sort of spiritual realm in which, as one believes, one's moral life is lived, a realm to whose *total* order, as one supposes, one could be false if one chose. One's mission, one's business, must ideally extend, in some fashion, to the very boundaries of this spiritual realm, so that, if one actually chose to commit one's supposed unpardonable sin, one could exist in this entire realm only as, in some sense and degree, an outcast,—estranged, so far as that one unpardonable fault estranged one, from one's own chosen moral health and fireside. At least this is how one resolves, in advance of decisive action, to view the matter, in case one has the precious privilege of being able to make such resolves. And I say that so to find one's self resolving, is to find *not* weakness and brooding, but resoluteness and clearness. Life seems simply blurred and dim if one can nowhere find in it such sharp moral outlines. And if one becomes conscious of such sharp outlines, one is not saying: "Behold me, the infallible judge of moral values for all mankind. Behold me with the absolute moral code precisely worked out." For one is so far making no laws for one's neighbors. One is accepting no merely traditional *tabus*. One is simply making up one's mind so as to give a more coherent sense to one's choices. The penalty of *not* being able to make such resolves regarding what would be one's own unpardonable sin, is simply the penalty of flabbiness and irresoluteness. To remain unaware of what we propose to do, never helps us to live. To be aware of our coherent plan, to have a moral world and a business that, in ideal, extends to the very boundaries of this world, and to view one's life, or any part of it, as an expression of one's own personal will, is to assert one's genuine freedom, and is not to accept any external bondage. But it is also to bind one's self, in all the clearness of a calm resolve. It is to view certain at least abstractly possible deeds as moral catastrophes, as creators of chaos, as deeds whereby the self, *if* it chose them, would, at least in so far, banish itself from its own country.

To be able to view life in this way, to resolve thus deliberately what genuine and thoroughgoing sin would mean for one's own vision, requires a certain maturity. Not all ordinary misdeeds are in question when one thinks of the unpardonable sin. Blunders of all sorts fill one's childhood and youth. What Paul conceived as our original sin may have expressed itself for years in deeds that our social order condemns, and that our later life deeply deplores. And yet, in all this maze of past evil-doing and of folly, we may have been, so far, either helpless victims of our nature and of our training, or blind followers of false gods. What Paul calls sin may have "abounded." And yet, as we look back, we may now judge that all this was merely a means whereby, henceforth, "grace may more abound." We may have learned to say,—it may be wise, and even our actual duty to say: "I will not brood over these which were either my ignorant or my helpless sins. I will henceforth firmly and simply resolve 'to get rid of them.' That is for me the best. Bygones are bygones. Remorse is a waste of time. These 'confusions of a wasted youth' must be henceforth simply ignored. That is the way of cheer. It is also the way of true righteousness. I can live wisely only in case I forget my former follies, except in so far as a memory of these follies helps me not to repeat them."

One may only the more insist upon this cheering doctrine of Lethe and forgiveness for the past, and of "grace abounding" for the future, when there come into one's life those happenings which Paul viewed as a new birth, and as a "dying to sin." These workings of "grace," if they occur to us, may transform our "old man" of inherited defect, of social waywardness, of contentiousness, and of narrow hatred for our neighbors and for "the law" into the "new life." It is a new life to us because we now seem to have found our own cause, and have learned to love our sense of intimate companionship with the universe. Now, for the first time, we have found a life that seems to us to have transparent sense, unity of aim, and an abiding and sustaining inspiration about it.

If this result has taken place, then, whatever our cause, or our moral opinions, or our religion may be, we shall tend to rejoice with Paul that we have now "died" to the old life of ignorance and of evil-working distractions. Hereupon we may be ready to say, with him, and joyously: "There is no condemnation" for us who are ready to walk after what we now take to be "the spirit." The past is dead. Grace has saved us. Forgiveness covers the evil deeds that were done. For those deeds, as we now see, were *not* done by our awakened selves. They were not our own "free acts" at all. They were the workings of what Paul called "the flesh." "Grace" has blotted them out.

I am still speaking not of any one faith about the grace that saves, or about the ideal of life. Let a man find his salvation as it may happen to him to find it. But the main point that I have further to insist upon is this: Whenever and however we have become morally mature enough to get life all colored through and through by what seems to us a genuinely illuminating moral faith, so that it seems to us as if, in every deed, we could serve, despite our weakness, our one highest cause, and be faithful to all our moral world at every moment,—then this inspiration has to be paid for. The abundance of grace means, henceforth, a new gravity of life.

For we now have to face the further fact that, if we have thus won vast ideals, and a will that is now inspired to serve them, we can imagine ourselves becoming false to this our own will, to this which gives our life its genuine value. We can imagine ourselves breaking faith with our own world-wide cause and inspiration. One who has found his cause, if he has a will of his own, can become a conscious and deliberate traitor. One who has found his loyalty is indeed, at first, under the obsession of the new spirit of grace. But if, henceforth, he lives with a will of his own, he can, by a wilful closing of his eyes to the light, *become* disloyal.

Our actual voluntary life does not bear out any theory as to the fatally predestined perseverance of the saints. For our voluntary life seems to us as it was free either to persevere or not to persevere. The more precious the light that has seemed to come to me, the deeper is the disgrace to which, in my own eyes, I can condemn myself, if I voluntarily become false to this light.

Now it is indeed not well to brood over such chances of falsity. But it is manly to face the fact that they are present.

I repeat that, in all this statement, I have presupposed no philosophical theory of free will, and have not assumed the truth of any one ethical code or doctrine. I have been speaking simply in terms of moral experience, and have been pointing out how the world seems to a man who reaches sufficient moral maturity to possess, even if but for a season, a pervasive and practically coherent ideal of life, and to value himself as a possible servant of his cause, but a servant whose freedom to choose is still his own.

What I point out is that, if a man has won practically a free and conscious view of what his honor requires of him, the reverse side of this view is also present. This reverse side takes the form of knowing what, for this man himself, it would mean to be wilfully false to his honor. One who knows that he freely serves his cause knows that he could, if he chose, become a traitor. And if indeed he freely serves his cause, he knows whether or no he could forgive himself if he wilfully became a traitor. Whoever, through grace, has found the beloved of his life, and now freely lives the life of love, knows that he could, if he chose, betray his beloved. And he knows what estimate his own free choice now requires him to put upon such betrayal.

Choose your cause, your beloved, and your moral ideal as you please. What I now point out is that so to choose is to imply your power to define what, for you, would be the unpardonable sin if you committed it. This unpardonable sin would be betrayal.

VIII

So far I have spoken of the moral possibility of treason. We seem to be free. Therefore it seems to us as if treason were possible. But now, *do* any of us ever actually thus betray our own chosen cause? Do we ever actually turn traitor to our own flag,—to the flag that we have sworn to serve,—after taking our oath, not as unto men, but as unto ourselves and our cause? Do any of us ever really commit that which, in our own eyes, is the unpardonable sin?

Here, again, let every one of us judge for himself. And let him also judge rather himself than his neighbor. For we are here speaking, not of customary codes, nor of outward seeming, but of how a man who knows his ideal and knows his own will finds that his inward deed appears to himself.

Still, apart from all evil speaking, the common experience of mankind *seems* to show that such actual and deliberate sin against the light, such conscious and wilful treason, occasionally takes place.

So far as we know of such treason at all, or reasonably believe in its existence, it appears to us to be, on the whole, the worst evil with which man afflicts his fellows and his social order in this distracted world of human doings. The blindness and the naïve cruelty of crude passion, the strife and hatred with which the natural social order is filled, often seem to us mild when we compare them with the spiritual harm that follows the intentional betrayal of great causes once fully accepted, but then wilfully forsaken, by those to whom they have been intrusted.

"If the light that is in thee be darkness, how great is that darkness." This is the word which seems especially fitted for the traitor's own case. For he has seen the great light. The realm of the spirit has been graciously opened to him. He has willingly entered. He has chosen to serve. And then he has closed his eyes; and, by his own free choice, a darkness far worse than that of man's primal savagery has come upon him. And the social world, the unity of brotherhood, the beloved life which he has betrayed,—how desolate he has left what was fairest in it. He has reduced to its primal chaos the fair order of those who trusted and who lived and loved together in one spirit!

But we are here little concerned with what others think of the traitor, if such traitor there be. We are interested in what (if the light against which he has sinned returns to him), the traitor henceforth is to think of himself. Matthew Arnold would say, "Let him think of his sin,"—that is, in this case, of his treason,—only in so far as is indispensable to the "firm resolve to get rid of it." We ask whether,—now that the traitor has first won his own light, and has defined by his own will his own unpardonable sin, and has then betrayed his cause, has sinned against his light and has done his little best to make chaos of his own chosen ideal and of his moral order,—we ask, I say, whether Arnold's rule seems any longer quite adequate to meet the situation.

Of course I am not venturing to assign to the supposed traitor any penalties *except* those which his own will really intends to assign to him. I am not acting in the least as his Providence. I am leaving him quite free to decide his own fate. I am certainly not counselling him to feel any particular kind or degree of the mere emotion called remorse. For all that I now shall say, he is quite free, if that is his desire, to forget his treason once for all, and to begin his business afresh with a new moral ideal, or with no ideal at all, as he may choose.

What I ask, however, is simply this: If he resumes his former position of knowing and choosing an ideal, if he also remembers what ideal he formerly chose, and what and how and how deliberately he betrayed, and knows himself for what he is, what does he judge regarding the now inevitable and endless consequences of his deed? And what answer will he now make to Matthew Arnold's kind advice:—"Get rid of your sin." He need not answer in a brooding way. He need be no Puritan. He may remain as cheerful in his passing feelings as you please. He may quite calmly rehearse the facts. He may decline to shed any tear, either of repentance or of terror. My only hypothesis is that he sees the facts as they are, and confesses, however cooly and dispassionately, the moral value which, as a matter of simple coherence of view and opinion, he now assigns to himself.

IX

He will answer Matthew Arnold's advice, as I think, thus: " 'Get rid of my sin?' How can I get rid of it? It is done. It is past. It is as irrevocable as the Archæan geological period, or as the collision of stellar masses, the light of whose result we saw here on earth a few years ago, when a new star flamed forth in the Constellation Perseus. I am the one who, at such a time, with such a light of the spirit shining before me, with my eyes thus and thus open to my business and to my moral universe, first, so far as I could freely act at all, freely closed my eyes, and then com-

mitted what my own will had already defined to be my unpardonable
sin. So far as in me lay, in all my weakness, but yet with all the wit and
the strength that just then were mine, I was a traitor.

That fact, that event, that deed, is irrevocable. The fact that I am the
one who then did thus and so, not ignorantly, but knowingly,—that fact
will outlast the ages. That fact is as endless as time.

And, in so far as I continue to value myself as a being whose life is
coherent in its meaning, this fact that then and there I was a traitor will
always constitute a genuine penalty,—my own penalty,—a penalty that
no god assigns to me, but that I, simply because I am myself, and take an
interest in knowing myself, assign to myself, precisely in so far as and
whenever I am awake to the meaning of my own life. I can never undo
that deed. If I ever say, 'I have undone that deed,' I shall be both a fool
and a liar. Counsel me, if you will, to forget that deed. Counsel me to do
good deeds without number to set over against that treason. Counsel me
to be cheerful, and to despise Puritanism. Counsel me to plunge into
Lethe. All such counsel may be, in its way and time, good. Only do not
counsel me 'to get rid of' just that sin. That, so far as the real facts are
concerned, cannot be done. For I am, and to the end of endless time
shall remain, the doer of that wilfully traitorous deed. Whatever other
value I may get, that value I retain forever. My guilt is as enduring as
time."

But hereupon a bystander will naturally invite our supposed traitor to
repent, and to repent thoroughly of his treason. The traitor, now cool
and reasonable once more, can only apply to his own case Fitzgerald's
word in the Omar Khayyam stanzas:—

> The moving finger writes, and having writ,
>   Moves on: nor all your piety nor wit
> Can lure it back to cancel half a line,
>   Nor all your tears wash out a word of it.

These very familiar lines were sometime viewed as Oriental fatalism. But
they are, in fact, fully applicable to the freest of deeds when once that
deed is done.

We need not further pursue any supposed colloquy between the traitor and those who comment upon the situation. The simple fact is that
each deed is *ipso facto* irrevocable; that our hypothetical traitor, in his
own deed, has been false to whatever light he then and there had and to

whatever ideal he then viewed as his highest good. Hereupon no new deed, however good or however faithful, and however much of worthy consequences it introduces into the future life of the traitor or of his world, can annul the fact that the one traitorous deed was actually done. No question as to whether the traitor, when he first chose the cause which he later betrayed, was then ethically correct in his choice, aids us to estimate just the one matter which is here in question,—namely, the value of the traitor as the doer of that one traitorous deed. For his treason consists not in his blunders in the choice of his cause, but in his sinning against such light as he then and there had. The question is, furthermore, not one as to his general moral character, apart from this one act of treason. To condemn at one stroke the whole man for the one deed is, of course, absurd. But it is the one deed which is now in question. This man may *also* be the doer of countless good deeds. But our present question is solely as to his value as the doer of that one traitorous deed. This value he has through his own irrevocable choice. Whatever other values his other deeds may give him, this one value remains, never to be removed. By no deed of his own can he ever escape from that penalty which consists in his having introduced into the moral world the one evil which was, at the time, as great an evil as he could then, of his own will, introduce.

In brief, by his own deed of treason, the traitor has consigned himself, —not indeed his *whole* self, but his self as the doer of this deed,—to what one may call the *hell of the irrevocable*. *All* deeds are indeed irrevocable. But only the traitorous sin against the light is such that, in advance, the traitor's own free acceptance of a cause has stamped it with the character of being what his own will had defined as his own unpardonable sin. Whatever else the traitor may hereafter do,—and even if he becomes and remains, through all his future life, in this or any other world, a saint,— the fact will remain: There was a moment when he freely did whatever he could to wreck the cause that he had sworn to serve. The traitor can henceforth do nothing that will give to himself, precisely in so far as he was the doer of that one deed, any character which is essentially different from the one determined by his treason.

The hell of the irrevocable: all of us know what it is to come to the border of it when we contemplate our own past mistakes or mischances. But we can enter it and dwell in it only when the fact "This deed is irrevocable," is combined with the further fact "This deed is one that, unless I call treason my good, and moral suicide my life, I cannot forgive myself for having done."

Now to use these expressions is not to condemn the traitor, or any one else, to endless emotional horrors of remorse, or to any sensuous pangs of penalty or grief, or to any one set of emotions whatever. It is simply to say: If I morally value myself at all, it remains for me a genuine and irrevocable evil in my world, that ever I was, even if for that one moment only and in that one deed, with all my mind and my soul and my heart and my strength, a traitor. And if I ever had any cause, and then betrayed it,—such an evil not only was my deed, but such an evil forever remains, so far as that one deed was done, the *only* value that I can attribute to myself precisely *as* the doer of that deed at that time.

What the pungency of the odors, what the remorseful griefs, of the hell of the irrevocable may be, for a given individual, we need not attempt to determine, and I have not the least right or desire to imagine. Certainly remorse is a poor companion for an active life; and I do not counsel any one, traitor or not traitor, to cultivate remorse. Our question is not one about one's feelings, but about one's genuine value as a moral agent. Certainly forgetfulness is often useful when one looks forward to new deeds. I do not counsel any one uselessly to dwell upon the past. Still the fact remains, that the more I come to take large and coherent views of my life and of its meaning, the more will the fact that, by my own traitorous deed, I have banished myself to the hell of the irrevocable, appear to me both a vast and a grave fact in my world. I shall learn, if I wisely grow into new life, neither to be crushed by any sort of facing of that fact, nor to brood unduly over its everlasting presence as a fact in my life. But so long as I remain awake to the real values of my life, and to the coherence of my meaning, I shall know that while no god shuts me, or could possibly shut me, if he would, into this hell, it is my own will to say that, for this treason, just in so far as I wilfully and knowingly committed this treason, I shall permit none of the gods to forgive me. For it is my precious privilege to assert my own reasonable will, by freely accepting my place in the hell of the irrevocable, and by never forgiving myself for this sin against the light. If any new deed can assign to just that one traitorous deed of mine any essentially novel and reconciling meaning,—that new deed will in any case certainly *not* be mine. I can do good deeds in future; but I cannot revoke my individual past deed. If it ever comes to appear as anything but what I myself then and there made it, that change will be due to no deed of mine. Nothing that I myself can do will ever really reconcile me to my own deed, so far as it was that treason.

This, then, as I suppose, is the essential meaning which underlies the traditional doctrine of the endless penalty of wilful sin. This deeper meaning is that, quite apart from the judgment of any of the gods, and wholly in accordance with the true rational will of the one who has done the deed of betrayal, the guilt of a free act of betrayal is as enduring as time. This doctrine so interpreted is, I insist, *not* cheerless. It is simply resolute. It is the word of one who is ready to say to himself, "Such was my deed, and I did it." No repentance, no pardoning power can deprive us of the duty and,—as I repeat,—the precious privilege of saying that of our own deed.

❧

THE PROBLEM OF CHRISTIANITY (1913)

ATONEMENT

The human aspect of the Christian idea of atonement is based upon such motives that, if there were no Christianity and no Christians in the world, the idea of atonement would have to be invented, before the higher levels of our moral existence could be fairly understood. To the illustration of this thesis the present lecture is to be largely devoted. The thesis is not new; yet it seems to me to have been insufficiently emphasized even in recent literature; although, as is well known, modern expositors of the meaning of the Christian doctrine of atonement have laid a constantly increasing stress upon the illustrations and analogies of that doctrine which they have found present in the common experience of mankind, in non-theological literature, and in the history of ethics.

I

The treatment of the idea of atonement in the present lecture, if it in any respect aids towards an understanding of our problem, will depend for whatever it accomplishes upon two deliberate limitations.

The first limitation is the one that I have just indicated. I shall emphasize, more than is customary, aspects of the idea of atonement which one could expound just as readily in a world where the higher levels of moral experience had somehow been reached by the leaders of mankind, but where Christians and Christianity were as yet wholly unknown.

My second limitation will be this: I shall consider the idea of atonement in the light of the special problems which the close of the lecture on "Time and Guilt" left upon our hands. The result will be a view of the idea of atonement which will be intentionally fragmentary, and which will need to be later reviewed in its connection with the other great Christian ideas.

It is true that the history of the Christian doctrine of the atonement has inseparably linked, with the topics that I shall here most emphasize, various religious beliefs, and theological interpretations, with which, under my chosen limitations and despite these limitations, I shall endeavor to keep in touch. But, in a great part of what I shall have to say, I shall confine myself to what I may call "the problem of the traitor,"—an ethical problem which, on the basis laid in the foregoing lecture, I now choose arbitrarily as my typical instance of the human need for atonement, and of a sense in which, in purely human terms, we are able to define what an atoning act would be, if it took place, and what it could accomplish, as well as what it could not accomplish.

Our last lecture familiarized us with the conception of the being whom I shall now call, throughout this discussion, "the traitor." We shall soon learn new reasons why our present study will gain, in definiteness of issue and in simplicity, by using the exemplary moral situation in which our so-called "traitor" has placed himself, as our means for bringing to light what relief, what possible, although always imperfect, reconciliation of the traitor with his own moral world, and with himself, this situation permits.

Perhaps I can help you to anticipate my further statement of my reasons for dwelling upon the unlovely situation of the hypothetical traitor, if I tell you what association of ideas first conducted me to the choice of the exemplary type of moral tragedy which I shall use as the vehicle whereby we are here to be carried nearer to our proposed view of the idea of atonement.

In Bach's Matthew Passion Music, whose libretto was prepared under the master's own guidance, there is a great passage wherein, at the last supper, Christ has just said: "One of you shall betray me." "And they all begin to say," so the recitative first tells us, although at once passing the words over into the mouths of the chorus, "Is it I? Is it I? Is it I?" And then there begins (with the use of the recurrent chorale), the chorus of "the Believers": " 'Tis I, *My* sins betray thee, who died to make me whole." The effect of this, as well as of other great scenes in the Passion Music,—the dramatic and musical workings in their unity, as Bach devised them, transport the listener to a realm where he no longer hears an old story of the past retold, but, looking down, as it were, upon the whole stream of time, sees the betrayal, the divine tragedy, and the triumph, in one,—not indeed timeless, but time-embracing vision. In this vision all flows and changes and passes from the sorrows of a whole world to the hope of reconciliation. Yet all this fluent and passionate life is one divine life, and is also the listener's, or, as we can also say, the spectator's own life. Judas, the spectator knows as himself, as his own ruined personality; the sorrow of Gethsemane, the elemental and perfectly human passion of the chorus: "Destroy them, destroy them, the murderous brood,"—the waiting and weeping at the tomb,—these things belong to the present life of the believer who witnesses the passion. They are all the experiences of us men, just as we are. They are also divine revelations, coming as if from a world that is somehow inclusive of our despair, and that yet knows a joy which, as Bach depicts it in his music drama, is not so much mystical, as simply classic in the perfection of its serene self-control.

What the art of Bach suggests, I have neither the right nor the power to translate into "matter-moulded forms of speech." I have here to tell you only a little about the being whom Mephistopheles calls "der kleine Gott der Welt," about the one who, as the demon says:—

> Bleibt stets von gleichem Schlag,
> Und ist so wunderlich, als wie am ersten Tag.

And I am forced to limit myself in this discourse to choosing,—as my exemplary being who feels the need of some form of atonement,—man in his most unlovely and drearily discouraging aspect,—man in his appearance as a betrayer. The justification of this repellent choice can appear, if at all, then only in the outcome of our argument, and in its later relation to the whole Christian doctrine of life. But you may now see what first suggested my using this choice in this lecture.

So much, however, it is fair to add as I introduce my case. The "traitor" of my discourse shall here be the creature of an ideal definition based upon facts set forth in the last lecture. I shall soon have to speak again of the sense in which all observers of human affairs have a right to say that there are traitors, and that we well know some of their works. But we have in general no right to say with assurance, when we speak of our individual neighbors, that we know who the traitors are. For we are no searchers of hearts. And treason, as I here define it, is an affair of the heart,—that is, of the inner voluntary deed and decision.

While my ideal definition of the traitor of whom we are now to speak thus depends, as you see, upon facts already discussed in our discourse on "Time and Guilt," our new relation to the being defined as a traitor consists in the fact that, at the last time, we considered the nature of his guilt, while now we mean to approach an understanding of his relation to the idea of atonement.

II

Two conditions, as you will remember from our last lecture, determine what constitutes, for the purposes of my definition, a traitor. The first condition is that a traitor is a man who has had an ideal, and who has loved it with all his heart and his soul and his mind and his strength. His ideal must have seemed to him to furnish the cause of his life. It must have meant to him what Paul meant by the grace that saves. He must have embraced it, for the time, with full loyalty. It must have been his religion, his way of salvation. It must have been the cause of a Beloved Community.

The second condition that my ideal traitor must satisfy is this. Having thus found his cause, he must, as he now knows, in at least some one voluntary act of his life, have been deliberately false to his cause. So far as in him lay, he must, at least in that one act, have betrayed his cause.

Such is our ideal traitor. At the close of the last lecture we left him condemned, in his own sight, to what we called the "hell of the irrevocable."

We now, for the moment, still confine ourselves to his case, and ask: Can the idea of atonement mean anything that permits its application, in any sense, however limited, to the situation of this traitor? Can there be any reconciliation, however imperfect, between this traitor and his own moral world,—any reconciliation which, from his own point of view, and for his own consciousness, can make his situation in his moral world essentially different from the situation in which his own deed has so far left him?

In the hell of the irrevocable there may be, as at the last time we pointed out, no sensuous penalties to fear. And there may be, for all that we know, countless future opportunities for the traitor to do good and loyal deeds. Our problem lies in the fact that none of these deeds will ever undo the supposed deed of treason. In that sense, then, no good deeds of the traitor's future will ever *so* atone for his one act of treason, that he will become clear of just that treason, and of what he finds to be its guilt. He had his moral universe; and his one act of treason did the most that he then and there could do to destroy that world and to wreck his own relation to its meaning. His irrevocable deed is, for his moral consciousness, its own endless penalty. For that deed he can never forgive himself, so long as he knows himself. And nothing that we can now say will change just these aspects of the matter. So much in the traitor's situation is irrevocably fixed.

But it is still open to us to ask whether anything could occur in the traitor's moral world which, without undoing his deed, could still add some new aspect to this deed,—an aspect such that, when the traitor came to view his own deed in this light, he could say: "Something in the nature of a genuinely reconciling element has been added, not only to my world and to my own life, but also to the inmost meaning even of my deed of treason itself. My moral situation has hereby been rendered genuinely better than my deed left it. And this bettering does not consist merely in the fact that some new deed of my own, or of some one else, has been simply a good deed, instead of a bad one, and has thus put a good thing into my world to be henceforth considered side by side with the irrevocable evil deed. No, this bettering consists in something more than this,—in something which gives to my very treason itself a new value; so that I can say, not: 'It is undone;' but 'I am henceforth in some measure, in some genuine fashion, morally reconciled to the fact that I did this evil.'"

Plainly, if any such reconciliation is possible, it will be at best but an imperfect and tragic reconciliation. It cannot be simply and perfectly destructive of guilt. But the great tragic poets have long since taught us that there are indeed tragic reconciliations even when there are great woes. These tragic reconciliations may be infinitely pathetic; but they may be also infinitely elevating, and even, in some unearthly and wondrous way, triumphant.

Our question is: Can such a tragic reconciliation occur in the case of the traitor? If it can occur, the result would furnish to us an instance of an atonement. This atonement would not mean, and could not mean, a clearing away of the traitor's guilt as if it never had been guilt. It would still remain true that the traitor could never rationally forgive himself for his deed. But he might in some measure, and in some genuine sense, become, not simply, but tragically,—sternly,—yet really, reconciled, not only to himself, but to his treason, and to its meaning in his moral world.

Let us consider, then, in what way, and to what degree, the traitor might find such an atonement.

III

The Christian idea of atonement has always involved an affirmative answer to the question: Is an atonement for even a wilful deed of betrayal possible? Is a reconciliation of even the traitor to himself and to his world a possibility? The help that our argument gets from employing the supposed traitor's view of his own case as the guide of our search for whatever reconciliation is still possible for him, shows itself, at the present point of our inquiry, by simplifying the issue, and by thus enabling us at once to dispose, very briefly—not indeed of the Christian idea of atonement (for that, as we shall see, will later reveal itself in a new and compelling form), but of a great number of well-known theological theories of the nature of atonement, so far as they are to help our traitor to get a view of his own case.

These theological theories stand at a peculiar disadvantage when they speak to the now fully awakened traitor, when he asks what measure of reconciliation is still for him possible. Our traitor has his own narrow, but for that very reason, clearly outlined problem of atonement to consider. We here confine ourselves to his view.

Calmly reasonable in his hell of the irrevocable, he is dealing, not with the "angry God" of a well-known theological tradition, but with himself. He asks, not indeed for escape from the irrevocable, but for what relative and imperfect tragic reconciliation with his world and with his past, his moral order can still furnish to him, by any new event or deed or report. Shall we offer him one of the traditional theological comforts and say: "Some one,—namely, a divine being,—Christ himself, has accomplished a full 'penal satisfaction' for your deed of treason. Accept that satisfying sacrifice of Christ, and you shall be reconciled."

The traitor need not pause to repeat any of the now so well-known theological and ethical objections to the "penal satisfaction" theories of atonement. He needs no long dispute to clear his head. The cold wintry light of his own insight into what was formerly his moral home and into what he has by his own deed lost, is enough to show him the mercilessly unchangeable outlines of his moral landscape. He sees them; and that is so far enough. "Penal satisfaction?" "*That*," he will say, "may somehow interest the 'angry God' of one or another theologian. If so, let this angry God be content, if he chooses. That does not reconcile me. So far as penalty is concerned:—

'I was my own destroyer and will be my own hereafter.'

I asked for reconciliation with my own moral universe, not for the accidental pacification of some angry God. The 'penal satisfaction' offered by another is simply foreign to all the interests in the name of which I inquire."

But hereupon let a grander,—let a far more genuinely religious and indeed truly Christian chord be sounded for the traitor's consolation. Let the words of Paul be heard: "There is now no condemnation for them that are in Christ Jesus, who walk not after the flesh, but after the spirit." The simply human meaning of those immortal words, if understood quite apart from Paul's own religious beliefs, is far deeper than is any merely technical theological theory of atonement. And our traitor will well know what those words of Paul mean. Their deepest human meaning has long since entered into his life. Had it not so entered, he would be no traitor; for he would never have known that there is what, for his own estimate, has been a Holy Spirit,—a cause to which to devote one's life,—a love that is indeed redeeming, and, when it first comes to us, compelling,—the love that raises, as if from the dead, the man who becomes the lover,—the love that also forces the lover, with its mysterious power, to die to his old natural life of barren contentions, and of distractions, and to live in the spirit. That love,—so the traitor well knows, redeems the lover from all the helpless natural wretchedness of the, as yet, unawakened life. It frees from "condemnation" all who remain true to this love.

The traitor knows all this by experience. And he knows it not in terms of mere theological formulas. He knows it as a genuinely human experience. He knows it as what every man knows to whom a transforming love has revealed the sense of a new life.

All this is familiar to the traitor. In his own way, he has heard the voice of the Spirit. He has been converted to newness of life. And *therefore* he has known what his own sin against the Holy Ghost meant. And, thereafter, he has deliberately committed that very sin. Therefore Paul's words are at once, to his mind, true in their most human as well as in their most spiritual sense. And just for that very reason they are to him now, in his guilt, as comfortless and as unreconciling as a death knell.

For they tell him of precisely *that* life which once was his, and which, so far as his one traitorous deed could lead to such a result, he himself has deliberately slain.

If there is to be any, even the most tragic, reconciliation for the traitor, there must be other words to be heard besides just these words of Paul.

IV

Yet there are expositors of the Christian idea of the atonement who have developed the various so-called "moral theories" of the atoning work of Christ. And these men indeed have still many things to tell our traitor. One of the most clearly written and, from a purely literary point of view, one of the most charming of recent books on the moral theory of the idea of atonement, namely, the little book with which Sabatier ended his life work, very effectively contrasts with all the "penal satisfaction" theories of atonement, the doctrine that the work of Christ consisted in such loving sacrifice for human sin and for human sinners that the contemplation of this work arouses in the sinful mind a depth of saving repentance, as well as of love,—a depth of glowing fervor, such as simply purifies the sinner's soul. For love and repentance and new life,—these constitute reconciliation. These, for Sabatier, and for many other representatives of the "moral theories" of atonement,— these are in themselves salvation.

I need not dwell upon such opinions in this connection. They are nowadays well know to all who have read any notable portion of the recent literature of the atonement. They are present in this recent literature in almost endless variations. In general these views are deep, and Christian, and cheering, and unquestionably moral. And their authors can and do freely use Paul's words; and on occasion supplement Paul's words by a citation of the parables. In the parables there is no definite doctrine of atonement enunciated. But there is a doctrine of salvation through loving repentance. Cannot our traitor, in view of the loving sacrifice that constitutes, according to tradition, Christ's atoning work, repent and love? Does *that* not reconcile him? May not the love of Christ both constrain and console him?

V

Once more, speaking still from his own purely human point of view, our traitor sadly simplifies the labor of considering in detail these various moral theories of atonement. The traitor seeks the possible, the relative, the inevitably imperfect reconciliation which, for one in his case, is still rationally definable. He discounts all that you can say as to the transforming pathos and the compelling power of love, and of the sacrifices. All this he long since knows. And, as I must repeat, all this constitutes the very essence of his own tragedy. He knew love before he became a traitor. He knew the love that has inspired heroes, martyrs, prophets, and saviours of mankind. All this he knew. And in his one traitorous deed he thrust it forth. That is the very heart of his problem. Repentance? Yes,—so far as he now has insight,—he has repentance for his traitorous deed. He has this repentance, if not as in the form of passionate remorse, still in the form of an irrevocable condemnation of his own deed. He has this repentance as the very breath of what is now his moral existence in the hell of the irrevocable.

As for amendment of life, and good deeds yet to come, he well knows the meaning of all these things. He is ready to do whatever he can. But none of all this doing of good works, none of this repentance, no love, and no tears will "lure back" the "moving finger" to "cancel half a line," or wash out a word of what is written. Once, when the great light first came, and the one who is now the traitor saw what life meant, his repentance—as he then indeed repented—reconciled him with his own life, and did so for precisely the reasons which Paul has explained. But that was his repentance for the former deeds of his folly, for the misadventures and the passions of his helpless natural sinfulness. He then repented, namely, of what he had done before the light came.

But *now* his state is quite other. We know *why* it is other. And we know, too, why the parables no longer can comfort the traitor. Their words can at most only remind him of what he himself best knows.

"Thou knewest," says the returning Lord to the traitor-servant in the parable of the talents; "thou knewest that I was a hard master." And as for our traitor,—so far as his one deed of treason could express his will,— it was the deed of one who not merely hid his talent in a napkin, but betrayed his Lord as Judas betrayed. Therefore if atonement is to mean for the traitor anything that shall be in any sense reconciling, he must hear of it in some new form. He is no mere prodigal son. His problem is that of the sin against the Holy Ghost.

Let us leave, then, both the "penal satisfaction" theories and the "moral theories" to address themselves to other men. Our traitor knows too well the sad lesson of his own deed to be aided either by the vain technicalities of the more antiquated of these theological types of theories, or by the true, but to him no longer applicable, comforts which the theories of the other—the moral type—open to his view.

Plainly, then, the traitor himself can suggest nothing further as to his own reconciliation with the world where, by his deed of betrayal, he once chose to permit the light that was in him to become darkness. We must turn in another direction.

VI

We have so far considered the traitor's case as if his treason had been merely an affair of his own inner life,—a sort of secret impious wish. But of course, while we are indeed supposing the traitor,—now enlightened by the view of his own deed,—to be the judge of what he himself has meant and done,—we well know that his false deed was, in his own opinion, no mere thought of unholiness. He had a cause. That is, he lived in a real world. And he was false to his cause. He betrayed. Now betrayal is something objective. It breaks ties. It rends asunder what love has joined in dear unity. *What* human ties the traitor broke, we leave to him to discover for himself. Why they were to his mind holy, we also need not now inquire. Enough,—since he was indeed loyal,—he had found his ties; —they were precious and human and real; and he believed them holy;— and he broke them. That is, so far as in him lay, he destroyed by his deed the community in whose brotherhood, in whose life, in whose spirit, he had found his guide and his ideal. His deed, then, concerns not himself only, but that community whereof he was a voluntary member. The community knows, or in the long run must learn, that the deed of treason has been done, even if, being itself no searcher of hearts, it cannot identify the individual traitor. We often know not who the traitors are. But if ours is the community that is wrecked, we may well know by experience that there has been treason.

The problem of reconciliation, then,—if reconciliation there is to be, —concerns not only the traitor, but the wounded or shattered community. Endlessly varied are the problems—the tragedies, the lost causes, the heartbreaks, the chaos, which the deeds of traitors produce. All this we merely hint in passing. But all this constitutes the heart of the sorrow of the higher regions of our human world. And we here refer such countless, commonplace, but crushing tragedies to these ruins which are the daily harvest-home of treason, merely in order to ask the question: Can a genuinely spiritual community, whose ideals are such as Paul loved to portray when he wrote to his churches,—can such a loving and beloved community in any degree reconcile itself to the existence of traitors in its world, and to the deeds of individual traitors? Can it in any wise find in its world something else, over and above the treason,—something which atones for the spiritual disasters that the very being of treason both constitutes and entails? Must not the existence of traitors remain, for the offended community, an evil that is as intolerable and irrevocable and as much beyond its powers of reconciliation as is, for the traitor himself, his own past deed, seen in all the light of its treachery? Can any soul of good arise or be created out of this evil thing, or as an atonement therefor?

You see, I hope, that I am in no wise asking whether the community which the traitor has assailed, desires, or does well either to inflict or to remit any penalties said to be due to the traitor for his deed. I am here speaking wholly of the possibility of inner and human reconciliations. The only penalty which, in the hell of the irrevocable, the traitor himself inevitably finds, is the fact: "I did it." The one irrevocable fact with which the community can henceforth seek to be reconciled, if reconciliation is possible, is the fact: "This evil was done." That is, "These invaluable ties were broken." This unity of brotherhood was shattered. The life of the community,—as it was before the blow of treason fell,—can never be restored to its former purity of unscarred love. This is the fact. For this let the community now seek,—not oblivion, for that is a mere losing of the truth; not annulment, for that is impossible; *but* some measure of reconciliation.

For the community, as I am now viewing its ideal but still distinctly human life, the question is *not* one of what we usually call "forgiveness." If "forgiveness" means simply an affectionate remission of penalty, that is something which, for a given community, may be not only humanly possible, but obviously both wise and desirable. Penalty is no remedy for the irrevocable. Forgiveness is often both reasonable and convenient. Nor need the question be raised as to whether the community could ever trust the traitor with the old hearty human, although always fallible, confidence. What the community can know is—not the traitor's heart, but the fact—manifest through the shattered ties and the broken spiritual life,—the fact that a deed of treason has been done. That the deed was the voluntary work of just this traitor, the community can learn only as a matter of probable opinion, or perhaps through the traitor's confession. But, just as the community cannot now search the traitor's heart, or know whether he will hereafter repeat his treason in some new form,—just so, too, it never has been able, before the deed of treason was committed, to search the hearts of any of its free and loyal members, and to know whether, in fact, its trust was wholly well founded when it believed, or hoped, that just this treason would never be committed by any one of the members whom it fondly trusted.

All the highest forms of the unity of the spirit, in our human world, constantly depend, for their very existence, upon the renewed free choices, the sustained loyalty, of the members of communities. Hence the very best that we know, namely, the loyal brotherhood of the faithful who choose to keep their faith,—this best of all human goods, I say,— is simply inseparable from countless possibilities of the worst of human tragedies,—the tragedy of broken faith. At such cost must the loftiest of our human possessions in the realm of the spirit be purchased,—at the cost, namely, of knowing that some deed of wilful treason on the part of some one whom we trusted as brother or as beloved may rob us of this possession. And the fact that we are thus helplessly dependent on human fidelity for some of our highest goods, and so may be betrayed,—this fact is due not to the natural perversity of men, nor to the mere weakness of those who love and trust. This fact is due to something which, without any metaphysical theory, we ordinarily call man's freedom of choice. We do not want our beloved community to consist of puppets, or of merely fascinated victims of a mechanically insistent love. We want the free loyalty of those who, whatever fascination first won them to their cause, remain faithful because they choose to remain faithful. Of such is the kingdom of good faith. The beloved community demands for itself such freely and deliberately steadfast members. And for that very reason, in a world where there is such free and good faith,—there can be treason. Hence the realm where the spirit reaches the highest human levels is the region where the worst calamities can, and in the long run do, assail many who depend upon the good faith of their brethren.

The community, therefore, never had any grounds, before the treason, for an absolute assurance about the future traitor's perseverance in the faith. After his treason, if indeed he repents and now begins once more to act loyally,—it may acquire a relative assurance that he will henceforth abide faithful. The worst evil is not, then, that a trust in the traitor, which once was rightly serene and perfectly confident, is now irrevocably lost. It is not *this* which constitutes the irreconcilable aspect of the traitor's deed. All men are frail. And especially must those who are freely loyal possess a certain freedom to become faithless if they choose. This evil is a condition of the highest good that the human world contains. And so much the community, in presence of the traitor, ought to recognize as something that was always possible. It also ought to know that a certain always fallible trust in the traitor can indeed be restored by his future good deeds, if such are done by him with every sign that he intends henceforth to be faithful.

But what is indeed irrevocably lost to the community through the traitor's deed is precisely what I just called "unscarred love." The traitor remains—for the community as well as for himself—the traitor,—just so far as his deed is confessed, and just so far as his once unsullied fidelity has been stained. *This* indeed is irrevocable. It is perfectly human. But it is unutterably comfortless to the shattered community.

It is useless, then, to say that the problem of reconciliation, so far as the community is concerned, is the problem of "forgiveness," not now as remission of penalty, but of forgiveness, in so far as forgiveness means a restoring of the love of the community, or of its members, towards the one who has now sinned, but repented. Love may be restored. If the traitor's future attitude makes that possible, human love ought to be restored to the now both repentant and well-serving doer of the past evil deed. But alas! this restored love will be the love for the member who *has been a traitor;* and the tragedy of the treason will permanently form part in and of this love. Thus, then, up to this point, there appears for the community as well as for the traitor, no ground for even the imperfect reconciliation of which we have been in search. Is there, then, any other way, still untried, in which the community may hope, if not to *find,* then to *create* something which, in its own strictly limited fashion, will reconcile the community to the traitor and to the irrevocable, and irrevocably evil, deed.

VII

Such a way exists. The community cannot undo the traitor's deed, and cannot simply annul the now irrevocable fact of the evil which has been accomplished. Penalty, even if called for, annuls nothing of all that has been done. Repentance does not turn backwards the flow of time. Restored and always fallible human confidence in the traitor's good intentions regarding his future deeds, is not true reconciliation. Forgiveness does not wash out a word of the record that the moving finger of treason has written. The love of the forgiving community, or of its members, for the repentant and now well-doing traitor, is indeed a great good; but it is a love that has forever lost one of its most cherished possessions,—the possession of a loyal member who, in the old times before the treason, not only loved, but, so far, *had steadfastly kept his faith*. By all these means, then *no* atonement is rendered to the community. Neither hatred nor penalty need be, from the side of the community, in any wise in question. But the fact remains: The community has lost its treasure; its once faithful member who, until his deed of treason came, had been wholly its own member. And it has lost the ties and the union which he destroyed by his deed. And, for all this loss, it lovingly mourns with a sorrow for which, thus far, we see no reconciliation. Who shall give to it its own again?

The community, then can indeed *find* no reconciliation. But can it *create* one? At the worst, it is the traitor, and it is not the community, that has done this deed. New deeds remain to be done. The community is free to do them, or to be incarnate in some faithful servant who will do them. Could any possible new deed, done by, or on behalf of, the community, and done by some one who is *not* stained by the traitor's deed, introduce into this human world an element which, as far as it went, would be, in whatever measure, genuinely reconciling?

VIII

We stand at the very heart and centre of the human problem of atonement. We have just now nothing to do with theological opinion on this topic. I insist that our problem is as familiar and empirical as is death or grief. That problem of atonement daily arises not as between God and man (for we here are simply ignoring, for the time being, the metaphysical issues that lie behind our problem). That problem is daily faced by all those faithful lovers of wounded and shattered communities who, going down into the depths of human sorrow, either as sufferers or as friends who would fain console, or who, standing by hearths whose fires burn no more, or loving their country through all the sorrows which traitors have inflicted upon her, or who, not weakly, but bravely grieving over the woe of the whole human world, are still steadily determined that no principality and no power, that no height and no depth, shall be able to separate man from his true love, which is the triumph of the spirit. That human problem of atonement is, I say daily faced, and faced by the noblest of mankind. And for these our noblest, despite all our human weakness, that problem is, in principle and in ideal, daily solved. Let us turn to such leaders of the human search after greatness, as our spiritual guides.

Great calamities are, for all but the traitor himself,—so far as we have yet considered his case,—great opportunities. Lost causes have furnished, times without number, the foundations and the motives of humanity's most triumphant loyalty.

When treason has done its last and most cruel work, and lies with what it has destroyed,—dead in the tomb of the irrevocable past,—there is now the opportunity for a triumph of which I can only speak weakly and in imperfectly abstract formulas. But, as I can at once say, this of which I now speak is a human triumph. It forms part of the history of man's earthly warfare with his worst foes. Moreover, whenever it occurs at all, this is a triumph, *not* merely of stoical endurance, nor yet of kindly forgiveness, nor of the mystical mood which, seeing all things in God, feels them all to be good. It is a triumph of the creative will. And what form does it take amongst the best of men, who are here to be our guides?

I answer, this triumph over treason can only be accomplished by the community, or on behalf of the community, through some steadfastly loyal servant who acts, so to speak, as the incarnation of the very spirit of the community itself. This faithful and suffering servant of the community may answer and confound treason by a work whose type I shall next venture to describe, in my own way, thus: First, this creative work shall include a deed, or various deeds, for which only just this treason furnishes the opportunity. Not treason in general, but just this individual treason shall give the occasion, and supply the condition of the creative deed which I am in ideal describing. Without just that treason, this new deed (so I am supposing) could not have been done at all. And hereupon the new deed, as I suppose, is so ingeniously devised, so concretely practical in the good which it accomplishes, that, when you look down upon the human world after the new creative deed has been done in it, you say, first, "This deed was made possible by that treason; and, secondly, *The world, as transformed by this creative deed, is better than it would have been had all else remained the same, but had that deed of treason not been done at all.*" That is, the new creative deed has made the new world better than it was before the blow of treason fell.

Now such a deed of the creative love and of the devoted ingenuity of the suffering servant, on behalf of his community, breaks open, as it were, the tomb of the dead and treacherous past, and comes forth as the life and the expression of the creative and reconciling will. It is this creative will whose ingenuity and whose skill have executed the deed that makes the human world better than it was before the treason.

To devise and to carry out some new deed which makes the human world better than it would have been had just that treasonable deed *not* been done;—is that not, in its own limited way and sense, a reconciling form, both of invention and of conduct? Let us forget, for the moment, the traitor. Let us now think only of the community. We know why and in what sense it cannot be reconciled to the traitor or to his deed. But have we not found, without any inconsistency, a new fact which furnishes a genuinely reconciling element? It indeed furnishes no perfect reconciliation with the irrevocable; but it transforms the meaning of that very past which it cannot undo. It cannot restore the unscarred love. It does supply a new triumph of the spirit,—a triumph which is not so much a mere compensation for what has been lost, as a transfiguration of the very loss into a gain that, without this very loss, could never have been won. The traitor cannot thus transform the meaning of his own past. But the suffering servant can thus transfigure this meaning; can bring out of the realm of death a new life that only this very death rendered possible.

The triumph of the spirit of the community over the treason which was its enemy, the rewinning of the value of the traitor's own life, when the new deed is done, involves the old tragedy, but takes up that tragedy into a life that is now more a life of triumph than it would have been if the deed of treason had never been done.

Therefore, if indeed you suppose or observe that, in our human world, such creative deeds occur, you see that they indeed do not remove, they do not annul, either treason or its tragedy. But they do show us a genuinely reconciling, a genuinely atoning, fact in the world and in the community of the traitor. Those who do such deeds solve, I have just said, not the impossible problem of undoing the past, but the genuine problem of finding, even in the worst of tragedies, the means of an otherwise impossible triumph. They meet the deepest and bitterest of estrangements by showing a way of reconciliation, and a way that only this very estrangement has made possible.

IX

This is the human aspect of the idea of atonement. Do we need to solve our theological problems before we decide whether such an idea has meaning, and is ethically defensible? I must insist that this idea comes to us, not from the scholastic quiet of theological speculation, but stained with the blood of the battle-fields of real life. For myself, I can say that no theological theory suggested to me this interpretation of the essential nature of an atoning deed. I cannot call the interpretation new, simply because I myself have learned it from observing the meaning of the lives of some suffering servants,—plain human beings,—who never cared for theology, but who incarnated in their own fashion enough of the spirit of their community to conceive and to accomplish such new and creative deeds as I have just attempted to characterize. To try to describe to you, at all adequately, the life or the work of any such persons, I have neither the right nor the power. Here is no place for such a collection and analysis of the human form of the atoning life as only a William James could have justly accomplished. And upon personal histories I could dwell, in this place, only at the risk of intruding upon lives which I have been privileged sometimes to see afar off, and briefly, but which I have no right to report as mere illustrations of a philosophical argument. It is enough, I think, for me barely to indicate what I have in mind when I say that such things are done amongst men.

All of us well know of great public benefactors whose lives and good works have been rendered possible through the fact that some great personal sorrow, some crushing blow of private grief first descended, and seemed to wreck their lives. Such heroic souls have then been able, in these well-known types of cases, not only to bear their own grief, and to rise from the depths of it (as we all in our time have to attempt to do). They have been able also to use their grief as the very source of the new arts and inventions and labors whereby they have become such valuable servants of their communities. Such people indeed often remind us of the suffering servant in Isaiah; for their life work shows that they are willing to be wounded for the sake of their community. Indirectly, too, they often seem to be suffering because of the faults as well as because of the griefs of their neighbors, or of mankind. And it indeed often occurs to us to speak of these public or private benefactors as living some sort of atoning life, as bearing, in a sense, not only the sorrows, but the sins of other men.

Yet it is *not* of such lives, noble as they are, that I am now thinking—nor of *such* vicarious suffering, of such sympathizing helpfulness in human woe, of such rising from private grief to public service,—that I am now speaking, when I say that atoning deeds, in the more precise sense just described, are indeed done in our human world. Sharply contrasted with these beneficent lives and deeds, which I have just mentioned, are the other lives of which I am thinking, and to which, in speaking of atonement, I have been referring. These are the lives of which I have so little right to give more than a bare hint in this place.

One's private grief *may be* the result of the deed of a traitor. That again is something which often seems to happen in our human world. One may rally from the despair due to even such a blow, and may later become a public benefactor. We all know, I suppose, people who have done that, and whose lives are the nobler and more serviceable because they have conquered such a grief, and have learned great lessons through such a conquest. Yet even *such* lives do not show exactly the reconciling and atoning power that I now most have in mind. Let me next state a mere supposition.

Suppose a community,—a modern community,—to be engaged with the ideals and methods of modern reform, in its contests with some of those ills which the natural viciousness, the evil training, and the treasonable choices of very many people combine to make peculiarly atrocious in the eyes of all who love mankind. Such evils need to be met, in the good warfare, not only by indignant reformers, not only by ardent enthusiasts, but also by calmly considerate and enlightened people, who distinguish clearly between fervor and wisdom, who know what depths of woe and of wrong are to be sounded, but who also know that only self-controlled thoughtfulness and well-disciplined self-restraint can devise the best means of help. As we also well know, we look, in our day, to highly trained professional skill for aid in such work. We do not hope that those who are merely well-meaning and loving can do what most needs to be done. We desire those who know. Let us suppose, then, such a modern community as especially needing, for a very special purpose, one who *does* know.

Hereupon let us suppose that one individual exists whose life has been wounded to the core by some of treason's worst blows. Let us suppose one who, always manifesting true loyalty and steadfastly keeping strict integrity, has known, not merely what the ordinary professional experts learn, but also what it is to be despised and rejected of men, and to be brought to the very depths of lonely desolation, and to have suffered thus through a treason which also deeply affected, not one individual only, but a whole community. Let such a soul, humiliated, offended, broken, so to speak, through the very effort to serve a community, forsaken, long daily fed only by grief, yet still armed with the grace of loyalty and of honor, and with the heroism of dumb suffering,—let such a soul not only arise, as so many great sufferers have done, from the depths of woe,— let such a soul not only triumph, as so many have done, over the grief that treason caused; but let such a soul also use the very lore which just this treason had taught, in order to begin a new life work. Let this life work be full of a shrewd, practical, serviceable, ingenious wisdom which only that one individual experience of a great treason could have taught. Let this new life work be made possible only because of that treason. Let it bring to the community, in the contest with great public evils, methods and skill and judgment and forethought which only that so dear-bought wisdom could have invented. Let these methods have, in fact, a skill that the traitor's own wit has taught, and that is now used for the good work. Let that life show, not only what treason can do to wreck, but what the free spirit can learn from and through the very might of treason's worst skill.

If you will conceive of such a life merely as a possibility, you may know why I assert that genuinely atoning deeds occur, and what I believe such deeds to be. For myself, any one who should supply the facts to bear out my supposition (and such people, as I assert, there are in our human world) would appear henceforth to me to be a sort of symbolic personality,—one who had descended into hell to set free the spirits who are in prison. When I hear those words, "descended into hell," repeated in the creed, I think of such human beings, and feel that I know at least some in our human world to whom the creed in these words refers.

X

Hereupon, you may very justly say that the mere effects of the atoning deeds of a human individual are in this world apparently petty and transient; and that even the most atoning of sacrificial human lives can devise nothing which, within the range of our vision, *does* make the world of the community better, in any of its most tragic aspects, than it would be if no treason had been committed.

If you say this, you merely give me the opportunity to express the human aspect of the idea of the atonement in a form very near to the form which, as I believe, the Christian idea of atonement has always possessed when the interests of the religious consciousness (or, if I may use the now favorite word, the subconsciousness) of the Church, rather than the theological formulations of the theory of atonement, have been in question. Christian feeling, Christian art, Christian worship, have been full of the sense that *somehow* (and *how* has remained indeed a mystery) there was something so precious about the work of Christ, something so divinely wise (so skilful and divinely beautiful?) about the plan of salvation,—that, as a result of all this, after Christ's work was done, the world as a whole was a nobler and richer and worthier creation than it would have been if Adam had not sinned.

This, I insist, has always been felt to be the sense of the atoning work which the faith has attributed to Christ. A glance at a great Madonna, a chord of truly Christian music, ancient or modern, tells you that this is so. And this sense of the atoning work cannot be reduced to what the modern "moral" theories of the Christian atonement most emphasize.

For what the Christian regards as the atoning work of Christ is, from this point of view, *not* something about Christ's work which merely arouses in sinful man love and repentance.

No, the theory of atonement which I now suggest, and which, as I insist, is subconsciously present in the religious sentiment, ritual, and worship of all Christendom, is a perfectly "objective" theory,—quite as "objective" as any "penal satisfaction" theory could be. Christian religious feeling has always expressed itself in the idea that what atones is something perfectly "objective," namely, Christ's work. And this atoning work of Christ was for Christian feeling a deed that was made possible only through man's sin, but that somehow was so wise and so rich and so beautiful and divinely fair that, after this work was done, the world was a better world than it would have been had *man* never sinned.

So the Christian consciousness, I insist, has always felt. So its poets have often, in one way or another, expressed the matter. The theologians have disguised this simple idea under countless forms. But every characteristically Christian act of worship expresses it afresh. Treason did its work (so the legend runs) when man fell. But Christ's work was so perfect that, in a perfectly objective way, it took the opportunity which man's fall furnished to make the world better than it could have been had man not fallen.

But this is indeed, as an idea concerning God and the universe and the work of Christ, an idea which is as human in its spirit, and as deep in its relation to truth, as it is, in view of the complexity of the values which are in question, hard either to articulate or to defend. How should we know, unless some revelation helped us to know, whether and in what way Christ's supposed work made the world better than it would have been had man not sinned?

But in this discussion I am speaking of the purely human aspect of the idea of atonement. *That* aspect is now capable of a statement which does not pretend to deal with any but our human world, and which fully admits the pettiness of every human individual effort to produce such a really atoning deed as we have described.

The human community, depending, as it does, upon its loyal human lovers, and wounded to the heart by its traitors, and finding, the farther it advances in moral worth, the greater need of the loyal, and the greater depth of the tragedy of treason,—utters its own doctrine of atonement as this postulate,—the central postulate of its highest spirituality. This postulate I word thus: *No baseness or cruelty of treason so deep or so tragic shall enter our human world, but that loyal love shall be able in due time to oppose to just that deed of treason its fitting deed of atonement.* The deed of atonement shall be so wise and so rich in its efficacy, that the spiritual world, after the atoning deed, shall be better, richer, more triumphant amidst all its irrevocable tragedies, than it was before that traitor's deed was done.

This is the postulate of the highest form of human spirituality. It cannot be proved by the study of mankind as they are. It can be asserted by the creative will of the loyal. Christianity expressed this postulate in the symbolic form of a report concerning the supernatural work of Christ. Humanity must express it through the devotion, the genius, the skill, the labor of the individual loyal servants in whom its spirit becomes incarnate.

As a Christian idea, the atonement is expressed in a symbol, whose divine interpretation is merely felt, and is viewed as a mystery. As a human idea, atonement is expressed (so far as it can at any one time be expressed) by a peculiarly noble and practically efficacious type of human deeds. This human idea of atonement is also expressed in a postulate which lies at the basis of all the best and most practical spirituality. The Christian symbol and the practical postulate are two sides of the same life,—at once human and divine.